Franz Boas among the Inuit of Baffin Island, 1883–1884:
Journals and Letters

Franz Boas among the Inuit of Baffin Island, 1883–1884

JOURNALS AND LETTERS

Edited and introduced by Ludger Müller-Wille

Translated by William Barr

UNIVERSITY OF TORONTO PRESS
Toronto Buffalo London

Franz Boas's original texts and material © American Philosophical Society.
Reproduced in translation with permission.

First published as *Franz Boas. Bei den Inuit in Baffinland 1883–1884. Tagebücher
und Briefe,* arranged, edited, and annotated by Ludger Müller-Wille. (Volume 1
of *Ethnologische Beiträge zur Circumpolarforschung,* ed. Erich Kasten.) Berlin:
Reinhold Schletzer Verlag 1994. English translation published by permission.

Printed in Canada

ISBN 0-8020-4150-7 (cloth)

Printed on acid-free paper

Canadian Cataloguing in Publication Data

Boas, Franz, 1858–1942
  Franz Boas among the Inuit of Baffin Island, 1883–1884 : journals and letters

  Translation of: Franz Boas bei den Inuit in Baffinland 1883–1884.
  Includes index.
  ISBN 0-8020-4150-7

  1. Boas, Franz, 1858–1942 – Journeys – Northwest Territories – Baffin
  Island. 2. Inuit – Northwest Territories – Baffin Island – Social life and
  customs. 3. Baffin Island (N.W.T.) – Social life and customs. I. Barr,
  William. II. Müller-Wille, Ludger, 1944– . III. Title.

  E99.E7B659813 1998   917.19′5042   C98-931821-4

This book has been published with the financial assistance of the Publications
Committee, University of Saskatchewan, and the Department of Geography,
McGill University.

University of Toronto Press acknowledges the financial assistance to its publishing program of the Canada Council for the Arts and the Ontario Arts Council.

Contents

Illustrations and maps follow page 112.

Foreword

I have always wanted to read my great-grandfather's Baffin Island journals and letters, so it was with enormous excitement and anticipation that I first opened the pages of this translation this past summer. Written more than a century ago, the bulk of Franz Boas's earliest ethnographic writings remained unedited and untranslated until only recently. The publication of Müller-Wille's edited and annotated volume of these texts in German in 1994 was aimed primarily at a German readership in order to reintroduce Boas's work to German scholars after it was banned by the Nazis in the 1930s. Now the translation of this volume into English makes these writings available to a much wider group of interested people. It also makes them available to contemporary Inuit, whose cultural traditions and legacy have always been of vital importance to their present lives.

Müller-Wille's skilful arrangement and sensitive editing of the Baffin Island material highlight the rich detail and insight with which Boas wrote about this field experience and its significance for him at the time. Moreover, Müller-Wille's introduction provides an important backdrop for our own appreciation of the original text. It is widely recognized that this trip signalled a crucial turning point for Boas personally, intellectually, and professionally, and that it was the primary context within which he developed his ethnographic field methods and began to articulate the more fundamental philosophical and moral attitudes that would form the core of his mature anthropological viewpoint. Yet until now few of us have had the privilege of reading for ourselves, in Boas's own words, how and under what circumstances this process took place.

Boas was a dauntingly prolific writer, and he generated an enormous amount of textual documentation of this trip, including journals, correspondence, a set of notebooks, and a letter-diary that he wrote to his future wife, Marie Krackowizer. The letter-diary is a special document because it is here that Boas begins to articulate elements of his anthropological position, even if they remain undefined. Beginning in early November 1883, his diaries include progressively more ethnographic detail and insight. This occurs in conjunction with his descriptions to Marie of daily life among the Inuit, and of his increasing accommodation to that life. As these ethnological observations become more frequent and more sophisticated, they also reflect more general anthropological insights. It is in this context that Boas articulated a position of cultural relativism: 'when I think ... of how a year ago I was among Berlin society and was following all the fine rules of "bon ton," and tonight am sitting in a snow house with Wilhelm and an Eskimo, eating a piece of raw, frozen seal meat, which first has been cut into pieces with an axe, and in addition am drinking hot coffee almost greedily, one can scarcely conceive of greater contrasts.'

Valerie Pinsky
American Museum of Natural History
New York, New York
12 February 1998

Preface to the Original German Edition

My first contact with Franz Boas and his life's work occurred during the winter term of 1965–6 at the Westfälische Wilhelms-Universität in Münster, when my professor in ethnology, Rüdiger Schott, emphasized in his first lectures, as he continued to do during my studies, Franz Boas's important contributions and his place in ethnology. When I later involved myself with northern peoples and especially with the Inuit of arctic Canada, Boas's work on the Inuit became an indispensable source. It was my research on Inuit toponymy in Nunavik and Nunavut (Canada) from the 1970s onwards that brought Boas closer to me both as a person and as a researcher. In 1883–4 he carried out the first extensive survey of place names among the Inuit of Baffin Island. In order to get a better understanding of his working methods, which he developed during his one and only period of field research among the Inuit in the Arctic, I began to study Franz Boas in both the literature and the archives, starting in Germany in 1982.

While I was perusing Boas's bequest at the American Philosophical Society in August 1983, the idea came to me of publishing in their entirety the journals and letters he wrote in the Arctic in 1883–4. Douglas Cole, co-author of an article on Boas (Cole and Müller-Wille 1984), who at that time was preparing an English translation of part of the letters that Boas had written for his fiancée, Marie Krackowizer (Cole 1983), recommended that I produce a complete edition of all the extant journals and letters Boas wrote in Baffin Island. I could not have imagined that this undertaking, with the interruptions filled with other projects, would last for more than ten years.

In August 1984 and January 1991 I had the opportunity to visit various places in Cumberland Sound, Franz Boas's arctic research area; my aim was to carry out place name surveys among the Inuit of Pangnirtung, based on his lists, in cooperation with Linna Weber Müller-Wille, and to collect oral history on the German Polar Station (1882–3) and on Boas himself. Apart from allowing us to peruse Franz Boas's personal and scientific legacies, these stays in Cumberland Sound gave us an insight into the atmosphere and into Boas's *modus operandi* during his field research among the Inuit in 1883–4.

During the past ten years many individuals and institutions have assisted me. I am grateful, firstly, to the colleagues in the archives and other institutions, where I always found people ready to assist me in locating and examining material. The institutions include the Bundesamt für Schiffahrt und Hydrographie [Federal Office for Navigation and Hydrography], Hamburg; the American Philosophical Society, Philadelphia; the Kommunalarchiv Minden [Minden Municipal Archives], Minden i. W.; Det Kongelige Bibliotek [The Royal Library], Copenhagen; Museum für Völkerkunde [Museum for Ethnology], Staatliche Museen Preussischer Kulturbesitz [State Museums for Prussian Cultural Heritage], Berlin; Landesarchive Schleswig-Holstein [Schleswig-Holstein Land Archives], Schleswig; Archiv der Humboldt-Universität [Humboldt University Archives], Berlin; and the libraries of the universities of Bonn, Kiel, and Marburg. The Geographisches Institut [Geographical Institute], Philipps-Universität (Marburg/L.), with its congenial circle of colleagues, where I was able to spend a sabbatical year in 1982–3, and the Department of Geography, McGill University, Montreal, where I have worked since 1977, have given me their support and appreciation in various ways.

There are many individuals whom I should identify, who knowingly or otherwise have contributed to my bringing to reality the publishing of these journals. I am indebted to all of them for their discussions, ideas, advice, and information. To the following I owe my sincere appreciation, even though they were not all directly connected with this project: Eenookie Akulukjuk, Allan Angmarlik, William Barr, Gerald L. Broce, Douglas Cole (d. 1997), Linda J. Ellanna (d. 1997), Peter Ernerk, Aksayook Etooangat (d. 1996), C.C. Knötsch (1987–92), John E. Lewis, John G. McConnell, Michael Müller-Wille, Rosie Okpik, Sherry H. Olson, Marius Tungilik, George Wenzel, Dennis J. Whelan, Heide W. Whelan, and the Inuit of Pangnirtung, Nunavut.

I am very grateful to Erich Kasten, editor of the series *Ethnologische Beiträge zur Circumpolarforschung* [Ethnological Contributions to Circumpolar Research], which was initiated with this volume, and to the Berlin publisher Reinhold Schletzer for their uncomplicated and patient collaboration. Through the efforts of Erich Kasten, Franz Boas's journals and letters were published in Berlin, where in 1882–3 and 1885–6 he collaborated with Adolf Bastian and others, and where in 1886 he obtained his Dr.habil. in the discipline of geography before emigrating to the United States of America.

Linna Weber Müller-Wille, my wife and colleague, and our children Ragnar, Gwen, and Verena have supported this project in their own way, showing the patience and encouragement without which I would have had great difficulty in managing the long hours at the microfilm reader and word processor. I owe them my special thanks.

This is the first time I have edited somebody else's private journals and letters. I hope that I have been fair to the author, especially since he is a prominent personality. I am not entirely certain whether I have come closer to Boas through his personal notes. From my own experience, I know that journals that are kept regularly do not contain everything.

This publication is dedicated to Franz Boas, but I also include in this dedication his servant Wilhelm Weike, the Scottish whaler and station manager James S. Mutch, and especially Boas's Inuit guides, such as Ssigna, Ocheitu, and Shanguja; and finally the 'cooneys,' the Inuit women who, inexplicably, too often remained nameless in Boas's notes. They all contributed to Boas's well-being, trials, and successes during his arctic sojourn, which resulted in the vast body of literature on the Inuit and their culture that Franz Boas compiled over the years.

Ludger Müller-Wille
Kelirikko, Brookfield, Vermont, and St-Lambert, Québec
20 July 1994

Preface to the English Edition

I stated in the introduction to the original German version that I hoped that the English translation of Franz Boas's Baffin Island diaries and letters, along with the excerpts from Wilhelm Weike's diaries, would make this important document for the history of anthropology available to a broader audience, including in particular the Inuit of southern Baffin Island, whose second language is English. The need for an English version is underscored by the current vogue to re-evaluate Boas's work in today's context with respect to his personal and scientific contributions – a form of revision that Boas's achievements have had to endure at various times since his death in December 1942.

Recent publications focusing on Boas are testimony to his lasting legacy as an extraordinary human being and a discerning scientist (see, for example, Cole in press; Stocking 1996). It is hoped that the presentation of his journal and letters from his early scientific period will cast additional light on his emergence as a major intellectual force in anthropology. In this connection, one has to realize that these journals and letters were written by Boas when he was between twenty-four and twenty-six years old – not by the established scientist he became in the prime of his academic career, as has often been assumed in assessments and re-evaluations of his scientific contribution.

I am grateful to William Barr of the Department of Geography, University of Saskatchewan, Saskatoon, for offering to undertake the translation, as he has done for many other manuscripts that are of historical importance to Canada's north and were written in languages other than English. He first embarked on this task in late 1994, just before the publication of the German original. I should like to thank him for his diligent and sensitive rendering of Boas's and Weike's German into English. Barr's efforts to find both a publisher and the funds to see this project through to fruition are also very much appreciated. His collegial attitude to discuss and review the English translation has resulted in a product with which both the author-editor and the translator can be satisfied.

During the final stages of manuscript preparation, I was able to make corrections and additions to my introduction and to the text written by Boas and Weike. Douglas Cole (in press), who continued to work on Boas, generously shared his information and unpublished manuscripts with me. I am grateful for his supportive collegiality. His sudden death in August 1997, at the time this book went to press, is a great loss to students of the history of anthropology. In late 1996 Bernd Gieseking of Minden/ Kassel, Germany, inspired me, through his inquisitive questions about Wilhelm Weike, Boas's servant in the Arctic, to bring out a stronger profile of this person who by happenstance had lived among the Inuit for one year. This has been achieved to some extent, though Weike's experience with Inuit lifestyles and the arctic environment still merits more attention and exploration. It is hoped that this will be carried out in the future. I am also grateful to the constructive comments and suggestions made both by the anonymous and the known reviewers of this text. For editorial and technical reasons some of the photos and maps published in the German version are not reproduced here.

The painting of Pangnirtung Fiord that appears on the back of the book jacket is the work of the late Maurice Haycock and is one of a collection of Haycock paintings owned by the Department of Geological Sciences, University of Saskatchewan. I wish to thank Dr Jim Basinger, head of that department, for permission to reproduce the painting.

It is a fortunate circumstance that Valerie Pinsky, Franz Boas's great-granddaughter, an anthropologist with the American Museum of Natural History in New York, where Boas himself worked, has agreed to write a foreword to this volume. What better way to close the circle! Her interest in this project has been stimulating, and I greatly appreciate the personal information and life dates on members of Boas's family which she and Lotte Urbach provided.

I wish to recognize the financial support of both the University of Saskatchewan, Saskatoon, and the Department of Geography at McGill University, Montreal, without which the translation would have been collecting dust for a few more years. Last but not least, Linna Weber Müller-Wille lent her support in straightening out topical questions and linguistic problems. I am most grateful to her.

Ludger Müller-Wille
Kelirikko, Brookfield, Vermont
6 July 1997

Franz Boas among the Inuit of Baffin Island, 1883–1884:
Journals and Letters

Introduction: Germans and Inuit on Baffin Island in the 1880s

The Simple Relationships between the Land and the People

In June 1883 Franz Boas (born Minden, 9 July 1858; died New York, 22 December 1942), aged twenty-four, left his home town of Minden in Westphalia in northwestern Germany, along with his servant Wilhelm Weike, to join the *Germania*, the ship that was to take them to Cumberland Sound (Tinixdjuarbing) in Baffin Island (Qikirtaaluk) in the North American Eastern Arctic. There Boas was to carry out a year's geographical/ethnographical research among the Inuit (singular: Inuk). This expedition, which followed the First International Polar Year (1882–3), was to prove decisive and trail-breaking for the development of ethnology in general (which later became cultural anthropology, as Boas understood it) and especially for the emergence of an ethnology of the arctic peoples of North America. Boas's objective, as he expressed it, was to investigate 'the simple relationships between the land and the people' (Boas 1885:62) with reference to the Inuit and their arctic habitat. He had explored this approach before beginning his field research by studying, on the basis of the available literature, 'the migrations of the Eskimo and their knowledge of the land they inhabited' in order to 'be able to establish a precise interconnection between the population of tribes, the distribution of food resources and the nature of the physical environment' (Franz Boas [FB]/Abraham Jacobi, 26 November 1882; see Boas 1883a, b).

In retrospect this, the first and only research trip that Boas spent among the Inuit, became personally and scientifically a key experience for him and ultimately one of special significance for the development of anthropology. Although this fact has been widely recognized in the literature (see Stocking 1965, 1992, 1996), so far no complete documentation has been presented of the notes Boas wrote in his native German between 1882 and 1884, the only texts being his numerous publications on the Inuit in both German and English (see Andrews et al. 1943) and some extracts from his letters and journals (Cole 1983; Cole and Müller-Wille 1984; Müller-Wille 1992). This omission is all the more surprising in that Boas influenced the academic and scientific life in the cultural sciences in North America in terms of both research and teaching (from *ca* 1890 until 1940) and thus was a prominent figure.

Hence, the aim of this publication is to effect, by editing all relevant journals, notes, and letters during Boas's first field research among the Inuit, a more complete picture of his early methodological approaches and techniques and his scientific development. In this sense, this edition must be seen first and foremost as a contribution to the history of anthropology, and especially to the discussion of ethnological field research methods and their ethical aspects. For example, the publication of the early field journals of Bronislaw Malinowski (1967) signified an important step in the re-evaluation of his work; this is now also the case with Boas (see Halpin 1994; Cole in press; Stocking 1996; and Stevenson 1997) with a renewed focus on the anthropology of Inuit in the Eastern Canadian Arctic. Secondly, Franz Boas's arctic journals are a valuable document on the history of the Inuit and of the Canadian Arctic at a period when deeply penetrating changes were influencing the way of life and living conditions of the Inuit. Thirdly, the journals and letters provide an insight into Boas's personal development and his relations with his family, his fiancée, his servant, and the Inuit and other residents of the Arctic.

As a precursor to Boas's original writings, I should like to discuss first the beginnings and early arrangements for his research in the Arctic in that they became a leitmotif for the investigations that followed; they attained the stature of classics in general anthropology in terms of their results and the resultant publications (Boas 1888, 1901–7), and they are still discussed in the literature as a basic model (see Smith 1984; Wenzel 1984; Dürr et al. 1992; Jacknis 1996). In this section I shall refer extensively to previously published works that have dealt with Boas's family background and Jewish heritage, his childhood and student career in Prussian Germany, and his first field research in the Arctic (Brilling 1966; Cole 1983, 1988, 1994, and in press; Cole and Müller-Wille 1984; Knötsch 1992a, b; Müller-Wille 1983a, 1992; Püschel 1983, 1988). Part of this introduction refers to discussions that I have elsewhere published in German (Müller-Wille 1994).

This edition of Boas's journals and letters (including excerpts from Wilhelm Weike's diaries) was deliberately presented first in the original German, Boas's mother-tongue, even though this meant that the range of their publication would be quite limited. The sources do not give any indication whether Boas ever considered publishing his personal notes, though it is evident that many passages from his journals and letters entered his publications (often verbatim) in both German and English, for example, the essays he submitted to the *Berliner Tageblatt*. At one point, before even reaching the Arctic, he contemplated writing a popular travel account to raise money and cover his expenses (FB/Marie Krackowizer [MK], 21 July 1883). In fact, he did pursue this idea with the German publisher F.A. Brockhaus in early 1886, but this book never materialized (F.A. Brockhaus/FB, 8 January 1886, Leipzig/Berlin, in Boas 1972). It is apparent that Boas was very eager to preserve this particular record of his life in his professional and private papers, which were deposited by his heirs after his death in 1942 with the American Philosophical Society. It is also apparent that Boas never planned to write an autobiography (see Cole in press).

By editing and publishing the original German texts, my aim was to preserve in Germany the memory and spiritual legacy of Franz Boas as an internationally recognized scientist and to bring his standing in German-language ethnology to deserved recognition. Having been defamed as a German Jew and academic by a number of German colleagues in the 1930s, this recognition was denied him because of the blind, racist mindset in German professional and especially ethnological circles during the Third Reich. Boas had enjoyed such recognition in Germany before 1933, during the greater part of his period of wide scientific activities in both the New and Old World (Andree 1969; Fischer 1990; Cole 1994).

The anti-Semitic attitudes in German universities extended back to the later part of the nineteenth century, when aspiring Jewish academics felt that they were not exactly welcome there. Boas's own experiences during his habilitation procedure in Berlin are testimony to the prevailing attitudes of the time (Cole 1994; Cole in press). That these were not isolated cases can be noted from the parallel academic career of one of Boas's Jewish contemporaries, Alfred Philippson (1864–1953), who stayed in Germany and became a geographer of renown and who, after retiring from the chair in geography at the University of Bonn in 1929, was shunned by his colleagues and incarcerated in Theresienstadt between 1942 and 1945, although he returned to live in Bonn after the liberation in May 1945 (Philippson's diaries, in Böhm and Mehmel 1996).

Even after 1945, Boas and his scientific contributions were barely acknowledged, if they were heeded at all, in German-language ethnology (though there are exceptions, see Rudolph 1968a, b), but they were recognized in North America, where the analysis, further development, and criticism of his ideas had never ceased (see, for example, Stocking 1968, 1974, 1992, 1996; *Études/Inuit/Studies* 1984; Hyatt 1990; D'Souza 1995; Cole in press). Thus, for example, at the First International Congress of Arctic Social Sciences, held at Quebec in October 1992, the first steps were taken towards commemorating the international Jesup North Pacific Expedition, which had been conceived by Boas and was led by him between 1897 and 1902, and which was memorialized one hundred years later as Jesup II, with similar themes, within the framework of an international and interdisciplinary program of research. This offers excellent proof that Boas's scientific plans and concepts are still effective today (Fitzhugh and Krupnik 1994). Hence, we must also welcome the fact that on the occasion of the fiftieth anniversary of Franz Boas's death (1992), several publications on his work appeared in Germany (Dürr et al. 1992; Rodekamp 1994).

Boas and German Polar Research in the Early 1880s

Boas's approach to polar research, geography, ethnology, and the Inuit has been described in detail elsewhere (see Cole and Müller-Wille 1984; Knötsch 1992a, b, 1993; Müller-Wille 1994). Boas himself mentioned that even as a boy (around 1868–9) he was enthused about the northern polar regions and the history of their exploration, and was reading books about them (Cole and Müller-Wille 1984:41; Cole 1988; Liss 1996). In the 1860s the fever for geographical discovery aimed at exploring the polar regions became rampant in the German-speaking countries, as it had already become a few decades earlier in other European countries, especially in Great Britain; this was exemplified by the two German attempts on the North Pole in 1868–9 and 1869–70 (Abel and Jessen 1954; Krause 1992). Thus, it comes as no surprise that young Franz Boas, with his training in natural history, was deeply interested in these events. His student years (1877–81) took him from Heidelberg via Bonn to Kiel, where he graduated Dr.phil. in physics with *magna cum laude* on 21 July 1881, at the age of barely twenty-three, having been taught by Gustav Karsten, his supervisor; his minor subjects were philosophy (Benno Erdmann) and geography (Theobald Fischer). He had already met the geographer Theobald Fischer in Bonn, where he took a lecture on polar geography with him, and he later studied under him in Kiel; Fischer influenced Boas through his lectures and seminars, and led him into polar research by stressing geographical issues with the focus on human environmental interactions. Fischer also became Boas's mentor during his time in Berlin after his arctic research, supporting and advising him in academic matters.

This period, the first few years after the founding of the Second German Reich (1871), was one of feverish international and national efforts to base polar research on the natural sciences. Major systematically planned and coordinated research schemes and networks were formulated and executed, aimed at effecting a deeply penetrating understanding of the physical conditions and interrelations in the Arctic that would provide clues for global conditions and change. This idea had been promoted in this sense for the first time in natural science circles in Europe in 1875 by Karl Weyprecht, an Austrian polar explorer and promoter of science (Weyprecht 1875; see Börgen 1882).

Under the energetic leadership of Georg von Neumayer (then head of the German Naval Observatory in Hamburg), the German Polar Commission, which had been founded to attain this nationally inspired goal, led the way in planning and organizing international collaboration and national contributions through stationary research programs within the framework of the First International Polar Year (IPY) in 1882–3, in which eleven nations with a total of fourteen research stations in both the Arctic and Antarctic participated (Barr 1983, 1985, 1992; Barr and Tolley 1982). In the summer of 1882 the German Polar Commission dispatched an expedition to South Georgia, a one-man operation to Labrador, and an eleven-man party (seven scientists and four workers) aboard the *Germania* to the north end of Cumberland Sound (Kingawa [K'ingua] Fiord/ Clearwater Fiord). Here, between September 1882 and September 1883, the scientific staff carried out planned and scheduled stationary experiments of various types, as well as natural science measurements synchronized with the other research stations of the IPY (Börgen 1882; Neumayer and Börgen 1886; Neumayer 1890, 1891).

The German party spent the year in a prefabricated hut at the German Polar Station at K'ingua. The station hired the Inuk Ocheitu as resident servant; he took up residence with his family in a tent and then a snow house barely 150 metres from the station. The Germans established relations (admittedly, very limited) with the indigenous Inuit and with the wintering Scottish and American whalers, whose crews included members of various peoples and races including a few Germans (Abbes 1884b, 1992). Some expedition members, apart from their work in the natural sciences, also compiled ethnographic notes on the Inuit and collected ethnographica; these were published both during and after Boas's sojourn on Baffin Island (Abbes 1884a, 1890; Ambronn 1883).

During the preparations for and execution of the International Polar Year, Boas completed his one-year compulsory military service near Minden (1881–2); in addition to his duties, he found enough time to plan his scientific career and to decide on geographical exploration from a fixed base among the Inuit in the uncharted regions of the 'British-American Arctic' (Cole 1988:129–31). At this time, it was still considered a compulsory initiation rite to venture into 'unknown lands' if one wanted to succeed in an academic career in geography, an issue of contention that later haunted Boas when obtaining the Dr.habil. at the University of Berlin in 1886 (Cole in press). Critical factors in the choice of location were the wintering whaling stations in Cumberland Sound, which had existed for some decades (Goldring 1986), especially the one on Kekerten Island which had been there since the 1860s (K'exerten/Qikirtait), and the German Polar Station at the north end of Cumberland Sound.

In addition, the German Polar Commission, under Georg von Neumayer, and other polar researchers such as Moritz Lindeman had generously promised Boas logistical help and had arranged contacts with Scottish whalers in Dundee and other ports and with the British Admiralty in London. The latter still played an important role in the North American Arctic, although Great Britain had transferred its claim to sovereignty over the Arctic Archipelago to the Dominion of Canada in 1880. As far as can be determined from the correspondence, Boas did not establish direct contact with Canadian authorities or institutions before his expedition. However, he did establish contact with polar researchers in the United States such as Emil Bessels (from Heidelberg), Heinrich Klutschak (from Prague), and Frederick Schwatka. He engaged in preparatory correspondence concerning the language of the Inuit (Inuktitut) with Hinrich J. Rink (Copenhagen) and with some German arctic scientists and explorers such as Moritz Lindeman (Bremen) and Paul Hegemann (Hamburg), the latter a captain on both of the German North Polar expeditions in the late 1860s.

In 1882–3 Franz Boas spent some months in Berlin, devoted to scientific preparation for his year of field research, with the aim of obtaining the support of scientific societies and established scientists such as Rudolf von Virchow and Adolf Bastian. He discussed his research plans with them – for example, how he might investigate the various aspects of the social, economic, and spatial organization of the Inuit, which underlay their seasonal rhythms; and the physical data of the arctic environment with its resources, which have an impact on human environmental relations. He learned topographic and cartographic techniques in order to be prepared for his intended terrain surveys, for which he drew mainly on the British Admiralty charts as a reference (Admiralty Charts 1847, 1853, and 1875). He also began to learn Inuktitut, principally from Greenlandic material and he improved his command of English. These preparations provided a wide base for the execution of the expedition and the field research, which clearly combined the then accepted working methods in the natural and human sciences and their modes of interpretation. This became a prominent attribute of the development of scientific procedures, one that let Boas become the 'trail-blazer of the modern science of humankind' (Dürr et al. 1992; Rennet 1992).

In terms of his practical preparations for wintering in the Arctic, Boas sought the advice of earlier German polar explorers (Cole and Müller-Wille 1984:42). He proceeded on the assumption that during his sojourn he would have to look after himself independently and would have to adapt to the local customs and way of life of the Inuit without any contact with the outside world, even though he would be able to use the German Polar Station, with the supplies and items of equipment that would be left behind there, and to rely on the Scottish whaling station on Kekerten Island as a support base. His equipment was 'state of the art' for its day: the finest measuring instruments (thermometer, anemometer), glass-plate camera, and theodolite, with which he achieved the most precise measurements for a topographic map, single-handed and often in the most difficult circumstances; also rifles, tent, boat, sledge, kerosene stove, clothing, foodstuffs (enough for two winterings), and other items that fully met the needs of polar research at that time. In addition, in the manner of the contemporary explorations among 'natives' in the emerging European colonies, Boas took along a large store of barter goods – knives, needles, beads, coffee, tobacco, and molasses – for payment of 'his Eskimos' as guides, translators, and informants.

To carry out his scientific work freely and without interruption, and for his own well-being, at the urging of his family Boas took Wilhelm Weike with him as his servant and handyman. Leutnant von der Goltz (no first name given, a member of a large and highly placed Prussian military dynasty), who had been recommended by the German Polar Commission and was expected to be Boas's assistant but who from the outset had seemed dubious to Boas, fortunately dropped out, without reason, shortly before the departure date.

Wilhelm Heinrich Christian Weike (born Häverstädt, 28 November 1859; died Berlin, early June 1917) was ten months younger than Boas and hailed from Häverstädt, a small farming village a few kilometres southwest of Minden i.W. One of three children, he had lost his father when barely a year old and grew up in Häverstädt, where he went to school for a few grades and worked on farms and for burghers in Minden (Bernd Giese-king, personal communication, April 1997). Since 1879 he had been employed as a servant in Boas's household (Cole 1988:131), and he was selected by Boas's father, who footed all his expenses, to keep Boas company in the Arctic and look after the daily chores. At Boas's request and with his instructions, Weike faithfully recorded in a diary his experiences among the Inuit, writing in simple, sober language, and extracts from this diary are included in this volume. During his sojourn he gradually acquired some knowledge of Inuktitut and English, and he taught his arc-tic contemporaries, such as James Mutch, some German; thus, as is appar-ent from his diary, he experienced no difficulty in communicating. At Christmas 1883 he froze a heel and several toes when on the ice of north-ern Cumberland Sound. He recuperated at the Scottish whaling station, which he did not leave between 7 January and 11 April 1884. His diary entries demonstrate that despite the barriers of language and his invalid condition, being a gregarious and quick-witted person he cultivated a close contact with the Inuit, both women and men, and became very familiar with their lifestyle. Weike certainly had a female friend; this is indicated in one of James Mutch's letters, where he writes: 'I hope William is happy with his new wife [Mathilde Nolting]. You had better tell him not to mention about Tookavy or she, Mrs. W., might be jealous if he should go with you again [to Baffin Island as Boas had tentatively planned for 1886]' (James Mutch/FB, 14 January 1886, Peterhead/Berlin, in Boas 1972).

Weike was indispensable to Boas, since he handled almost all practical matters for him. Relations between the two were clearly those of master and servant. Boas addressed Weike (whose name he even sometimes mis-spelled as *Weicke* [FB, 27 April 1883]), by using the formal 'you' and his first name, Wilhelm. In turn, Weike used solely the generally expected formal address, 'Herr Doctor' ('Herr Dr.' or 'Hr. Dr.' in his diary), which the Inuit keenly adapted to 'Doctoraluk' (big doctor) as their nickname for Boas (FB, 31 October 1883). To the Inuit and whalers, Weike was Willie or William.

Wilhelm Weike contributed, if not always consciously, to the advancement of academic science, as did the Inuit who shared with Boas their expertise, a contribution that has not always been appropriately acknowledged. In addition, Weike's diary provides an interesting angle on the conduct of scientific fieldwork in anthropology, seen from the perspective of a person quite unrelated to the subject.

On 17 and 18 June 1883, respectively, Franz Boas and Wilhelm Weike arrived in Hamburg to take passage on the *Germania* of the German Polar Commission, which sailed on 20 June for Baffin Island under Captain A.F.B. Mahlstede and his crew of four men to evacuate the personnel of the German Polar Station at K'ingua. For young Boas, this voyage meant the beginning of a scientific enterprise which ultimately took him to Columbia University in New York, where for decades, as a professor in the Department of Anthropology, he expounded the basics and outlines of the 'science of man' (i.e., cultural anthropology), as both a teacher and a researcher. For the even younger Wilhelm Weike, it was an extraordinary, singular event in cross-cultural experience, which he drew on during his life in Minden and later in Berlin.

Human Environmental Relations in the Arctic: The Ecological Approach

The 'initiation trip' (*Erstlingsreise*, Boas 1894:97) – Boas's first and only field research among the Inuit – has been analysed elsewhere in terms of its practical and technical aspects (Cole and Müller-Wille 1984). The journals, letters, and notes of Boas and some of his contemporaries, which are printed here chronologically, convey in the greatest possible detail the working methods and lifestyle that Boas adopted and pursued during his stay among the Inuit. In my view, his intensive field research methods are characterized by two conspicuous aspects that have had an influence on the scientific development of cultural anthropology as an academic discipline in general:

1 the observation, analysis, and interpretation of human environmental relations in the Arctic, i.e., the Inuit's organization of the utilization of space and resources in a seasonal rhythm under specific natural and geographical conditions;
2 the development and use of ethnological and geographical (interdisciplinary) modes of operation, which led to a cultural-anthropological field research method.

In discussing these aspects one must take into consideration that at this time, during the early 1880s, Boas was starting his scientific career and at this point was standing at the juncture of various professional directions, all of which were initially of great interest to him; for example, physics, psychophysics, physical geography (including topography and cartography), anthropogeography, physical anthropology, linguistics, folklore, and general ethnology. The year of his first field research, 1883–4, became for him a transition, step by step, from physical geography to anthropogeography and finally to ethnology, or rather to anthropology – Boas's 'science of man' in the widest sense. This evolution also entailed a personal change, which clearly reveals itself in his private papers during the period of more than two years covered in this documentation (Cole 1983, 1988, and in press; Cole and Müller-Wille 1984). The personal changes were related to Boas's increasingly competing loyalties: to his family (his parents and sisters in Germany), his fiancée in the United States, his *Heimatgefühl*, sense of cultural identity with Germany, and finally his serious commitment to *Wissenschaft*, knowledge and science. He knew that he had to set priorities and thus make choices by which he clearly would lose but also gain.

Under the banner of the prevailing discussions at German universities, especially in Berlin, in geography (Carl Ritter, Theobald Fischer, Friedrich Ratzel, and Ferdinand Freiherr von Richthofen), zoology (Ernst Haeckel, who in 1869 introduced the concept of 'ecology' for describing the 'external physiology of animals'), ethnology (Adolf Bastian), and physical anthropology (Rudolf von Virchow), Franz Boas had identified as the program for his field research the investigation of the dependence of humankind on natural factors and the conditions of the natural environment (FB/MK, 27 April 1883; Kluckhohn and Prufer 1959; Massin 1996). Even though Boas does not use the concept and term 'ecology' in his early writings, in retrospect his thematic and theoretical orientation may be described as 'rudiments of cultural ecology' (Wenzel 1984), since he was tackling the analysis of the involvement of people in their own social structure in relation to the natural environment.

In his early preparatory studies of the literature on the Inuit of the 'Arctic American archipelago,' Boas addresses the hypothesis that population distribution, migratory movements, types of settlement, and resource use among the Inuit are influenced by fluctuations in the natural conditions, or, to cite Boas himself, that humankind is dependent on 'changes in the climate and ice conditions in those regions'; and 'above all ... the distribution of the living areas of the Eskimos is dependent on the favourable nature (or otherwise) of hunting conditions' (Boas 1883a:121–2). It is important to note that Boas clearly pointed out the linkages between human activity and climatic and even global change. Later, as a result of his extensive fieldwork and by recording oral traditions by interviewing the Inuit, Boas confirmed these interpretations of the relationship between humankind and environment in the Arctic, which he had published even before his sojourn among the Inuit (Boas 1883a–c).

On the other hand, it should be stressed that before his field research, Boas approached this deterministic evaluation with a certain scepticism and emphasized 'that conclusions of this type cannot be adequately supported by the known facts' (Boas 1883a:119). Yet he later unequivocally established the direct connection between natural environmental conditions and human behaviour when he proposed that there was a relationship between ice conditions, seal populations, and distribution and hunting potential as far as the Inuit were concerned, this potential being in accordance with the Inuit's pattern of settlement, type of economy, and even social organization (Boas 1888:417; Smith 1984; Wenzel 1984).

During his sojourn on Baffin Island, Boas carried out an extremely multifaceted and, in the modern sense, interdisciplinary scientific program. He had to familiarize himself with the environment, the people, and the logistics of travelling on water, ice, and land in order to attain his ambitions as a young scientist in the border zone between geography and ethnology. His diary entries, which in many places contain reflections of this type, provide a clear impression of this process. At the beginning of his stay in the Arctic, physical-geographical observations, logistical preparations for travelling, and other technical and practical matters predominate.

Relations with the Inuit, the indigenous population, and the few Europeans, the Euro-Canadians and Euro-Americans at the two whaling stations on Kekerten and on a whaling ship at Naujateling, assumed an important role as Boas learned both English and Inuktitut, though by his own admission he never mastered the latter adequately. The constant travelling by boat, then later exclusively by dogsled and on foot, kept Boas fully occupied, leaving precious little time for the recording of data. It appears that his brief visits in solely Inuit settlements at Anarnitung and Saumia between December 1883 and March 1884 and in the final weeks before his departure from K'ivitung at Davis Strait in late August 1884 gave him the opportunity really to feel his way into Inuit society and language (as is revealed in his diary entries by his frequent use of Inuktitut).

In this regard, Wilhelm Weike seems to have had an easy social relationship with the Inuit, enjoying outings, hunting, and games despite the chores involved in looking after Boas's practical affairs.

The topographic surveys, which led to Boas's cartographic masterpiece, printed by the renowned Justus Perthes publishing house in Gotha (Boas 1885: plate 1, insert 1–6), and the documentation of place names from oral tradition (1885:90–5), which he began right from the beginning and carried out consistently and in detail with the Inuit, are the expression of his research initiative at grasping human environmental relations in the arctic habitat of the Inuit. This is one of the scientific contributions, surviving to the present, which Boas has given to the representation and analysis of environmental knowledge and geographical perception of the Inuit.

Hence, during his field research, Boas was particularly anxious to gather data both on the natural environmental conditions and on the Inuit's social, economic, and spatial organization. These topics represented a widely cast and extensive research program for one person, even though his servant Wilhelm Weike, the manager of the Scottish whaling station James Mutch, and numerous Inuit, both women and men, assisted him with the practical aspects. James Mutch became indispensable for his many helpful translations (from English to Inuktitut and vice versa) and for the interpretation of Inuit culture. Quite a few Inuit were conversant with the whaler's version of English, which was thus the lingua franca for all parties.

Boas collected data on the weather and the sun's position, on tidal fluctuations, and on ice conditions, as well as on topography. The latter took precedence; he travelled almost uninterruptedly around the southeastern coastal areas of Baffin Island to make observations of the terrain and carry out topographic surveys; these Boas augmented with maps drawn by the Inuit, some of which he published (1885, 1888). His surveys then took shape as the first map of this area that was based on exact geodetic measurements, and its validity endured well into the twentieth century.

In order to gain access to the human dimension of the natural environment, Boas began his field research by intensively and systematically recording the geographical knowledge of the Inuit; in return for payment in goods and food, he had them draw maps, and he recorded all the place names they knew, both on maps and on paper; this rapidly expanded his Inuktitut vocabulary. Boas had noted the importance of place names for the interpretation of human environmental relations when he was discussing the areas of utilization and patterns of settlement cannot deny that Boas achieved his access to people, services, and places, as well as obtaining dogs and data, through the incentive and even pressure tactics of offering and withholding payments and 'trade goods' such as rifles, ammunition, knives, tobacco, and foodstuffs, which he used extensively for this purpose. As a generous gesture after his return to Germany, Boas arranged through the Scottish whaling company that thirty pounds of tobacco be sent to James Mutch at Kekerten to be distributed to all his Inuit acquaintances so that they would not forget him (Crawford Noble/FB, 7 and 19 July 1885, Dundee/Minden, in Boas 1972).

Journals and Letters, 1882–1884: The Source Material

Franz Boas's journals, records, and letters, as well as excerpts from Wilhelm Weike's diary, written both before and during their one-year expedition (1883–4) among the Inuit of the Canadian Arctic, are published here in English translation as completely as was feasible, apart from passages of a purely private nature, which have been excluded. These documents represent a testimonial to Boas's developing research initiatives in geography and ethnology (anthropology) and are also a reflection of his working methods and his relations with the Inuit and other residents of southern Baffin Island. A few limited extracts from these records have been published earlier in English and German (Cole 1983; Müller-Wille 1992). This publication includes the records which Boas himself considered journals *sensu stricto*, as well his personal letters, which were in fact an extension of his journals; they thus form the corpus of 'journals and letters' as described below.

Franz Boas's personal notes and publications on the Inuit of the Arctic are very extensive. During his stay in Baffin Island (for details, see Cole and Müller-Wille 1984; Knötsch 1992a, b, c; Müller-Wille 1983a, 1992, 1994), Boas kept a variety of journals and notebooks, field journals, itineraries, catalogues of ethnographic collections, and letter-journals, which he called his data books (FB/MK, 24 February 1884). In addition, he made numerous maps and sketches. He took a total of forty-eight photographs (glass plates) between 27 June 1883 and 30 April 1884, of which only one-third have survived, owing to poor developing techniques and to Boas's ineptitude in photographic matters. Seven of these plates are published in this volume.

In total, the manuscript material of Boas's 1883–4 writings housed in his professional and private bequest at the American Philosophical Soci-

of the Neitchillik [Netsilik] Inuit (1883b). On the basis of the map thus produced (1885: plate 1) and the associated list of place names (1885:90–5), he was able to extract, represent, and interpret the arctic environment from the point of view of the Inuit, the indigenous people of this area.

The place names and the additional information that Boas collected provided information on the Inuit's current and historical settlement patterns, migratory movements, distribution and utilization of resources (marine and terrestrial mammals), population distribution and density, and linguistic and social relationships. The approach via toponymy, as an expression of the close relationship between humankind and environment, and finally via the 'stories and songs' he recorded, provided Boas with unique access to the language and culture of the Inuit, which he used to produce an extensive ethnographical glossary, *The Central Eskimo* (1888), a work that is still considered a classic of Inuit anthropology. Using these methods, Boas was pursuing a clearly ecological initiative, which invariably saw humankind in relation to the natural environment.

The diversity and intensity of the ethnological-geographical works that Boas produced in his early years between 1883 and 1888 represent an expression of the research approach which he developed during his one-year sojourn in the Arctic among the Inuit but which he applied only conditionally in his later years among the indigenous peoples along the Canadian Northwest Coast (see Rohner 1969; Kasten 1992). In practice, Boas never again immersed himself as intensively in another culture through active participation as he did with 'his Eskimos' in the Arctic. Still, he continued his interest in the Inuit and the Arctic by maintaining an extensive correspondence not only with James Mutch, who kept him informed of changes in Cumberland Sound and on Baffin Island until the early 1920s (see Boas 1972) but with other arctic whaling captains, all of which resulted in further publications (Boas 1901–7).

Fieldwork Methods: 'I am now truly just like a typical Eskimo.'

The personal, social, linguistic, and economic situation relating to Franz Boas's first field research has been discussed at length elsewhere (Cole and Müller-Wille 1984; Knötsch 1992a). However, four types of working method need to be emphasized here, in that they were applied by Boas during his ethnological-geographical work and led both to extraordinary results, which were realized in numerous influential scientific publications (Andrews et al. 1943), and to a refinement of the ethnological research methods of his time.

1 *Participatory observation* as an ethnological research method, whereby Boas adapted to the living conditions of the Inuit, learned their language, and as far as possible participated in all activities, especially embracing the lifestyle in the arctic environment, in order to gain an insight into the culture of the Inuit. Boas did not later expand on this research method or develop it further in his research, but he transmitted it to his students. Thus, this early methodological contribution to anthropological field research was recognized only much later within the discipline, though ethnologists who have worked among the Inuit have referred to it variously (Wenzel 1984; Knötsch 1992b).

2 *Systematic and structured interviews* with experts among the Inuit in order to cover particular aspects of their culture (for example, toponymy, geographical knowledge, language structure and vocabulary, myths, stories, behaviour, etc.). Boas conducted these interviews at the whaling stations, in snow houses, and in tents, recording and copying the information and texts into his diaries or notebooks.

3 *Systematic mapping and surveys* (topographic surveys) of a quantitative nature covering population distribution, settlement patterns and migratory movements, hunting practices, and the spatial use of resources. On the basis of the maps and data compiled by Boas, historical analyses can be carried out today of the changes in land use among the Inuit during the last century. His database is extremely precise and thus represents a valuable source.

4 *Recording oral traditions*, which were then preserved and are used today by the Inuit as a historical source to enhance and develop their culture and language. Thus, to some degree Boas's book, *The Central Eskimo* (1888, see also 1901, 1907), has become the encyclopedia of the Inuit in Cumberland Sound and along the west shore of Davis Strait, for it illustrates how their ancestors lived and thought prior to the pervasive influence of Christian missions and Canadian government institutions (Angmarlik 1984; Stevenson 1997). This is possible today only because Boas recorded this information in detail more than 115 years ago.

In general, as suggested above, Franz Boas's research among the Inuit became the key event in terms of his later scientific development (Stocking 1965). Quite apart from the rigorous methods of research in natural sciences in which he had been trained, Boas had to learn in the Arctic how to familiarize himself with the society, culture, and language of the Inuit. this undertaking he was following the example of Charles F. Hall (1865 whom he read extensively and who had adopted the motto 'Living as a Eskimo with the Eskimos' (Boas 1885:36). The Prague explorer Heinrich Klutschak (1881, 1987) was also an important model for Boas. Klutschak lived among the Inuit of the Central Arctic between 1878 and 1880 with the Schwatka expedition while searching for the Franklin expedition. Boas had read both his and Hall's books before setting out for the Arctic.

The expedition led by Frederick Schwatka adapted the Inuit lifestyle entirely and travelled extensively with the Inuit on the tundra in the Central Arctic without being dependent on supplies from outside (Barr, in Klutschak 1987:xxx). The title of Klutschak's book, *Als Eskimo unter Eskimos* (As an Inuk among the Inuit) (1881), can thus be seen to some degree as the leitmotif for Boas's research mode and lifestyle in the Arctic. Thus, Boas noted proudly and compellingly in the letter-journal he wrote for his fiancée Marie Krackowizer, who was then living in New York, 'As you see, my Marie, I am now truly just like an Eskimo; I live like them, hunt with them, and count myself among the men of Anarnitung [an Inuit winter settlement]. Moreover I scarcely eat any European foodstuffs any longer but am living entirely on seal meat and coffee' (see text, FB/ MK, 15 February 1884; see Cole 1983; Cole and Müller-Wille 1984:54). Boas viewed himself as being integrated and accepted as a 'participant observer' within Inuit society in order to learn to understand their cultural expressions and philosophy of life.

Although Boas stayed frequently at the Scottish whaling station at Kekerten (which he used as his operational base) between mid-September 1883 and early May 1884, he and Wilhelm Weike spent the bulk of the year living 'like an Inuk' with the Inuit in snow house and tent camps while travelling around Cumberland Sound and the west shore of Davis Strait. Franz Boas was very anxious to be accepted by the Inuit, even though he had trouble and difficulties with the language and logistics (for example, sledging, buying dogs, procuring caribou skins and seal meat) and even though, in the minds of the Inuit, he was linked to the spread of diphtheria and influenza, which had been brought in by the whalers shortly before. His journals contain much proof of this connection. After some adaptation and a certain amount of effort, Boas came to respect the lifestyle of the Inuit, whom he saw personally as partners. As he noted, 'Eskimos are far from being uncivilized' (FB/parents, sisters, 3 October 1883), an early expression of his cultural relativism, which only later bore fruit in his publications and teachings. On the other hand, one ety embraces 200,000 words. Boas was obsessed with safeguarding his journals, letters, and notes. He produced copies of almost everything he wrote. Thus, the material in his bequest is as complete as it can be. Furthermore, his early correspondence concerning his stay with the Inuit in Baffin Island is scattered in many places and has turned up in archives in Germany, Denmark, and the United States.

Since, for reasons of safety, Boas copied most of his records during his sojourn in the Arctic, one cannot always be sure when and where he made the original entries. The conditions under which he wrote were often extreme; for example, he had to thaw his ink to be able to write his journal in his sleeping bag in an igloo or to note down long lists of numbers for topographical surveys and determinations of positions on the sea ice during his extended journeys in Cumberland Sound at temperatures that dropped to $-48°$C. The security and warmth of the Scottish whaling station at Kekerten with the affable James Mutch – a Scot who was married to an Inuk and was fluent in Inuktitut – represented a pleasant change and a welcome haven.

The texts edited here were taken either direct from the originals, which I examined and transcribed in the archives I visited, or from microfilms or photocopies provided by the archives. The transcriptions were edited only when absolutely necessary, and this is always noted in the text. In this edition, the source of each text is precisely identified by a code in brackets (see below) at the beginning of each item. This was deemed essential in order to distinguish the various layers of journal entries and their exact location in the complex of handwritten material that has survived in the Boas papers.

American Philosophical Society (APS)
105 South Fifth Street, Philadelphia, PA 19106-3386

The APS holds in its manuscript collections the Franz Boas Papers, including personal and professional material given to the APS by the heirs of Franz Boas in the late 1940s. This collection contains a wealth of original material. The documents, photos, sketches, and maps are published here with the express permission of the American Philosophical Society as granted in letters of 14 November 1983 and 21 February 1984 (Stephen Catlett) and 9 December 1993 and 12 January 1994 (Beth Carroll Horrocks). The society's literary copyright to these texts will not be influenced by this publication.

Franz Boas Family Papers [APS:FBFP],
Files B:B61p and B:B61.5 (microfilm 1445)

FRANZ BOAS [FB], DIARIES, JOURNALS, AND ITINERARIES

[BN]
First black notebook, 20 June – 15 August, 28 August – 9 September, 19 September – 14 October 1883, and 13 March 1884 (black hardcover, 10 × 16 cm)

[Notebook]
Second black notebook, 16 July – 14 August, 28 August – 4 September 1883, 19 September 1883–2 February 1884 (black hardcover, 10 × 16 cm).

[D]
First diary with printed dates, two days per page, divided by a line, 28 March – 5 April, 28–9 May, 2–20 June, 4–8 September, 3–4 and 15–17 October 1883, 1–11 January, 7–12 February, 11–20 March, and 6 May – 5 June 1884 (black hardcover, 10 × 16 cm).

[D2]
Second diary with printed dates, two days per page, divided by a line, 1 January – 25 April, 6 May – 24 July, and 27 July – 30 August 1884 (black hardcover, 10 × 16 cm)

WILHELM WEIKE [WW], DIARY

[WW]
Diary, 10 June 1883 – 1 September 1884 (originally bound, now a collection of loose sheets, 17 × 20 cm, 445 pages; fair copy of the original diary with possible corrections copied in German script for Franz Boas in 1885–6 in Berlin)
   Wilhelm Weike, Franz Boas's servant in 1883–4 (born 28 November 1859, died in Berlin in early June 1917) kept his diary daily with only a few breaks. The original was probably retained by Weike, but his bequest could not be traced in Berlin, where he moved in 1886 with Boas's parents and sister Antonie (Boas) Wohlauer. He was married to Mathilde Nolting in Minden in 1885; they did not have any children (FB/James Mutch, 26 July 1917, Bolton Landing/Peterhead, in Boas 1972).

FRANZ BOAS, LETTERS

[FB/parents, sisters]
Franz Boas to his parents, father Meyer Boas (born 10 November 1823 in Minden, died 21 February 1899 in Berlin) and mother Sophie (Jette) Boas, née Meyer (born 12 July 1828 in Minden, died 12 July 1916 in Berlin), and to his three sisters, the eldest Antonie (Toni) (born 12 July 1854 in Minden, died *ca* 1932 in Germany; married Wohlauer), Hedwig (Hete) (born 16 May 1863 in Minden, died 2 October 1949 in the United States; married Richard Lehmann), and Anna Margaret (Aenne) (born 21 August 1867 in Minden, emigrated to Brazil between 1935 and 1937, died in Rio de Janeiro 26 September 1946; married Urbach), in Minden i.W., 12 May 1882 – 20 September 1884 (notebooks perforated down the left side, 16 × 20 cm)

In these sporadically written letters, which he called 'polar letters' written by 'your polar bear' (FB/parents, sisters, 25 November 1883), Boas covered events from time to time.

[FB/MK]
Franz Boas to his fiancée, Marie Anna Ernestina Krackowizer of New York (born 3 August 1861, died 16 December 1929 in New York), living in Stuttgart 1881–3; engaged 28 May 1883 in Germany, and married 10 March 1887 in New York; letters between 27 April 1883 and 12 September 1884, with only a few gaps (copy pads, 8.5 × 17.5 cm, perforated down the left side, collections of loose sheets)

These private letters, which Boas wrote fairly regularly, also served as a field diary from mid-December 1883. For Boas these letters became the most important mental refuge during his arctic sojourn; he expressed his inner feelings in them (Cole 1983).

During his absence from Germany, Boas was able to send or receive letters only a few times. Before the winter of 1883–4, this occurred on 22 June 1883 off Heligoland via the pilot boat and on 27 June in Pentland Firth off the island of Stroma via a fishing boat; he sent letters on 16 September direct to Hamburg with the *Germania* and on 3 October with the *Catherine* via Dundee (Scotland) to Minden i.W. and to New York. After wintering, he dispatched material with whalers via Scotland to Germany on 27 August 1884, and on 8 and 21 September 1884 he sent letters and telegrams from St John's and New York. He delivered the letter-journals for his fiancée to her personally on 23 September 1884, after his arrival in New York, at Lake George in upstate New York, where the Krackowizer family had its summer home.

Boas Professional Papers [APS:BPP]

The following letters, which are also published here, are from Boas's scholarly bequest at the APS (see also Boas 1972):

FB/Abraham Jacobi, 26 November 1882
Moritz Lindeman/FB, 21 December 1882
Paul Hegemann/FB, 20 February 1883
Crawford Noble/FB, 12 May 1883

Boas Print Collection [APS:PC]

FRANZ BOAS PRINT COLLECTION, B:B61, NO. 1–34

Photos and reproductions of Boas's family, of his stay in Baffin Island, and from his professional career (ca 1865–1942). There are sixteen plates (dated July–October 1883) of varying quality in the collection; seven of them are published here.

Bundesamt für Seeschiffahrt und Hydrographie (BSH)
Bibliothek, Postfach 30 12 30, D-20305 Hamburg, Germany. (Formerly Deutsche Seewarte, then Deutsches Hydrographisches Institut und Bundesamt für Schiffsvermessung)

Documents of the International Polar Commission and the German Polar Commission (DPK = Deutsche Polar-Kommission) and the stations of the northern, Labrador, and southern expeditions within the framework of the International Polar Year 1882–3 (Müller-Wille 1983b). Publication of the archival material from the original documents is by express approval of the BSH as per letter of 19 January 1994 and 20 May 1997 (Ingrid Koslowski).

[BSH:DPK]

Deutsche Polar-Kommission, Northern Expedition, K'ingua Station, Cumberland Sound of the Neitchillik [Netsilik] Inuit (1883b). On the basis of the map thus produced (1885: plate 1) and the associated list of place names (1885:90–5), he was able to extract, represent, and interpret the arctic environment from the point of view of the Inuit, the indigenous people of this area.

The place names and the additional information that Boas collected provided information on the Inuit's current and historical settlement patterns, migratory movements, distribution and utilization of resources (marine and terrestrial mammals), population distribution and density, and linguistic and social relationships. The approach via toponymy, as an expression of the close relationship between humankind and environment, and finally via the 'stories and songs' he recorded, provided Boas with unique access to the language and culture of the Inuit, which he used to produce an extensive ethnographical glossary, *The Central Eskimo* (1888), a work that is still considered a classic of Inuit anthropology. Using these methods, Boas was pursuing a clearly ecological initiative, which invariably saw humankind in relation to the natural environment.

The diversity and intensity of the ethnological-geographical works that Boas produced in his early years between 1883 and 1888 represent an expression of the research approach which he developed during his one-year sojourn in the Arctic among the Inuit but which he applied only conditionally in his later years among the indigenous peoples along the Canadian Northwest Coast (see Rohner 1969; Kasten 1992). In practice, Boas never again immersed himself as intensively in another culture through active participation as he did with 'his Eskimos' in the Arctic. Still, he continued his interest in the Inuit and the Arctic by maintaining an extensive correspondence not only with James Mutch, who kept him informed of changes in Cumberland Sound and on Baffin Island until the early 1920s (see Boas 1972) but with other arctic whaling captains, all of which resulted in further publications (Boas 1901–7).

Fieldwork Methods: 'I am now truly just like a typical Eskimo.'

The personal, social, linguistic, and economic situation relating to Franz Boas's first field research has been discussed at length elsewhere (Cole and Müller-Wille 1984; Knötsch 1992a). However, four types of working method need to be emphasized here, in that they were applied by Boas during his ethnological-geographical work and led both to extraordinary results, which were realized in numerous influential scientific publications (Andrews et al. 1943), and to a refinement of the ethnological research methods of his time.

1 *Participatory observation* as an ethnological research method, whereby Boas adapted to the living conditions of the Inuit, learned their language, and as far as possible participated in all activities, especially embracing the lifestyle in the arctic environment, in order to gain an insight into the culture of the Inuit. Boas did not later expand on this research method or develop it further in his research, but he transmitted it to his students. Thus, this early methodological contribution to anthropological field research was recognized only much later within the discipline, though ethnologists who have worked among the Inuit have referred to it variously (Wenzel 1984; Knötsch 1992b).
2 *Systematic and structured interviews* with experts among the Inuit in order to cover particular aspects of their culture (for example, toponymy, geographical knowledge, language structure and vocabulary, myths, stories, behaviour, etc.). Boas conducted these interviews at the whaling stations, in snow houses, and in tents, recording and copying the information and texts into his diaries or notebooks.
3 *Systematic mapping and surveys* (topographic surveys) of a quantitative nature covering population distribution, settlement patterns and migratory movements, hunting practices, and the spatial use of resources. On the basis of the maps and data compiled by Boas, historical analyses can be carried out today of the changes in land use among the Inuit during the last century. His database is extremely precise and thus represents a valuable source.
4 *Recording oral traditions*, which were then preserved and are used today by the Inuit as a historical source to enhance and develop their culture and language. Thus, to some degree Boas's book, *The Central Eskimo* (1888, see also 1901, 1907), has become the encyclopedia of the Inuit in Cumberland Sound and along the west shore of Davis Strait, for it illustrates how their ancestors lived and thought prior to the pervasive influence of Christian missions and Canadian government institutions (Angmarlik 1984; Stevenson 1997). This is possible today only because Boas recorded this information in detail more than 115 years ago.

In general, as suggested above, Franz Boas's research among the Inuit became the key event in terms of his later scientific development (Stocking 1965). Quite apart from the rigorous methods of research in natural sciences in which he had been trained, Boas had to learn in the Arctic how to familiarize himself with the society, culture, and language of the Inuit. In this undertaking he was following the example of Charles F. Hall (1865), whom he read extensively and who had adopted the motto 'Living as an Eskimo with the Eskimos' (Boas 1885:36). The Prague explorer Heinrich Klutschak (1881, 1987) was also an important model for Boas. Klutschak lived among the Inuit of the Central Arctic between 1878 and 1880 with the Schwatka expedition while searching for the Franklin expedition. Boas had read both his and Hall's books before setting out for the Arctic.

The expedition led by Frederick Schwatka adapted the Inuit lifestyle entirely and travelled extensively with the Inuit on the tundra in the Central Arctic without being dependent on supplies from outside (Barr, in Klutschak 1987:xxx). The title of Klutschak's book, *Als Eskimo unter Eskimos* (As an Inuk among the Inuit) (1881), can thus be seen to some degree as the leitmotif for Boas's research mode and lifestyle in the Arctic. Thus, Boas noted proudly and compellingly in the letter-journal he wrote for his fiancée Marie Krackowizer, who was then living in New York, 'As you see, my Marie, I am now truly just like an Eskimo; I live like them, hunt with them, and count myself among the men of Anarnitung [an Inuit winter settlement]. Moreover I scarcely eat any European foodstuffs any longer but am living entirely on seal meat and coffee' (see text, FB/MK, 15 February 1884; see Cole 1983; Cole and Müller-Wille 1984:54). Boas viewed himself as being integrated and accepted as a 'participant observer' within Inuit society in order to learn to understand their cultural expressions and philosophy of life.

Although Boas stayed frequently at the Scottish whaling station at Kekerten (which he used as his operational base) between mid-September 1883 and early May 1884, he and Wilhelm Weike spent the bulk of the year living 'like an Inuk' with the Inuit in snow house and tent camps while travelling around Cumberland Sound and the west shore of Davis Strait. Franz Boas was very anxious to be accepted by the Inuit, even though he had trouble and difficulties with the language and logistics (for example, sledging, buying dogs, procuring caribou skins and seal meat) and even though, in the minds of the Inuit, he was linked to the spread of diphtheria and influenza, which had been brought in by the whalers shortly before. His journals contain much proof of this connection. After some adaptation and a certain amount of effort, Boas came to respect the lifestyle of the Inuit, whom he saw personally as partners. As he noted, 'Eskimos are far from being uncivilized' (FB/parents, sisters, 3 October 1883), an early expression of his cultural relativism, which only later bore fruit in his publications and teachings. On the other hand, one cannot deny that Boas achieved his access to people, services, and places, as well as obtaining dogs and data, through the incentive and even pressure tactics of offering and withholding payments and 'trade goods' such as rifles, ammunition, knives, tobacco, and foodstuffs, which he used extensively for this purpose. As a generous gesture after his return to Germany, Boas arranged through the Scottish whaling company that thirty pounds of tobacco be sent to James Mutch at Kekerten to be distributed to all his Inuit acquaintances so that they would not forget him (Crawford Noble/FB, 7 and 19 July 1885, Dundee/Minden, in Boas 1972).

Journals and Letters, 1882–1884: The Source Material

Franz Boas's journals, records, and letters, as well as excerpts from Wilhelm Weike's diary, written both before and during their one-year expedition (1883–4) among the Inuit of the Canadian Arctic, are published here in English translation as completely as was feasible, apart from passages of a purely private nature, which have been excluded. These documents represent a testimonial to Boas's developing research initiatives in geography and ethnology (anthropology) and are also a reflection of his working methods and his relations with the Inuit and other residents of southern Baffin Island. A few limited extracts from these records have been published earlier in English and German (Cole 1983; Müller-Wille 1992). This publication includes the records which Boas himself considered journals *sensu stricto*, as well his personal letters, which were in fact an extension of his journals; they thus form the corpus of 'journals and letters' as described below.

Franz Boas's personal notes and publications on the Inuit of the Arctic are very extensive. During his stay in Baffin Island (for details, see Cole and Müller-Wille 1984; Knötsch 1992a, b, c; Müller-Wille 1983a, 1992, 1994), Boas kept a variety of journals and notebooks, field journals, itineraries, catalogues of ethnographic collections, and letter-journals, which he called his data books (FB/MK, 24 February 1884). In addition, he made numerous maps and sketches. He took a total of forty-eight photographs (glass plates) between 27 June 1883 and 30 April 1884, of which only one-third have survived, owing to poor developing techniques and to Boas's ineptitude in photographic matters. Seven of these plates are published in this volume.

In total, the manuscript material of Boas's 1883–4 writings housed in his professional and private bequest at the American Philosophical Soci-

ety embraces 200,000 words. Boas was obsessed with safeguarding his journals, letters, and notes. He produced copies of almost everything he wrote. Thus, the material in his bequest is as complete as it can be. Furthermore, his early correspondence concerning his stay with the Inuit in Baffin Island is scattered in many places and has turned up in archives in Germany, Denmark, and the United States.

Since, for reasons of safety, Boas copied most of his records during his sojourn in the Arctic, one cannot always be sure when and where he made the original entries. The conditions under which he wrote were often extreme; for example, he had to thaw his ink to be able to write his journal in his sleeping bag in an igloo or to note down long lists of numbers for topographical surveys and determinations of positions on the sea ice during his extended journeys in Cumberland Sound at temperatures that dropped to −48°c. The security and warmth of the Scottish whaling station at Kekerten with the affable James Mutch – a Scot who was married to an Inuk and was fluent in Inuktitut – represented a pleasant change and a welcome haven.

The texts edited here were taken either direct from the originals, which I examined and transcribed in the archives I visited, or from microfilms or photocopies provided by the archives. The transcriptions were edited only when absolutely necessary, and this is always noted in the text. In this edition, the source of each text is precisely identified by a code in brackets (see below) at the beginning of each item. This was deemed essential in order to distinguish the various layers of journal entries and their exact location in the complex of handwritten material that has survived in the Boas papers.

American Philosophical Society (APS)
105 South Fifth Street, Philadelphia, PA 19106-3386

The APS holds in its manuscript collections the Franz Boas Papers, including personal and professional material given to the APS by the heirs of Franz Boas in the late 1940s. This collection contains a wealth of original material. The documents, photos, sketches, and maps are published here with the express permission of the American Philosophical Society as granted in letters of 14 November 1983 and 21 February 1984 (Stephen Catlett) and 9 December 1993 and 12 January 1994 (Beth Carroll Horrocks). The society's literary copyright to these texts will not be influenced by this publication.

Franz Boas Family Papers [APS:FBFP],
Files B:B61p and B:B61.5 (microfilm 1445)

FRANZ BOAS [FB], DIARIES, JOURNALS, AND ITINERARIES

[BN]
First black notebook, 20 June – 15 August, 28 August – 9 September,
19 September – 14 October 1883, and 13 March 1884 (black hardcover,
10 × 16 cm)

[Notebook]
Second black notebook, 16 July – 14 August, 28 August – 4 September
1883, 19 September 1883–2 February 1884 (black hardcover, 10 × 16 cm).

[D]
First diary with printed dates, two days per page, divided by a line,
28 March – 5 April, 28–9 May, 2–20 June, 4–8 September, 3–4 and
15–17 October 1883, 1–11 January, 7–12 February, 11–20 March, and
6 May – 5 June 1884 (black hardcover, 10 × 16 cm).

[D2]
Second diary with printed dates, two days per page, divided by a line,
1 January – 25 April, 6 May – 24 July, and 27 July – 30 August 1884 (black
hardcover, 10 × 16 cm)

WILHELM WEIKE [WW], DIARY

[WW]
Diary, 10 June 1883 – 1 September 1884 (originally bound, now a collection of loose sheets, 17 × 20 cm, 445 pages; fair copy of the original diary
with possible corrections copied in German script for Franz Boas in
1885–6 in Berlin)
    Wilhelm Weike, Franz Boas's servant in 1883–4 (born 28 November
1859, died in Berlin in early June 1917) kept his diary daily with only a
few breaks. The original was probably retained by Weike, but his
bequest could not be traced in Berlin, where he moved in 1886 with
Boas's parents and sister Antonie (Boas) Wohlauer. He was married to
Mathilde Nolting in Minden in 1885; they did not have any children
(FB/James Mutch, 26 July 1917, Bolton Landing/Peterhead, in Boas
1972).

FRANZ BOAS, LETTERS

[FB/parents, sisters]
Franz Boas to his parents, father Meyer Boas (born 10 November 1823 in Minden, died 21 February 1899 in Berlin) and mother Sophie (Jette) Boas, née Meyer (born 12 July 1828 in Minden, died 12 July 1916 in Berlin), and to his three sisters, the eldest Antonie (Toni) (born 12 July 1854 in Minden, died *ca* 1932 in Germany; married Wohlauer), Hedwig (Hete) (born 16 May 1863 in Minden, died 2 October 1949 in the United States; married Richard Lehmann), and Anna Margaret (Aenne) (born 21 August 1867 in Minden, emigrated to Brazil between 1935 and 1937, died in Rio de Janeiro 26 September 1946; married Urbach), in Minden i.W., 12 May 1882 – 20 September 1884 (notebooks perforated down the left side, 16 × 20 cm)

In these sporadically written letters, which he called 'polar letters' written by 'your polar bear' (FB/parents, sisters, 25 November 1883), Boas covered events from time to time.

[FB/MK]
Franz Boas to his fiancée, Marie Anna Ernestina Krackowizer of New York (born 3 August 1861, died 16 December 1929 in New York), living in Stuttgart 1881–3; engaged 28 May 1883 in Germany, and married 10 March 1887 in New York; letters between 27 April 1883 and 12 September 1884, with only a few gaps (copy pads, 8.5 × 17.5 cm, perforated down the left side, collections of loose sheets)

These private letters, which Boas wrote fairly regularly, also served as a field diary from mid-December 1883. For Boas these letters became the most important mental refuge during his arctic sojourn; he expressed his inner feelings in them (Cole 1983).

During his absence from Germany, Boas was able to send or receive letters only a few times. Before the winter of 1883–4, this occurred on 22 June 1883 off Heligoland via the pilot boat and on 27 June in Pentland Firth off the island of Stroma via a fishing boat; he sent letters on 16 September direct to Hamburg with the *Germania* and on 3 October with the *Catherine* via Dundee (Scotland) to Minden i.W. and to New York. After wintering, he dispatched material with whalers via Scotland to Germany on 27 August 1884, and on 8 and 21 September 1884 he sent letters and telegrams from St John's and New York. He delivered the letter-journals for his fiancée to her personally on 23 September 1884,

after his arrival in New York, at Lake George in upstate New York, where the Krackowizer family had its summer home.

Boas Professional Papers [APS:BPP]

The following letters, which are also published here, are from Boas's scholarly bequest at the APS (see also Boas 1972):

FB/Abraham Jacobi, 26 November 1882
Moritz Lindeman/FB, 21 December 1882
Paul Hegemann/FB, 20 February 1883
Crawford Noble/FB, 12 May 1883

Boas Print Collection [APS:PC]

FRANZ BOAS PRINT COLLECTION, B:B61, NO. 1–34

Photos and reproductions of Boas's family, of his stay in Baffin Island, and from his professional career (*ca* 1865–1942). There are sixteen plates (dated July–October 1883) of varying quality in the collection; seven of them are published here.

Bundesamt für Seeschiffahrt und Hydrographie (BSH)
Bibliothek, Postfach 30 12 30, D-20305 Hamburg, Germany. (Formerly Deutsche Seewarte, then Deutsches Hydrographisches Institut und Bundesamt für Schiffsvermessung)

Documents of the International Polar Commission and the German Polar Commission (DPK = Deutsche Polar-Kommission) and the stations of the northern, Labrador, and southern expeditions within the framework of the International Polar Year 1882–3 (Müller-Wille 1983b). Publication of the archival material from the original documents is by express approval of the BSH as per letter of 19 January 1994 and 20 May 1997 (Ingrid Koslowski).

[BSH:DPK]

Deutsche Polar-Kommission, Northern Expedition, K'ingua Station, Cumberland Sound

No. 289. Station journal of the German Polar Commission at K'ingua Fiord, Cumberland, kept by the station director, Dr Wilhelm Giese, 24 April – 16 October 1883; entries for 30 August and 7–16 September 1883 are published here.

12J. Documents pertaining to the affairs of Dr Boas, arranged by the president of the German Polar Commission, Professor Georg von Neumayer; 24 May 1883 – 6 November 1885.

Transcribing and Editing the Texts

I transcribed the manuscript texts from the original or from microfilms and photocopies at the APS in Philadelphia (August 1983); at St Lambert, Québec (July–September 1983, December 1989, October–November 1992, August 1993, December 1993 – January 1994, and June–July 1994); at Dartmouth College, Hanover, New Hampshire (summer 1989); and at the University of Colorado, Boulder (July 1997). In May 1997, in preparation for the English edition, I transcribed some additional texts from Weike's diary. Boas used predominantly the Roman script but with remnant influences of the German Gothic script. Some short sections of his records, mainly in the notebooks and collection catalogues, are written in shorthand, which he had learned in the mid-1870s. These sections were not deciphered, since they did not form part of the journals and letters. Boas wrote his entries in both pencil and ink. With the exception of a very few words, all the texts could be transcribed. All the other sources (Weike's diary, the Deutsche Polar-Kommission material, etc.), were written in German script.

The dominant principle adopted for the transcription was to maintain the text exactly as it was composed and written. Words underlined by Boas are shown here in italics. Boas went through the Prussian school system between 1864 and 1877 – in other words, years before the Prussian (German) orthography reforms, which were finally enacted in 1902. His manner of writing and punctuation, in some cases extremely idiosyncratic, as well as some grammatical errors have been faithfully reproduced here. Spelling and grammar have been corrected and commas introduced only where absolutely necessary; these instances are identified by square brackets. Since Boas hardly ever used paragraphs in his journals, I have introduced them for greater ease of understanding and to maintain the flow.

While sifting through the material, I discovered that Boas kept journals and letters that were parallel to each other or were copied from one to another daily or after a certain time for safety's sake. Thus, there emerged several strata of entries, which frequently are precise repetitions, though in other cases they diverge markedly from one another. Hence, I have compared all the texts that can be considered as journals *sensu stricto* (see the above list), and I have identified all the passages that complement one another chronologically and in terms of events and information, including Weike's diary. Some repetition has therefore been inevitable. I also looked through the other collections of material, such as notebooks, collection catalogues, his 'Ethnographic Book,' and lists of words and names, which also are located in the Boas bequest; they are cited in only a few cases as a source of information (for example, in the case of personal names).

The corpus of the 'journals' thus identified has been transcribed and compared by me in strict chronological sequence. The resultant text represents chronologically all the entries that Boas and/or Weike wrote during their stay in the Arctic. It consists of the following:

1 From the Franz Boas Family Papers: [Notebook], [BN], [D], and [D2], then [FB/parents, sisters], [FB/MK] and finally [WW]. The first four sources may be seen as the professional journals. The letter-journals and Weike's diaries are, by contrast, of a purely private nature, except when Boas mixed both journals and letters to his fiancée, as in December 1883.

   The [FB/MK] correspondence is the longest document; Boas wrote almost one-third of it during the voyage from Hamburg to Baffin Island. Here, just as in the letters to his parents and sisters, passages have been excluded which contain personal remarks and amorous comments and which in my opinion ought not to be published here in view of their intimate nature. These passages are clearly identified in the text.

2 Sections from Weike's journal [WW] were used to expand the text for the days when Boas did not make any entry or where the information in Weike's journal was lacking in Boas's. Weike's journal consists of 445 closely written pages (*ca* 50,000 words); hence, for reasons of space, no attempt was made to publish it in full here, though this is certainly a task that ought to be tackled at a later date as the interest in Weike's perspective increases (Gieseking 1997).

3 From the Boas Professional Papers: After perusing the professional cor-

respondence, I selected certain letters that related to Boas's research plans and the field research, and I have inserted them chronologically into the text.

4 From the archival material of the Deutsche Polar-Kommission: This section includes extracts from the station journal of the German Polar Station at K'ingua and from relevant correspondence that is to be seen as augmenting Boas's entries in order to convey the course of events from the viewpoint of the German Polar Station.

The date and day of the week of each journal entry and letter are always noted in full. In this connection, the date has been retained in its original rendering throughout and, where necessary, expanded to its full form in brackets. For the sake of clarity, the text has been visibly divided into months and days; each day is identified by a new heading and the date and day emphasized in bold type. In addition, the text has been broken up into chapters whose headings relate to trips, locations, and major events. My aim here was to facilitate easier access to the chronological sequence of events and the geographical location during Boas's stay on Baffin Island. Inserted after some of the headings and occasionally between the entries are my own explanatory comments, which are given in italics in order to distinguish them from the text.

Various symbols and abbreviations are used in the text in order to make the original source more explicit; glossaries and lists at the end of the book contain further elucidations of words and names, including those of dogs, ships, and boats. The exact sources are identified in brackets. For letters, the sequence is sender slash recipient; place sent from slash place received in; date of letter.

[text]	Information, translations, expansions of the text, explanations and elucidations provided by the editor [LMW] or translator in English [WB]. These sections are not part of the original text.
[D: .. text]	Inserted text derived from the source specified
[place name]	As rendered by Boas (1885:90–5)
[proper name]	As rendered by Boas (1885, 1894)
[I. *nuna* = land]	Inuktitut word or sentence in italics, spelling after Schneider 1985 or, when identified by Boas after his published Inuktitut word list (Boas 1894), with English translation (see glossary)
{text}	Text stroked out in the original by Boas

.. text ..	Text beginning or ending in mid-sentence, or trans-posed
(...)	Original text passages not transcribed
...	Illegible passages
[?]	Unclear, undocumented, or unverifiable information

Particular attention was paid to personal names and place names included in the original text. These are European (predominantly English) and Inuktitut names, which Boas and also Weike often rendered in varying versions; here they are all presented faithfully in their original variations. It should be noted that Boas transcribed Inuktitut names (and also some English and Scottish names) phonetically, just as he heard them. It was only at the end and after completion of his investigations that he standardized the spelling of Inuktitut, which he adapted to the official Greenlandic orthography at that time on the advice of Hinrich J. Rink (see Boas 1885, 1894).

The European proper names were easy to identify and verify, but substantial difficulties arose with the proper names of the Inuit, since Boas used interchangeably both the indigenous name and the English names which the whalers used for some of the Inuit as substitutes and nicknames. By comparing the different sources, I was able to find in most cases the Inuktitut and English names for each individual Inuk, though some English nicknames for the Inuit could not be matched with Inuit names. Boas's Inuktitut vocabulary, in which he published a total of 274 proper names (Boas 1894), served as a source and guideline. The names taken from this list are printed here in square brackets in the text and are connected with the names used in the original.

All the English and Inuktitut place names used by Boas are also faithfully recorded in their variations and have been located and identified on the basis of the place name index and the map (Boas 1885:90–5, plate 1). The Inuktitut and English names given in square brackets in the text and index come from that publication; the letter x used here by Boas is equivalent to the German *ch*-sound, or in today's standardized Inuit orthography a *q*. In *The Central Eskimo* (1888) the spelling was changed, again creating considerable orthographic confusion for the writing of Inuit place names derived from Boas's surveys. Further information on place names has been taken from other available sources (Goldring 1985; Goldring et al. 1984; Müller-Wille and Weber Müller-Wille 1984).

The Inuktitut name of both the American and Scottish whaling stations, bastardized by the whalers as Kekerten, Kickerton, or Kikastan

(1. *qikirtaq, qikirtait* = island, islands), referred to the island on which the stations were built, the stations themselves, and the surrounding archipelago. Over quite a long period, Boas inexplicably wrote this name variously (and in parallel) in his records as either Kikkerton or Kikkerten; he eventually decided on the first of these forms and later opted for K'exerten in the map and the list of place names (1885).

Boas used a large number of abbreviations in his German writings. In the English version these are generaly spelled out unless they are commonly recognizable as standard abbreviations. Boas used both standard metric German and British Imperial measurements; where necessary, they are explained.

Franz Boas and the Inuit Today

Boas's early ethnological-geographical research among the Inuit of Baffin Island has become the foundation of modern Inuit anthropology, to which Inuit and other researchers repeatedly refer. Boas's publications represent an extraordinary and enduring contribution to the analysis of cultural development and change in a particular physical environment. Hence, it is not surprising that Boas's writings are still studied and evaluated in arctic social sciences, even though he occupied himself with the Inuit for only the first third of his long scientific career, which lasted more than sixty years. In the current social and political climate of relations between aboriginal peoples and outsiders' interests in their lands, the significance of Boas's legacy is that respect must be paid to cultural distinctness and differences, to the position of minorities, and above all to the equality of races, whether they be Jews, Germans, or Inuit, in order to uphold, maintain, and enhance common human rights.

The Inuit of southern Baffin Island have seen many changes during the last 150 years. Waves of outsiders – whalers, missionaries, government officials, scientists of various types, international if ephemeral tourists, and an increasing number of *qallunaat* who have become permanent residents in 'Inuit land,' Nunavut – have come, gone, stayed, and left their traces. When Boas and Weike sailed into Pangnirtung Fiord in early October 1883, their Inuit guides – Ssigna (also Jimmy), Utütiak (Yankee), and Nachojaschi – hardly knew the area and knew only a few place names. At that time Pangnirtung, the small promontory dotted with prehistoric sites jutting into the fiord, was apparently not often frequented by local Inuit. Today, after a varied history of some seventy years of human settlement starting with the *qallunaat*'s interests in the early 1920s, Pangnirtung is a densely populated, technologically very modern living space for more than 1,200 people, Inuit and *qallunaat* alike, crowded into a spatially limited residential area that is split by the indispensable airstrip. By contrast, the Kekerten Islands, which were the centre of population and activity in Cumberland Sound as Boas saw it in the 1880s, are today a national historic site preserving the remnants of the cultural contact that Inuit and whalers, as well as external scientists, shared for a brief period (Northwest Territories n.d; Stevenson 1997). The following texts written by Franz Boas and Wilhelm Weike are a testimony to the events of this particular period in the history of relations between Inuit and *qallunaat* as seen from the outside. They provide, albeit to a limited extent, some insight into the conditions and circumstances of the Inuit.

(Introduction translated by William Barr; revised and adapted for the English version by the author in May–August 1997)

Abbreviations

APS	American Philosophical Society
BN	first black notebook
BPP	Boas Professional Papers
BSH	Bundesamt für Seeschiffahrt und Hydrographie
BT	*Berliner Tageblatt*
D	first diary
D2	second diary
DPK	Deutsche Polar-Kommission
E	English
FB	Franz Boas
FBFP	Franz Boas Family Papers
G	German
I	Inuktitut
LMW	Ludger Müller-Wille, editor
MK	Marie Krackowizer
Notebook	second black notebook
PC	Boas Print Collection
WB	William Barr, translator
WW	Wilhelm Weike's diary

JOURNALS AND LETTERS

May 1882 – September 1884

Period of Preparation in Germany, 1882–1883

Formulating and Securing the Research Plans

Boas's plans and preparations for his research trip to the Inuit of Baffin Island can be clearly deciphered in the letters he wrote or received prior to his stay in the Canadian Arctic, from the fall of 1882 onwards. The following represent only a small selection, but they give an overview of the extensive and complex preparations that Boas undertook.

[FB/sisters; Minden/Paris; while serving as a one-year conscript, Boas complains of the inaction in the military and is counting the days to his discharge.]
[**14 May 1882**]   (...) The only thing is that from time to time I can read something about *my* Eskimos, and take notes on them. (...)

[APS:BPP, FB/Abraham Jacobi (a doctor, married to Boas's mother's sister); Berlin/New York]
26 November 1882   (...) In the event that you remember my last letters and our conversations from the summer before last [1881], you already know that my research plans have become quite definite. Currently I intend a project which certainly entirely fits my general train of thought, but which at the same time will serve me as my habilitation thesis. Specifically I am investigating the migrations of the Eskimo and their knowledge of the country they inhabit, and of nearby regions, in the hope of being able to demonstrate a precise interconnection between the size of the groups, the distribution of foodstuffs and the natural environment. I shall be publishing minor collections of material over the course of the winter in the *Zeitschrift der Gesellschaft für Erdkunde zu Berlin* [Boas 1883a, b], and will send them to you in due course. (...)

My most determined wishes are directed towards the American polar regions[,] and as far as is possible, I am very well equipped for this. I am completely conversant with the literature on these regions, as the minor works that will appear in the next few months will reveal [see above]. In addition I am learning everything here that is necessary for scientific trips and finally, the main aspect as far as I am concerned, I am learning the Eskimo language, and have already made relatively good progress. If I actually succeed in getting there, my main research area will be the migrations of the Eskimo.

I am now making great efforts here to interest the appropriate circles in my project; here I have got to know [Rudolf von] Virchow, [Adolf] Bastian and other influential personalities; I am in contact with a gentleman in Bremen [Moritz Lindeman] and another in Copenhagen [Henry Rink], who are authorities in this area, and have made contact with the Scottish whalers [with Crawford Noble of Dundee]. In addition I shall attempt to take advantage of the experiences of two New York residents E. [Emil] Bessels [from Heidelberg] and [Heinrich] Klutschak [from Prague] (two Germans), but I do not have their addresses yet. Naturally I do not yet know whether my efforts will produce practical successes; but there is interest in my studies. Precisely because I have these goals so strongly in mind, I would very much have liked to be over there, since I know that the interest in the American North is at present very strong there.

I have developed my plans to such an extent that I can tell you them exactly. On the W. [west] side of Davis Strait, i.e. opposite Greenland, Baffin Island [I. *Qikirtaaluk* = big island] extends to about 74°N. On the west coast [actually northeast coast, WB] of the island, at about 73°N lie Ponds Inlet [Torsuxateng] and Eclipse Sound [Tununirn]. Here there is the Eskimo settlement of Kaparoktolik [K'aparoktelling], whose occupants make trading trips overland every year to Igloolik [Igdlulik], a settlement on Fury and Hecla Strait (70°N; 80°W from Gr. [Greenwich]). The local Eskimos are familiar with the unknown east shore of Foxe Channel to about 60°N 75°W, and this area is also visited by the Inuit of Cumberland Sound [Tinixdjuarbing]. Hence if one entirely adapts to the Eskimo lifestyle, as [Charles F.] Hall and [Frederick] Schwatka did, it is possible without any difficulty to cover this stretch [with or without Inuit accompaniment]. The cost is really the critical factor.

I have made the calculations and find that I can definitely do everything for $500–600. I will spend $175 on astronomical instruments and chronometers, $175 on rifles and ammunition, $100 on emergency supplies and trade goods, $25 for building a sledge. The latter items are perhaps not necessary at all. Total $475. I am estimating that the remainder will be needed for such costly items as clothing, my passage etc. It depends on whether I succeed in prevailing on the owners of a whaling ship to provide me with transport very cheaply. From here I would have the opportunity of getting there for next to nothing with the government ship [*Germania*] which is evacuating our polar station from Cumberland Sound. But there is also an expedition ship going north from your side too [first *Alhambra* then *Proteus*; Barr 1985][;] it will be taking provisions for the station at Lady Franklin Bay [under Adolphus Greeley], and can possibly put me ashore at a suitable spot.

Perhaps you have connections with the American Geographical Society, and perhaps can greatly help me, since its patronage would as good as guarantee success for my plan. Thus, via this society Hall and Schwatka received from private individuals in a very short time almost everything they needed for their travels, and Schwatka needed, moreover, not quite $500. Given the limited funds (by comparison to their needs) which I require, this would naturally be much easier. If at all possible, please try to do what you can for me. (...)

I hope to achieve quite a lot through this trip, apart from the scientific success that I have promised myself; in that due to it I would immediately be accepted among geographical circles and in demand to contribute a word with regard to polar research as a practically experienced traveller, while I wish to interest the ruling societies in the research method that I have in mind, as being the only means whereby these fairly great areas can be thoroughly studied without major cost or danger, and if several such travellers are travelling at the same time[,] our knowledge of meteorology, magnetic conditions and hydrography will be better furthered than by expensive expeditions.

Finally may I also ask you not to relay anything about this to my parents and sisters, since they would be unnecessarily alarmed. (...)

[APS:BPP, Moritz Lindeman (patron of German polar voyages)/FB; Bremen/Berlin]
21 December 1882 (...) It is very gratifying that your voyage is financially assured! *But stay with the Germania.* The whalers *all* cruise the coast 'off shore.' One cannot count on them coming close enough to land to be able to land someone. You might possibly cruise around for the entire summer aboard a whaler, even if the whalers were to take a passenger. I would greatly doubt it, but if so, you would probably have to pay a *consider-*

able price. At the same time there would be *no question* of any obligation to land the passenger at any specific time. The British whaling fleet sails from Dundee. (...)

[FB/parents; Berlin/Minden]
13 1 83 (...) You can now indulge yourselves in the thought that I shall be going away in any case. I have applied first to the German Polar Commission, in order to reach the German station directly, which I might use as a good refuge and starting point. Bastian has applied to them for me, and I hope I shall soon get a reply as to the ship's sailing time and much else. (...)

Last night I dreamed I had become engaged and that my fiancée did not want to let me go north to the Eskimos at all; this threw me into the most unpleasant mood!! (...)

23 1 1883 (...) You must certainly be curious to learn whence I shall be getting some money. My sources are as follows. Last Friday I very impertinently wrote a letter with the following content to Herr Rudolf Mosse, owner of the *Berliner Tageblatt.* I presented my plan to him and requested 2500 marks for the trip, from which I promised him reports. I drew his attention to the fact that I was offering him for a minuscule sum (what effrontery!) the advantages which the *New York Herald* had derived from [Henry Morton] Stanley [the African traveller] for a great outlay of money and time, and that my journey would cause a sensation in every way, since through it the last still-unknown coastal areas of Arctic America would be identified, and since, moreover the type of travel would be unusual (Further shamelessness!). Then I boasted of my contacts and asked for a reply. Immediately a letter arrived on the Saturday from the editor-in-chief Dr. A. Levysohn, who summoned me for an interview for yesterday; in particular he wanted to know more detail about the 'scientific patrons' of my enterprise. Since I could not attend an interview yesterday, I wrote to him and made an appointment for today. There I learned that Herr Mosse would probably be inclined to agree to my proposal; he simply wanted to know how I would prepare myself and wanted to know my contacts. (...)

They would now like just a short article from me in the form of an essay which I shall make as elegant and popular as possible. I now have almost no doubt but that I will get the money. This afternoon I shall start on the article, the arrival of a ship at an Eskimo village, with the colour laid on thick. (...)

On 2 February 1883 Boas concluded a preliminary contract with the Berliner Tageblatt (BT). *For the sum of 3,000 reichsmarks, underwritten by his father, he was obliged, after three trial pieces on recent developments in German geography and the discovery of the Northwest Passage, to send* BT *a total of fifteen articles on his researches among the Inuit in the Arctic; these would be published exclusively in* BT *between August 1883 and April 1885 (see complete listing in Müller-Wille 1984). Thereby his expedition was financially secure.*

[APS:BPP, Paul Hegemann (captain on the Second German North Pole Voyage, 1869–70)/FB; Hamburg/Berlin]
20 2 1883   (...) On behalf of Capt. Mahlstedt [Mahlstede of the *Germania*] I am to inform you, that an Eskimo receives 32 lbs of ship's biscuit, 1 gallon of molasses, 2 lbs coffee and 12 oz. of tobacco as payment for 4 weeks. (...)

The Third German Geographers' Conference in Frankfurt a. M.

With his entry of 28 March 1883, Boas began his variously handled diaries, correspondence, journals, itineraries, and notebooks, which he continued until 20 September 1884, shortly before reaching New York.

[D]
[28 March] Wednesday   Left for Frankfurt at 7. Did not meet up with Müller in Göttingen at noon. Travelled on; went to bed in the evening here [Frankfurt, WB] too tired to go to the meeting.

[29 March] Thursday   Opening of the [Third German] Geographers' Conference. At the executive meeting. [Friedrich] Ratzel's lecture on the polar regions [Ratzel 1883]. Much to write for the [*Berliner*] *Tageblatt.* In the evening attended a dinner at the Zoological Garden. Boring. Met the Gotha gentlemen [from the Justus Perthes publishing house] as well as Müller-Beeck from Berlin. Otherwise I knew nobody. Got to know a teacher from Jena. Viewed an exhibition. Interesting.

[30 March] Friday   Terrible sessions, awfully much to write. In the palm garden in the evening. [Hermann von] Wissmann was there. Got to know [Alfred] Kirchhoff Halle, and some other uninteresting people. Spoke to Breusing Bremen and [Otto] Finsch. Quite a fine evening.

[**31 March**] **Saturday**   Frankfurt, Geographers' Conference. Munich chosen for the site of the conference for 1884. Lecture by [Richard] Lehmann on knowledge of the German Fatherland. Make an attempt to establish a [geographical] society in Minden? [Albrecht] Penck. Influence of water on the earth's surface. Hühl spoke, but superficially. Müller-Beeck spoke. At noon again went to see the director from Trier. The Pariser Hof. Before that travelled around with Cram who was ill. In the afternoon I reported to Berlin [to the *Berliner Tageblatt*] for the last time, thank God! Thus I had no time to go to the theatre for the special performance. Wissmann's lecture.

Logistical Preparations for the Sojourn in the Arctic

On 1 April Franz Boas paid a formal call on Marie Krackowizer's mother in Stuttgart. On 2 April he visited Perthes' cartographic establishment in Gotha: 'Soon finished, since not much there.' Then he travelled via Jena and Weimar to Berlin and back to Minden. On 28 May in Minden, 'in the arbour' in his parents' garden, he received a letter from Marie Krackowizer in Stuttgart in which she accepted his proposal of marriage. Previously, on 27 April 1883, he had formulated for Marie – 'Estimable young lady!' – his expedition and research plans with an accompanying map.

[FB/MK; Minden/Stuttgart]
[**27 April 1883**]   (...) Today I am keeping my promise, in that I am sending you a map of the area through which I will be travelling, as well as a short sketch of my intended journeys. You must not think that in reality I shall follow this plan exactly. If I see that some part of the trip is impracticable, or that another is more rewarding than the one intended now, I will undoubtedly adapt it to the changed circumstances. I am also pondering a great deal as to whether it is not advisable to abandon the second trip completely, and rather to spend the time on a careful exploration of Cumberland Sound. In any case what I am sending you is the plan of the trip as far as I can judge at present.

One thing, which I have not been able to state publicly and which I am happy to share with you, is the purpose my trip represents for me scientifically, since I am afraid that otherwise you might conclude from the entire enterprise that I am an adventurous spirit, when in fact I am not. The material I want to collect up there, which will mainly pertain to the migration areas and routes of the [Inuit] bands, will provide me with a basis for an investigation of the dependence of the peoples' migration areas on natural boundaries; this in turn will be only a preliminary study for general questions from the area of peoples' lives, and thus the results of this trip will be of the highest significance. (...)

I have selected Cumberland Sound as the starting point for the trip I shall be undertaking in the coming summer.

The shores of this bay are occupied by an Eskimo band that totals about 400 people [in 1883–4 Boas counted 245 Inuit; see Boas 1885:70, 1888:426]. These admittedly do not live in permanent settlements, but they assemble every winter at some stations at which some families stay all year. The largest of these at present are Kikkerton [K'exerten], Neianta-lik [Naujateling] and Nugumiut. Whereas in winter the Eskimos catch mainly seals, in summer they move up the large fiords to hunt caribou, shoot birds and catch salmon. They then penetrate into the interior as far as Lake Kennedy [Nettilling], which is distinguished by its fish and game resources. Occasionally they make trading trips along the west coast of Baffin Island as far as Iglulik. In addition Cumberland Sound is now used very widely by Scottish and American whalers; they generally begin the spring fishery off the entrance of the Sound in May, then they sail north and return in the fall for a second fishery. Some of these ships, especially Americans, winter on the southwest shore of the sound in order to be on hand for the spring fishery when the ice still denies the ships access. On one of the islands in the Sound, Kikkerton, opposite Irvine Inlet [Nettil-ling], is located a Scottish whaling station, whose personnel are perma-nent residents. In the innermost arm, Kingawa [K'ingua] Fiord a German polar station is in operation at present, one of the circumpolar stations established for the year 1882–83; these have primarily been carry-ing out meteorological and magnetic observations.

While I shall be relying on these contacts, I propose to follow the fol-lowing travel schedule, although naturally it will be subject to probable changes and adaptations depending on circumstances obtaining on the spot.

On about 20 June I shall leave Hamburg on board *Germania*, Captain Mahlstede, in order to travel to Kingawa. *Germania* belongs to the Ger-man Polar Commission and is heading over there to evacuate the seven scientists and their 4 servants who comprise the station staff. On her out-ward voyage the ship will call at Kikkerton; there, backed by recommen-dations from the owner [Crawford Noble] of the Scottish station, I shall secure the help of the resident personnel and hire some Eskimos for my further researches. I will travel with them to Kingawa, where I shall take over the station buildings and the inventory, instruments etc. and will unload my own things. My companion, Herr [Leutnant Graf] von der Goltz will stay at Kingawa and will receive precise instructions from me as to what he should do. [The lieutenant, whose first name could not be established, resigned shortly afterwards for unexplained reasons. The von der Goltz were a renowned Prussian family whose many male members served in the military.]

I myself will set off with my servant Wilhelm Weicke [Weike] and the Eskimos for Lake Kennedy, from where I shall try to reach the west coast of Baffin Island; I want to try to follow this coast to Fury and Hecla Strait, on the shores of which the Iglulik band of Eskimos have their residence. From here I want to try to take an Eskimo back with me to Kingawa; he should be able to show me the shortest route to the Baffin Bay coast [the northern extension of Davis Strait] and to Kingawa.

If I stay there over winter we will make ethnographic collections and detailed studies of the language, customs and manners of the Eskimos, and make surveys in the immediate neighbourhood of Kingawa. In the spring we three, accompanied by Eskimos, will set off by the shortest route to Iglulik, where we want to stay as long as possible. From there we will try to push through to Ponds Bay [Torsuxateng] via a route regularly used by the Eskimos, in order to get to know the bands in this area too. From here we will return south along the Baffin Bay coast as fast as possible, but depending on travel conditions, so as to be at Kingawa in approximately July [1884]. We will spend the remainder of the time until the whalers sail, in Cumberland Sound, then return in fall with a whaling ship.

[FB/MK; Minden/Stuttgart]
[28 May 1883]   Dear Fräulein! (...) I shall be back in the fall of 1884, but if I do not come then, I will be coming out in the fall of 1885. If I am not back then, some accident has befallen me and you should not expect me to return. (...)

In May 1883 Boas was in correspondence with whalers in Scotland and with the German Polar Commission in Hamburg in order to secure his travel plans as well as his accommodation, equipment, and supplies in Baffin Island.

[APS:BPP, Crawford Noble (owner of the Kekerten whaling station)/FB; Aberdeen/Berlin; original in English]
12 May 1883   Doctor, I will forward your letter to Mr. James Mutch [head of the Scottish station] but we have resolved not to send away the

steamer [*Catherine*] till about the 25 July. If the Germania leaves about the 20 June the chances are that you will get to the mouth of the inlet before the ice is cleared away. Should you find a big pack it might be well for you to run across to East Greenland and remain there for a short time till the pack clears away. Some seasons you could have great difficulty in getting through the pack of the ice before the middle to end of August but it is quite possible that you may get in about end of July.

Kindly tell Mr. Mu[t]ch and also Mr. John Roach at the American station on Kickerton Island that they may be looking for our vessel about 20 August and also say to Mr. Roach that we are sending out provisions to him for his station and will bring home what produce he may have.

[BSH:DPK; FB/Georg Neumayer (president of the German Polar Commission); Hamburg]
Hamburg, **24 May 1883**   This summer I intend to make a research trip to Cumberland Sound to study the conditions of the local Eskimos and to explore the west coast of Baffin Island.

To implement this trip I am requesting the gracious support of the German Polar Commission with regard to the following points:

1. Permission to make the crossing on board *Germania* and instructions to Captain Mahlstede to advance my goals, as far as this is in accordance with the purposes for which *Germania* is being sent out.
   In addition, provision of
2. Means of transport such as a tent and sledge.
3. Two complete fur suits.
4. Equipment and materials for hunting and fishing.
5. Provisions, namely up to
   500 lb of No. 2 ship's biscuit and fine rye bread
     60 lb butter
     60 lb salt beef
     60 lb salt pork
   140 lb wheat flour, double kiln-dried
     20 lb beans, brown
     20 lb beans, white
     20 lb peas, green
     20 lbs lentils
     20 lbs pearl barley
     10 bottles vinegar
   100 lbs Austral.[ian] beef
     40 lbs mutton

>   30 lbs corned beef
>   10 bottles lemon juice
> 6. Instruments, namely
>   Artificial horizon (glass and mercury),
>   A lever watch,
>   A mercury barometer,
>   Two thermometers,
>   An aneroid barometer.

Finally I am requesting permission to keep any materials that might be useful to me, such as snow shovels, cooking equipment and household equipment.

>   Hoping for a well-disposed reply,
>
>   Yours sincerely,
>   Dr. Franz Boas

The supplies requested by Boas were those of the German Polar Station, which was wintering at the north end of Cumberland Sound in 1882–3. Although the German Polar Commission approved Boas's request for these items and arranged for them to be transferred to him, the list could not be filled in toto, as is shown by the receipt signed by Boas on 15 September 1883 (see below); Boas also received free passage for Wilhelm Weike and himself on board the Germania.

[D]

On 5 June Boas was practising revolver shooting in Minden and as a result developed a buzzing in his ears; on the sixth he was in Hannover and took care of some matters there. Back in Minden on 7 June, he received a flag from Marie on which 'Vorwärts!' (Forward!) was embroidered; it was intended for his boat, which he named Marie.

[**9 June, Sunday**]   (...) Letter to (...) Neumayer, concerning living at the Naval Observatory [in Hamburg]. To [Rudolf] Mosse [*Berliner Tageblatt*], about whether he wanted to take on the journey entirely. My idea is to make a name for myself so that, when I come back, I can enter into a relationship with the *New York Herald* so that I can marry Marie in two years. This must work out! Then after six months I *must* go to Alaska. Forward! (...)

Boas left Minden by train at 1 a.m. on 11 June, reaching Hamburg at 7 a.m., in order to make the final preparations for his expedition. He stayed at the Kronprinzen Hotel.

[11 June] **Monday**   Hamburg. Arrived here at 7 a.m. Got things in some sort of order at the Kronprinzen, then to Stücken's to see about clothes and to Rickers. My things are all here. Back to Stücken's and Bandegiet's [provision stores]. Then to *Germania*, and spoke to [Kapitän A.F.B.] Mahlstede. My things will be repacked here. To the Naval Observatory, where I have got a room. Slept at the Kronprinzen for a while, then to the Naval Observatory in order to see Professor [Neumayer] again. (...) Hegemann visited me at my room. I am dead tired and am going to bed (4 p.m). I hope I'll soon have things finished and can get home by Thursday. In the evening back home and wrote to Marie. No letter for me. In the evening went to have something to eat with Neumayer.

[12 June, **Tuesday**]   In the morning went to Ricker's to pack things. Clothes still have to be lined, and an inventory taken. Ordered a revolver. At noon on board the *Frisia* with Hegemann. Did not meet Tilly. Spoke with Neumayer early this morning. Was at the Market, ate lunch, bought stationery and in the evening was invited to Hegemann's in Eisenbüttel. Went home with Mahlstede. Letter from Marie and one from home. (...)

Boas spent Tuesday, 13 June, in Hamburg, packing.

[14 June] **Thursday**   Travelled to Kiel! Visited Streit first, then Bojos. Spent noon and afternoon with [Profesor Theobald] Fischer, who is very cordial. Visited [Profesor Benno] Erdmann, but not poor Frau Steenfedt! Well, when I come back I can make up for that (on 19 May 1884). Wrote to Marie at the station.

On Friday, 15 June, Boas travelled from Kiel to Minden via Hannover.

[16 June, **Saturday**]   Last night wrote to Marie from Hannover to overcome the difficult leave-taking. It is really hard!

Wilhelm Weike, at the instigation of Franz Boas, had begun his diary in Minden i. W. on 10 June 1883.

[WW]
It was a very warm day; our beds have all been dispatched, and the other items that were still here. Dr. Boas is travelling back to Hamburg tonight, and I shall be following later, because I still have so much to do there.

[D]

[17 June] Sunday Reached Hamburg this morning, ran around a lot and at noon went out with Neumayer to a social gathering at Rickers' estate outside Hamburg. It was his birthday. I cannot say that I feel comfortable in these circles! Naturally the company toasted me and, despite myself I also toasted Kingawa. Unfortunately I got home too late in the evening, and thus could not fetch Papa, and so he had to come with Wilhelm [Weike].

[WW]

(...) My departure from Minden became very precipitate; it was already 12 o'clock when news came that I was to come; so I first had to pack and then I still had some things to take care of in town, and all of this in a rush; it was not long before I had to leave; our friends were at the station to see me off. How beautiful the countryside looks with the splendour of flowers in the grain fields.

Monday, 18 June When one lives in a small town one has no concept of life in the big city; all the rushing about and chasing in the streets with the horse trams and other conveyances, and when one sees the commercial activity, and the trade and traffic from one house to another.

Tuesday, 19 June There was still a lot to take care of and things to haul on board; since I was already sleeping on board there was a great deal to do before I got to bed. At 8 o'clock I went with H. [Herrn] Koch [the cook Adolf Lange of the *Germania*] back to Altona; we came home very early; it was very fine.

On Board the Germania from Hamburg to Baffin Island, June – July 1883

Across the North Sea and the Atlantic

[D]
[**20 June**] **Wednesday** Farewell, my dear homeland! Dear homeland, adieu!

[BN]
20th. *Germania* is lying in the inner Jonashafen next to *Irene*, directly below the Naval Observatory. Still a great deal to take care of in the morning. On board at 11, where I met Hegemann. The group is gradually assembling: 16 men: Neumayer and Rühnecke; the people from the Astronomical Observatory, Prof. von Bernuth, Oberstleutnant [lieutenant colonel] von Arnim, Papa's escort and a friend of Neumayer. The harbour pilot guided us slowly out, towed by the tug *Helgoland*. The captain was the last to come on board. In the stream by about 1.30. The Naval Observatory over there is quite crowded. Cheers from there, the seamen's hostel and Wiener's Hotel. Had breakfast in two shifts. Beautiful trip down river; by 11 at Cuxhaven where I went ashore once again and wrote letters.

21st [June, Thursday] Neumayer's birthday. Papa left around noon. Neumayer and Rickers took me back aboard; Hegemann and Fülscher had stayed aboard. Took our leave of them at 10. Organized my cabin and unpacked some boxes. Since there is no steam tug available, and a foul wind, we are still at anchor. Went to bed early in the evening.

The departure of Boas, but with no mention of Weike by name, was duly reported in the regional newspaper Minden-Lübbecker Kreisblatt *(1883) as the fourth item under 'Local Reports' on Tuesday, 26 June 1883. The text was most likely submitted by Boas's father.*

[*Minden-Lübbecker Kreisblatt*, 26 June 1883]
Our citizen, Herr Dr. Franz Boas, began last week, accompanied only by a servant, a research trip into the arctic regions of North America lasting one and a half years to study the geographical, ethnographical and meteorological conditions of these regions not yet explored by science. A ship, equipped by the Geographical Society that will pick up the members of the meteorological station on Labrador [*sic*], will take him to his destination. Herr Dr. Boas intends to reside among the Eskimos for quite a long period and to participate in their migrations. Renowned scholars have great hopes, expecting rich scientific results from this expedition. We hope that this can be realized and that the young researcher will return safely to his home.

[BN]
22nd [June, Friday]   At 2 a.m. we weighed anchor and were towed out by the steam tug *Helgoland*. We gave the pilot some final letters. The tug towed us to off the mouth of the Elbe, then we sailed out against a foul wind on a NWerly course for 5 hours. Soon Helgoland was in sight, and we tacked off it twice. The wind is slackening; I am quite seasick. By evening we are north of Norderney; we can still see the Wangeroog light, and the mainland between Norderney and Baltrum; then we tacked and on the morning of the 23rd we were again northwest of Helgoland. Very smooth; almost flat calm. We lay working, so as not to get among the English fishing boats, a whole fleet of which are lying here. At 9.30 a.m. the waves are travelling at 5 seconds to the NNW. Calm. A slight swell perceptible from the S. Calm all day; we are drifting around northwest of Helgoland. Towards evening a light breeze from the S arose and we can make progress. At 9.30 p.m. there is a triple swell. (...)
    Around midnight Helgoland [showed] a light again. 22nd. Very quiet, but we are making progress with a favourable SW wind. A magnificent day. We caught and ate many gurnard. At 3.00 p.m. an errant butterfly came on board, the last sign of the receding land. In the morning a fishing boat was in sight. We set up observations with a sling psychrometer.

[FB/MK; first entry in the letter-diary for his fiancée, Marie Krackowizer]
23rd June 1883 [Saturday]   My dearest! Today I am starting to write my

diary for you, and first of all I have to tell you how much I love you! I am always thinking of you, my Marie[,] and wait longingly for the time I shall be with you again. I sent you my last greetings yesterday via the pilot, who left us off the mouth of the Elbe. (...)

Early yesterday morning we came in sight of Helgoland; at noon it lay before us in bright sunshine with its steep cliffs and friendly houses. In the afternoon we sailed west along the Frisian islands, and only turned back when we sighted the dunes of Norderney to the south of us around 7 o'clock. The area to leeward was alive with fishing boats, which lay before us in large numbers, and numerous ships that were heading out from the Weser or Elbe.

Sunday, 24 [June]   Today is a magnificent morning. A very light breeze is blowing from the southeast, so we are making progress in the desired direction. The water is so clear and quiet, and the air so soft and warm that it is a real joy. At midnight last night we lost sight of the light on Helgoland and thereafter there was nothing to see but water and sky. (...)

Since yesterday I have been giving Wilhelm instruction in English; I hope he will have learned something before we arrive over there. So far he is doing quite well; he is able and willing, and thus I am really satisfied with him. I am quite surprised at how well one lives here on board ship. Almost better than we landsmen are accustomed to. At 7 a.m. we have breakfast, consisting of coffee, bread and butter, beef steaks, fish, etc. At 12 noon, usually soup made from pulses and meat with potatoes; port is served with this. At 3 o'clock coffee with bread and butter; at 7 again a hot dinner, potatoes, meat, bread and butter and cold cuts with tea. This is really living well! And at the same time I am always in the open air, with the beautiful sky above, the wide sea all around me and heaven in my heart! (...)

8 p.m. I have just calculated, to my dismay, that I have only 576 sheets like this one, so I won't be able to write to you like this the whole time. But I am afraid that later it won't be as much as now. Once the work begins, or if the weather becomes stormy, I'll probably have to give up writing. (...)

How I am looking forward to reading your letters which will reach me via Aberdeen, among the Eskimos. (...)

[BN]
25 [June, Monday]   In the early morning the water was light blue. A breeze arose so that by noon we were making 5 knots and later 7. On the

Dogger Bank the water is green. The morning was overcast; clear in the afternoon. At 7 p.m. the wave length was 11 m, wave height 1 m, direction ESE magn. Course NW; speed 5½ knots. Dark green. Speed 8 seconds.

[FB/MK]

(...) I have just been teaching Wilhelm some more English. But he has a frightfully hard head, which it is difficult to get anything into. But that is not surprising since he really has never learned anything.

Today I want to describe for you something of our ship's company. First of all there is the captain [A.F.B. Mahlstede, from Bremerhaven]: an old man who has grown up with the sea. On land he was high-spirited and inclined to all sorts of pranks; loved to drink his 'icebreakers' (a sort of grog) with his companions and generally had a good time. But at the same time he never abandoned the real North German composure. If I wanted to chat with him about this or that, e.g. to ask how much the Eskimos might charge for their services, his answer would be: 'Oh, that varies.' 'Well, you can give me an approximate amount, surely.' 'Ooh, one can't say exactly.' 'How much do they ask for a dog, say?' 'Oh, sometimes they're quite cheap.' And I had to chat to him for probably two hours in order to get any information.

Here at sea he is quite different. He doesn't drink a drop and concentrates entirely on his ship. He is always quiet and calm, but one can see how purposeful he is about everything. I shall never forget seeing him sleeping yesterday. His weathered face, framed by a long grey-blond beard, the complete picture of an old sea wolf, which is what they call him in Hamburg. I would trust his word entirely.

The mate [Wilhelm Wenke from Bettingbühren, Amt Elsfleth] is quite different: a genial young man of about 32–33. He too has the quiet, calm seaman's manner and if the three of us are sitting at table together, we sometimes sit so quietly that not a single word is exchanged. One instinctively behaves around people as they generally behave, and when I see a seaman it seems quite normal to me to keep quiet for half an hour before speaking to him. The mate is pleasant in every way. He shows and explains everything to me; brings to my attention any oddities, for which seafarers have a superb eye; in short he shows me just what I can only wish for.

In addition there are two young seamen on board [Anton Andresen from Sweden and Wilhelm Wincke from Rostock], a carpenter [F. Carl Johansen from Kiel] and a cook [Adolf Lange from Magdeburg], and we two passengers. I eat with the captain and the mate. (...)

What I am doing now is far from being optimal. For the sake of a scientific idea that I favour, I am rushing away from everybody to bury myself with messieurs les Esquimaux, but science alone is not the most beloved thing in life! Oh! I see myself sitting in the middle of chatting to you and would like to stay for a long time; you are the only reason for this. (...)

[BN]

26 [June, Tuesday]   Overcast in the morning. A fresh breeze out of the SE. At 10 8¾ knots. Wave direction ESE. Course NWbN. Wave velocity 10 seconds. Estimated wavelength 30–40 m. In the morning blue, afternoon green. Seasick again. Clear weather in the evening. Encountered a Norwegian herring boat. Rough sea.

27 [June, Wednesday]   At 7.45 a.m. the Scottish coast appeared through the fog, about 25 nautical miles away. More birds and sails again. The water a deep dark green. (...)
We crossed the Firth of Moray [Moray Firth] and at noon were in sight of the Scarabian [Grampian] Mountains and Warrow [Mormond] Hill. Passing the northern beach of Sinclair Bay [Sinclair's Bay] we pushed into the Pentland Firth against the current, leaving the Pentland Skerries to starboard [on the north], and sailed through between Stroma and Swona. A fishing boat from Stroma came alongside; it took our mail to forward it to London. [Here Boas also received letters from his fiancée and his parents.] In a few hours we were south of Turn [Tor] Ness [on the island of Hoy], having thus sailed through the Pentland Firth. 2 photographic exposures: one of the boat departing and the other of Dunnett Head and the sunset. [These plates did not survive.]

28 [June, Thursday]   A stiff breeze from WSW; very seasick. The Scottish coast still in sight in the morning (Cape Wrath). Later Lewis Isle [Isle of Lewis] to the south and Rona to the north came into sight. A rough sea all day, with rain and a strong wind. In the evening took in the topgallant sail and the ... topsail. Still many divers, gulls and gannets in sight.

29th [June, Friday]   Calmer weather. Wind and sea subsiding rapidly. Water ... dark green; it was light brown early in the morning, and subsequently a deep blue. The wind is dropping rapidly. Saw the first mollys [fulmars].

[FB/MK]

(...) We have a substantial start on the Aberdeen ship [the supply ship *Catherine* did not sail until 25 July], and we may hope that if the ice is open, we will get there well ahead of her. I am now greatly looking forward to meeting the people at the German station. How eagerly all the gentlemen will read through all their letters. (...)

I do not know whether I have already written to you that Leopold Ambronn [deputy head of the polar station], brother of my oldest student friend [the botanist Hermann Ambronn, at Heidelberg with Boas] is also at Kingawa. As a result I have recently written to the brother, from whom I hadn't heard a word for 6 years, and thus have found an old friend whom I had long since given up for lost. (...)

[BN]

30th June [Sunday]   Almost calm. Made a trial with the sling psychrometer and cleaned my revolver, as I did yesterday evening. In the morning the first porpoises and killer whales were seen near the ship. The wind is swinging gradually more into the east. At 8 a.m. we lowered a 75 cm diameter disc of white painted canvas. It was visible to 6.5 fathoms. Little motion in the sea. At 12 noon a slight halo around the sun. Heavy clouds on the evening of the 29th in the NW sky; above cirrus clouds, which display intense rainbow colours, quite irregularly distributed; behind all this is a deep blue sky. On the afternoon of the 30th the water was dark green. (...) 30th June. In the morning some dolphins near the ship.

[FB/MK]

(...) You know, despite all the sadness associated with such a parting, it is wonderful for me to have now attained *one* goal of my dreams. Fifteen years ago [in 1868, when he was nine or ten] I dreamed of participating in a polar expedition; now I have attained this; I am on my way yet so differently from what I had dreamed of. I am not heading out under the orders of a friend, but am dependent on myself. Not simply inspired by geographical exploration, but with quite definite scientific goals! My thoughts are not always on my science; no, my love, my Marie, they are on you in my heart, and of creating a future around *us*, beloved. Can you believe that this is much better like this than when I first dreamed of an arctic expedition? I can't believe it; earlier I often thought I was a flop, but now everything has turned out so well that I myself am often amazed.

I thank you for how all my plans have been fulfilled and for how I have won your love! If only my luck continues to be favourable, and I can enfold you in my arms in New York in the fall of 1884. The last two years seem almost like a dream to me, but they began with the trip to the Harz [on which Boas met Marie for the first time in 1881]. First there, then a month of diligent work in Berlin, and as a soldier in Minden. My efforts and hopes of getting to Baltimore [where he had applied to Johns Hopkins University], and always in the background this trip in mind; can you believe me that at the same time I was also thinking of you? When this collapsed, the vain efforts with Gotha [to find a situation as a cartographer]; the winter in Berlin, the initially unsuccessful, then successful efforts towards my trip; the pains of parting and the finest thing of all, our love. Can you believe that everything appears just a gaily coloured dream? (...)

[BN]
1 July [Sunday]   A dismal day, cold and rainy. Water green.

2nd July [Monday]   At 7 a.m. a long tree trunk, with roots but no bark, was seen drifting. At 8 the water was blue-green; later glass-green. Dull and rainy. In the evening a short blink of sunshine.

3rd July [Tuesday]   Saw a jaeger; some sun at noon; water glass-green. It is clearing up somewhat. At 3 a piece of driftwood on which a bird was sitting.

4th [July, Wednesday]   Making only slow progress. At noon a *Phoca groenlandica* was seen and was probably storm-driven. In the evening a number of porpoises, much more agile than those seen earlier. Many gulls at the same time. The wind is swinging into the north. It is still very dull; the sun breaks through the fog occasionally for only a few moments.

Thursday 5th July   Still a lot of fog. At noon two fulmars near the ship, similar to sandpipers, according to the captain; a goose flying towards the NW. At 5 p.m. the water was a deep blue.

[FB/MK]
(...) I have now begun a task that I was unable to complete in Minden, namely to combine all my scientific plans and to summarize them. I am afraid that otherwise I will no longer remember anything of all this when I come home. I am sending them to my friend Rudolf Lehmann in Berlin, who is to look after them until I come back. But I am keeping a copy for myself. If I get bored during the winter I already know what I will be

doing. I have completed the outline for a book on psychophysics, a new philosophical discipline, at which I have been working quite a lot, and I will be able to work at it then. In any case it depresses me somewhat to have suddenly disappeared in the middle of my work on the psychophysical literature. (...)

[BN]
Friday 6th [July]   A freshening wind. A lot of spray across the deck. In the afternoon the sea is a *pure* deep green. On the morning of the 7th the water colour is still the same. (...)

7 July [Saturday]   Overcast weather. In the morning the water was still pure green, later greenish blue. At 2.30 p.m. a pure blue. In the evening a dark blue-green. From the 7th on the air bottles were not first rinsed and dried. The wind is becoming stronger; at 9 took a reef in the topsail.

Off Greenland

8th July [Sunday]   From 4 to 7 a.m. a severe gale out of the E (magn[etic]); under reefed mainsail, schooner, ... sail. The cabin battened down. I am very seasick. Towards noon it is smooth and calm. At 9.30 ... sighted [Greenland] 35–40 miles away, through the fog. At 3 land was clearly in sight; by evening the high mountains and glaciers of Greenland were clearly visible. 50 miles away. In the afternoon a whale sighted. All day we were angling for birds. In the evening we could hear the muttering of a storm.

[FB/MK]
(...) Tomorrow we will probably pass from the Atlantic into the Arctic Ocean (to celebrate my birthday). (...)

[D]
[9 July, Monday]   Here's to me! Ipsissimus! [Boas was celebrating his birthday; he was 25 years old.]

[WW]
The gale became steadily stronger; one wave after another swept on board. One could not sleep for the rumbling, until things came to life on board again; I then got dressed. I had some things for the Doctor [Boas],

since it was his birthday, and I passed them to him; at this point he looked at his watch; it was 3.30 and the storm was raging terribly; this lasted until around 10 o'clock.

[BN]

10 July [Tuesday]   At 3.45 a.m. waves breaking on the ice were heard; and at 5.30 some floes were seen. The land [Greenland] can be seen only vaguely; much rain and fog. At 11 we could again hear surf on the ice. Water blue; calm. {11th July} In the afternoon the transparency of the blue water was 14 fathoms (with a white disc of 75 cm diameter). Inclined at 5° due to the wind. Disappeared at a depth of $14\frac{1}{2}$ fathoms.

[FB/MK]

(...) At about 3 o'clock the land came in sight again. We could see the high mountain peaks only vaguely though the fog and rain; the white glaciers would peep out, then quickly disappear in the dense mist. We also heard the first whale blowing near the ship; but I did not get a sight of it. In the evening it became quite clear over the land and the bold mountain forms were visible; the ice-covered slopes gleamed at us from a distance, beckoning and waving. This was the first alpine landscape I had seen, and indeed it is a wonderful sight. (...)

[BN]

11th July [Wednesday]   Early in the morning sighted ice some 7 miles to leeward; drifted this distance of 7 miles in $2\frac{1}{2}$ hours. By 11 o'clock it could be seen to windward, since we had passed it around 9 (photograph no. 2, underexposed). At 11 it extended from SSW to NNE close astern of the ship; on a bearing of 85° at a distance of 5–6 nm [nautical miles]. Thus it is drifting away from the land. In the morning we also saw an iceberg. Collected some terns: and algae with a drift net. The ice is now drifting towards the S (true) against the wind (which is very light). At 12 we encountered a strip of foam that lay parallel to the ice; they had both been swept to the same position by two opposing currents. Both were aligned SSW-NNE (magn.). Collected algae and animals.

[FB/MK]

(...) This afternoon I read my birthday letters again. It is too funny to see how everyone firmly believes that I have gone out to attain fame and honour. Not true; they don't know me at all, and I would stand very low in my own estimation if that was the *purpose* for which I was investing trouble and effort. You know that I am aiming for something higher than this and that this trip is only a means (in every sense) to that goal. And in so far it is perhaps correct that I am seeking *recognition* for my achievements from outside, because for my further purposes I must attain the situation that my word, which I can throw in the balance for the sake of my ideas, is accepted as that of a man of action. But that is all that comes to mind when I think of recognition. Empty fame is worth nothing to me. (...)

[BN]
12th [July, Thursday]   Water olive-green in the evening. In the morning a moderate gale from the south.

13th [July, Friday]   No ice.

[WW]
Nothing.

[BN]
14th [July, Saturday]   A fair wind; since yesterday the water again green and blue. A fine day; constantly on deck.

15th [July] Sunday   The sun is breaking through[,] very cold, 2°C. Fair wind. At 6 a.m. an iceberg in the far distance. At noon an iceberg. Several in the evening. At 7.30 icefields and icebergs from N to NW and soon to W, extending SW–NE (...) 1 mile away to the NW; an iceberg to the east 170′ high and 570′ long. The pack ice ends to the WSW (...) Ice appeared ahead somewhat later, at 7.45. (...)

[FB/MK]
(...) Today it is extremely cold, only 2°C, but I am sitting on deck as I write to you. Only today I put on my Eskimo boots, since otherwise it would be too cold on deck. (...)

From 16 July onward, entries are continued in both the Notebook and the Black Notebook [BN].

In the Drift and Pack Ice
off Baffin Island,
July–August 1883

[Notebook]

16th July [Monday]   At 10 o'clock the ice was bearing ENE–WSW. At 6 a.m. there were mirages[.] Water appeared to be lying beyond the ice. Our course since yesterday evening, on the basis of the position of an iceberg N5$\frac{1}{2}$E. At 10.30 the ice to the NNE is farther away than in the vicinity. At 11.00 the ice bore NE$\frac{1}{2}$N–W$\frac{1}{2}$S. Farther away at N$\frac{1}{2}$E. At 12 the ice NNE–W$\frac{1}{2}$N. Farther away at N$\frac{1}{2}$E. Since 11 we've been heading south away from the ice. At 6.30 p.m. the ice lay from SE through N to W. To the north it is visible only from the masthead. Cape Mercy [Uibarun] is visible from aloft N$\frac{1}{2}$E about 60 miles away. At 7.30 the ice lay S$\frac{1}{2}$E–W through N. At 8.30 SE–WSW through N; to the NNW it is 1500' away. At 9.30 NW–SE$\frac{1}{2}$E. At 9 Cape Mercy appeared refracted at about NE. At 9.45 the ice, as seen from the masthead extended to the south, where it appeared to end. The iceberg that we passed at noon was determined to be 250' high and 750' long. Data: speed 2$\frac{1}{2}$ knots; angle with the ship's median initially 5°. (...)

17th July 1883 [Tuesday]   At 9 a.m. an iceberg. Data: speed 3$\frac{1}{2}$ knots. As we passed it was 80–90 m away. Passed it between 8.59 and 9 03' 5". It was 1000' long and 56' high. (...). The ice drifted with it 3 N. miles to the WNW in 5 hours. In the morning everything was still all clear. By 9 in the midst of ice floes. Nearby the iceberg we measured yesterday bears SW$\frac{1}{2}$W (...) 10.30. Ice edge runs SSW–NNE; ice visible to the WNW from the masthead so that we are lying in a bay. (...) The end of the ice at noon SE$\frac{1}{2}$E. At 4 ESE–N$\frac{1}{2}$W; at 4.30 from the masthead through E to S$\frac{1}{2}$W. At 5 N through E to S. (...)

[BN]
(...) At 9 [p.m.] the coast of Greenland came in sight. Apparently in the vicinity of Frederiksdal [Nanortalik]; we passed the latter (...), then stood off again. A severe storm with heavy, wild seas. By 11.30 the storm was slackening and by 12 it was quite light. The ship is working heavily. (...)

[Notebook]
The cause of the thundering in the ice. The waves surge into the under-cut water line, and the deeper this is cut, the louder the noise. The smaller floes have almost all a large ice-foot which extends under water; above this they are very markedly undercut. The foot appears greenish; the deeper in the water the more intense the colour; by reflection this also makes the side surfaces of the floes appear green. The colour of the ice itself is generally sky blue. This appears only when one is looking at ice that is saturated in water, which makes it transparent enough to let in the light penetrating from above through the white upper surface. The dry surface always appears white. When waves break over the edge, they often make the floes appear green. On the night of the 17th to ..

.. **the 18th [July, Wednesday]**   there was a lot of ice in sight. On the evening of the 18th after sunset there was a rainbow, cut off at the horizon.

19th [July, Thursday]   In the morning fairly heavy weather.

Boas made no entry on Friday, 20 July, and Weike merely recorded, 'Nothing on Friday and Saturday.'

[Notebook]
21st [July, Saturday]   Icebergs in sight in the afternoon; in the evening counted 10 ahead of the ship. One appears to measure 270' and another 1300'.

[FB/MK]
(...) In my report for the *Berliner Tageblatt* I have brought us safely to the Greenland coast[,] we have survived the storm of 8 July and it is now about to clear up, and Greenland and the rough ice will come in sight. Then I will write another report about Kikkerton and Kingawa. I must keep them carefully for my own use, since they are to be reworked into my book on the trip. I think that I should already have it half finished when I come back, since I have to get some work done during the winter. (...)

Boas's entry for 22 July listed only a large number of positions.

[Notebook]
23rd [July, Monday]   (...) It appears that the ice to the SW and the large bergs are drifting SW while the part by which we were lying around 5 was motionless so that to the SW of this part a deep bay has formed. 2–6 o'clock, we sailed $\frac{1}{2}$ a mile from the ice edge, which lies to starboard. At 6.15 over 1 mile away. The iceberg I photographed in the morning is bearing WSW; and the end of the drift ice NW. At 7.30 the ice is moving farther and farther away from our starboard side. At 8 from N to S$\frac{1}{2}$E to ESE fairly free from ice (as seen from the masthead).

24th [July, Tuesday]   (...) 3.40 a.m. From this point onwards the ice edge inclines away to the east.

[BN]
We are drifting among the ice. At 2 a ring around the sun. We are again sailing in ice-free water. A light breeze and a quiet sea. The ice had packed together more. At 9.30 fairly clear water. Drifting off the ice with sails set. Light breeze; clear sky. We sailed along the pack ice.

25 July [Wednesday]   Fickle and variable breeze; we are cruising off the ice. Light breeze; clear sky, intersecting wave patterns. Fickle breeze, clear sky. Fog on the horizon. Thick fog. Drifting with sails set.

26 July [Thursday]   Drifting with sails set. Thick fog. Around 1 calm, light frost. (...) Sounded but no bottom with 150 fathoms.

[Notebook]
27th [July, Friday]   At 8 a.m. large, open floes from SW to SE. From E to SW apparently very close. NW–N the same. At 10 the water was green-blue, transparent to 15 fathoms. The lowered disc floats. At 9 WSW–NNW.

[BN]
Found a piece of driftwood. Depth 190 fathoms; yellowish mud and stones.

[FB/MK]
(...) We have now been at sea for 35 days. When will we get to Kikkerton at least? I am longing to get to the work that lies ahead. I have already

abandoned the fall trip to Iglulik; it will be too late by the time we get to Kingawa. Where am I going to winter? With the Scots or the Americans? This trip is really a true test of patience. (...)

[Notebook]
28th [July, Saturday]   Many icebergs in sight in the morning. From 4 a.m. we've been sailing along the ice; later thick fog and rain. Passed an iceberg with a peculiar channel.

[BN]
Tacking and dodging off the ice.

[Notebook]
29th [July, Sunday]   Remarks on icebergs and the ice edge.

Photographed and sketched an iceberg; around 9 ice in sight; clear and sunny. At 10.30 NNE–WNW. I can distinguish three especially characteristic shapes of icebergs. Tabular bergs with sharply truncated edges, often slanting plateaux, mountains and pinnacled mountains. Different from these are totally rounded bergs, which have probably capsized. They are always undercut at the water line so that here the water breaks beneath one's feet. If a piece breaks off, they change their point of equilibrium and these edges emerge above water, often steeply inclined. With time they become rounded off, but remain recognizable for a long while. Sometimes these lines intersect. They appear quite often to merge into vertical faces, the cause of which is probably the undercutting of the water line. With an overcast sky the colour of icebergs appears white, the shadows a pure blue, but with a greenish tone along the water line; with a clear sky, by contrast they have sharp, grey shadows, generally darker than the background. Icebergs at a great distance usually appear greener than they are in fact; probably due to the effect of strong refraction, which elevates them. Refraction makes all the shadows appear elongated in a vertical direction, so that bergs and the ice edge acquire a wall-like appearance. One usually sees these forms, elongated in a vertical direction, sharply truncated at the top, probably as a mirror image of the water line? Or then it might be a vague, reversed mirror image, as is indicated by the commonly projecting edges. Clear mirror images, lying above the actual objects, are more rare, as also are those where one cannot see the object itself at all.

Compared to sea ice, snow on the land always appears a yellowish shade, never bluish. The ice edge runs W–SW. Cape Mercy almost always retains its solid appearance, although the wind frequently blows strongly from N and NE. Two [directions] appear ... to produce a current [setting] N, and hence this can probably explain the form of the ice edge. The bay that extends towards Cape Mercy has survived the whole time we have been cruising here, although on 1st August it became wider towards the SW, while the ice there drifted away. During the first few days there was almost no ice drifting around that had broken away from the ice edge, but on the 28th fairly large floes were visible and on the 30th fields and large floes were drifting around. The floes are usually attacked by the ice [sea, WB] in such a way that high pinnacles are left upright at the ends, associated with a tongue below water. One usually also sees archways broken right through floes. The ice always appears blue where light is shining through it and it is always more striking when the contrast with the blue sky ceases.

Like the floes the icebergs never display rounded forms, but always remain sharp and jagged. Pan floes commonly show not only a [broken-off] edge but also an ice-foot perforated in such a way that the surface stands on several legs, like a table. A mushroomlike shape, as in tables supported by several legs, is also commonly encountered in the floes. Floes too commonly display old water lines as well. Pans rarely project more than 2′ above water, and their depth below water is hard to estimate. On top they commonly display ice tables with legs etc.; I have also noticed these on tabular bergs. At 8 many bergs in sight. (...)

30 July [Monday]   N–NE at a great distance. The land is visible, but severely distorted by refraction. Many floes and icebergs. We are sailing along the ice. It is freezing on the rigging; below the temperature is above 0°. In the evening the land is again visible, deformed by refraction.

31st July [Tuesday]   Drifting near the land. Since the 30th constant red refractions; occasionally the {ice} land on the far side of the sound is visible. On the evening of the 31st we were sailing along an open ice edge.

[BN]
Light breeze; thick fog clearing at 3; clear sky; much ice and icebergs in the vicinity. At 8 a large ice field to the W. Fickle breeze; around noon calm. Dodging and drifting off the ice. Had a light breeze from the NE; no opening to be seen west of the ice. At 4 took a bearing on Cape Mercy. (...)

[Notebook]
1 August [Wednesday]   5 p.m. The land is well in sight. (...) At 2 p.m. severe refraction. Part of the ice edge has broken away. We are again seeing the conspicuously shaped berg of the evening of 30 July. At 8 a.m. ice. SE$\frac{1}{2}$E–WSW through north. At 2.30 pm took two photos of mirages. At 6.30 C. Mercy N$\frac{1}{2}$W.

[BN]
(...) We've been sailing northward and southward along the ice edge; no open water towards the land. At 4 took a bearing on C. Mercy. Undeveloped photos: 1. Mirage, 2 August; 2. Shattered iceberg and ice edge, 3 August at 3.30 p.m. 3. Iceberg and floes on morning of 5 August. 4. Pack ice and floes on morning of 5 August. 5. Loose ice on evening of 5 August. 6. and 7. plate of 4 August. (...)

[WW]
[**2 August, Thursday**]   Dodging about. [Boas does not make any entry this day.]

[BN]
3rd Aug. [Friday]   Noon. With the prevailing wind the ice is setting strongly out of the [Sound]. Since the start of the period that we have been dodging here, the ice edge has broken up greatly. Today many very small, loose pieces are drifting around off the ice edge. The fog that prevailed here a few days ago, despite its duration, was very shallow, so one could always see the blue sky.

4th Aug. [Saturday]   The maximum height of mirages is 8–10′. At 6 Cape Mercy was no longer visible; the water line of the inverted mirror image is 16′ high.

5th August [Sunday]   In the afternoon we were sailing through much loose ice. The flat, rafted floes are about 1 m above water, and often less. Where they are higher they always have a wide foot. Very commonly the floes are broken in the middle, so all that is left standing are columns at the corners. Such pieces may tower 10′ and more out of the water. Pieces 2 m high are very common. Arches have commonly been broken through them. Mushroom-shaped forms are frequent. In some cases this may be rafted ice, but such shapes can also be produced by disintegration of the floes above water. The small floes have almost always antler-shaped tops.

The pack ice is now much more open. Whereas earlier, when distorted by refraction it appeared wall-like, there are now many patches of water within it. For more than two days the wind has been off the land. Large fields and much loose ice have drifted away. By comparison with the nearby ice it always appears yellowish, when the sun is in the south almost reddish-purple, always with something of a yellowish shade.

[FB/MK]
(...) Over 6 weeks at sea is a rather long time! I am now quite accustomed to shipboard life, although at first it was very difficult for me. When I describe it for you, you will scarcely believe it, it is so intriguing here. The seamen all go about in the most ragged clothes they possess. Tattered coats, boots that are almost falling apart are their normal attire. There is fresh water available for washing only once per week. Since soap does not lather with salt water and one simply moves the dirt from one place to another, you can imagine how we all look by Saturday. A coal man is clean by comparison! And one needs only to lay hold of something on board ship, and one is as black as night again; although things are scrubbed daily, the soot from the stove and dirt from the rigging etc. make every-thing black. There is always a major wash-fest on Sunday; this is also the only day when everyone appears newly washed. I always save the water in which I rinse my photographs and thus can wash in fresh water at least every second day. The seamen generally dispense with washing entirely for the entire week. (...)

I am now very accustomed to eating a lot of bacon and salt meat, and bite quite readily into a piece of bacon, something I could not have done during the first few days or weeks. I scarcely miss bread, because the ship's biscuits now taste quite good to me and I am always unbelievably hungry. We get coffee at 7 o'clock and at 11.30 I am always waiting for lunch because by then I am very hungry. We have quite a fixed menu: Sunday: pudding with syrup, then fresh meat and vegetables (tinned). Monday: brown beans and bacon. Tuesday: peas and salt meat with potatoes. Wednesday: salt meat and fresh vegetables, then pudding (from Sunday). Thursday: peas and bacon. Friday: beans and salt meat. Saturday: pearl barley with plums and dried cod. At first I found this terrible. You can smell it from one end of the ship to the other; but now I like even this, and scarcely notice the smell any more. In short, I am quite accustomed to all these amenities (How will I get along later on land?[)]

6th August [Monday]   We have now been trying in vain for two days to push through to the west and have had no success, since whenever we could sail into the ice it soon became so close that we had to turn back as quickly as possible. But one thing is certain; during the past few days it has slackened greatly. We are now sailing towards Cape Mercy again; after 2 hours it came in sight again, but unfortunately there is ice to be seen ahead. How long will we be able to keep cruising here! (...)

It was stupid that I did not have more photos taken of me before I left Germany! Now you are always looking at a picture of me when I did not even know you yet. Then it occurred to me that I could produce one myself and quickly had Wilhelm photograph me for you. I will make a print of it for you. (...)

We are again about 60 miles from Cape Mercy and will be lying off the ice again for the night. Today we sailed through streams of open ice a few times.

7th August [Tuesday]   This evening I can send you only a brief greeting since it is late and my lamp is threatening to go out. This morning we were off Cape Mercy again, but could not make any progress because everything was full of ice. Now we have fog again and as a result have sailed far offshore again to reach open water. Despite this there are still many icebergs here as well as [loose] pieces, with which we collide occasionally which produces a real shock. (...)

I have now completed 17 photos, which I shall send back home so that you can imagine how I have seen everything. Yesterday and today I have caught up with a lot of work that I still had to do: completed sketches, wrote up my journal, wrote letters, developed photos etc.[,] so I was totally occupied; at the same time I ran on deck quite often because there is always plenty to see here. Thus I scarcely get any proper peace while working, since I am always afraid that I will miss something; it would be a fine tale to go off on a voyage of discovery and not keep one's eyes open. A few days ago I hoped that we would be at Kikkerton by tomorrow, but that hope has just been disappointed again. One learns patience here! (...)

[ww]
Wednesday, 8 August On the 6th and 7th there was a tolerable breeze but we had to search for open water. On the evening of the 7th we encountered fog, which lasted all day on the 8th and it also fell calm, which makes for jolly travelling; sleeping is the major pastime.

Neither Boas nor Weike made any entry on 9 August.

[Notebook]

10th August [Friday]   At 9.15 ice 6 n. miles to starboard. From the mast-head one can see that there is a bay ahead. At 10 ice all around; the only opening is astern. At 12.30 in the ice. Until 8 p.m. ice to starboard.

[FB/MK]

(...) I really am a very wicked person, in that I have not written to you for 2 days. My cabin looks terrible now and I have done so much work in those two days that I did not get round to writing to you. Specifically I have unpacked all my things for the fall journey and fitted my boat out fully. This morning we hoisted it on deck and now it is also to be chris-tened [*Marie*]. Then we had to hoist all possible chests and boxes out of the hold, open them and close them up again. Provisions had to be taken out; dishes unpacked and repacked, books packed etc. Even my civilian suit has now happily been stowed away and I have been transformed totally into a seaman. Now I only wish that we would reach the Sound soon! Yesterday and the day before there was dense fog[,] today it is fairly clear again and we are coming somewhat closer to land. But here again our progress is halted, since just now, at 10 a.m. we reached the ice edge. What will be the outcome when we are still lying around here on 10 August! I really am seriously concerned about it. How are my things to get to Kikkerton and what can I begin this fall, when we will be arriving so late! And if we don't get there at all, what then? An unsuccessful northern expedition would cause me real grief! And what a disappointment it would be for me! (...)

It would be fine if I were to see you, dearest, this fall, but it would be a *very* heavy disappointment to return without any success. What should I do then? I would have to produce a fairly major geographical work very quickly and habilitate myself as a Privatdocent [qualification for profes-sorship in the German university system] and at the same time complete my psychophysical work. (...)

[Notebook]

11th August [Saturday]   3 p.m.; ice 5 miles to NNE. At 3.30 a.m. ice. At 5 sailed round a point then at 5.20 it bore NNE. Ice to starboard only $\frac{1}{2}$ a n. mile away. At 5.35 at the ice, which is now drifting SW. At 7 at the ice; at 8 tacked about $\frac{1}{2}$ a n. mile from the ice. A moderate number of small floes.

12th August [Sunday]   At 7 a.m. ice 5 n. miles to port. At 7.40 ice 4 n.

miles to NNE; farther away to the N and barely visible to the NNW. Ice to the W. To the east a point of ice about 7 n. miles away. To the NNW 4 miles. The ice to the W consists only of pieces. At 8.15 at the ice, from the point of which it falls off to starboard. At 12 noon ice from E to NW; to the SW much loose ice. At 1.00 ice $\frac{1}{2}$ a n. mile ahead. At 4 ice from starboard to ahead. At 6.30 the ice is extending to the NE. At 7.15 ice to port, somewhat astern. From 4 to 7 we were sailing along the ice edge.

13th Aug. [**Monday**]   At 4 a.m. the ice extends round to the N. At 8.30 p.m. ice from starboard, ahead and round to E.

[FB/MK]
(...) A year ago today *Germania* ran into the Sound [when she was bringing the polar station personnel to K'ingua] but today we can't even think of it. (...)

[Notebook]
14th [**August, Tuesday**]   At 5 a.m. in the ice. We then sailed round a point that formed an angle of about 50°; the ice edge extends from NE to SW and later moved more towards N. At 12.40 the ice was entirely out of sight. At 5.30 ice to the NW, 3 n. miles away. At 6 a point of ice 3 n. miles away at W$\frac{1}{2}$N, from which it falls off to the W. [BN] At 7 Cape Mercy.

Here the entries in the Notebook are interrupted until 28 August.

[FB/MK]
(...) Early today we again had a strong east wind and heavy seas, which lets us conclude that there is a lot of open water. Unfortunately, however, it was very gloomy and we could barely see a couple of miles. In the afternoon the wind slackened completely and finally, around 7 o'clock the fog dispersed, at least up above, and suddenly Cape Mercy emerged quite close by. We've never been so close to it before; it is 3 German miles away; the nearest bay in the coast is only 2 German miles away [Ka'xodlutang or Kaxodlúin]. But in front of this there is still some ice lying; about 1 German mile southwest of us the ice forms a corner, where we can perhaps circumvent it. (...)

Today I packed away my finished photographs; there are now 24 of them [of the 48 plates that Boas had with him, of which only 16 survived], which, however, you will also receive. I have made copies of all of them; they are not all good, but they do include some flawless plates. (...)

[BN]
15 August [Wednesday]   The ice is moving along the coast until just
about $10\frac{1}{2}$ nautical miles ahead of the ship then it begins ..

The text in the Black Notebook breaks off here in mid-sentence and does not con-
tinue again until 28 August.

[FB/MK]
16th [August, Thursday]   Yesterday I again did not get around to writing
to you. We were steering towards land and approached very close to it
and I seized the opportunity to survey the land somewhat. Thus I had
plenty of work all day, and in the evening I attempted to work out my
observations, but I have not got very far. We had great hopes of making
some progress, but around 11 o'clock everything was suddenly full of ice.
But we have got farther than ever before. One could see deep into the
Sound and one could even make out the land on the opposite shore
clearly. Around Cape Mercy the land is snow-free except for the deep
crevices in the rocks; farther north by contrast everything appears to be
full of snow and ice. Yesterday we were very disappointed that we could
not get any farther, for we hoped with great confidence that the Sound
was fairly free of ice. We encountered a quite colossal iceberg here; it was
only about 50' high but 0.7 n. miles long and 0.2 wide; isn't that incredi-
ble? Today we had much rain and fog. It was totally calm earlier, but now
a fresh east wind has arisen which, we hope, will drive away the ice.

17th [August, Friday]   It is really sad that we are making no progress at all.
Every day we make new attempts to find an opening in the ice but there is
never any available. Today we again got to within 2 German miles of the
land, but then everything came to nought again. There is ice all around
and it lies here just as closely packed as at the start. We are now hoping constantly for an east wind, which ought to drive away this ice, so that we can
at least sail around Cape Mercy, but nothing ever comes of this. In the
morning the wind is always blowing fairly strongly, but in the afternoons
and evenings it is calm again. I am now making an effort to get the most
exact picture possible of the land, but I have still not got an angular mea-
surement, which I have not yet been able to get accurately enough. Until
I get one, I cannot work much out though, even so, I can obtain very
approximate values. Yesterday and today I was engaged in observations
almost all day, but it has not produced much because fog set in every time,
making my observations useless. When will we finally get there? (...)

18 August [Saturday]   Today I really had a lot of work. From 6 a.m. until sunset I was taking bearings and sketching constantly to be able to compile my map properly. All this is a major task, but I am delighted that I have something to do. Now we are advancing somewhat farther every day and hope that perhaps tomorrow we will finally be able to get round Cape Mercy. Today, finally, I was able to get some observations with the help of the sun and moon, so my observations are now on a more secure basis. Today I was quite annoyed that I had not been able to make any progress with these observations, but now my problems are over, since I have a sufficiency of them. But the calculations are terrible. I have plenty of work for the winter here. It would be good if I could work them out right now, but this is not possible since I cannot observe and work everything out. The [British] chart [Admiralty Chart 235, 1875] agrees very poorly with the actual positions of the points and I am very impatient to see how the new picture of things will emerge. I am always awake as soon as there is anything to observe, because I hope very much to be able to plot the entire coastline at least superficially. (...)

This evening I am really tired. It is 11 o'clock and I have been working and freezing all day, so I have a right to be tired. Here, it is really a trick to observe, sketch and especially write. This evening my fingers were really just icicles rather than human members when I was sketching the coast. (...)

Early today we suddenly heard a loud clap of thunder with a totally clear sky, followed by a protracted echo, which died away in a dull rumbling. An iceberg, at least 10 n. miles away from us, had collapsed and the land and the surrounding icebergs were reflecting the noise, broken into numerous echoes. This was the first time that we had heard this noise, or rather this thunder, at such a loud volume! It was a very fine day today. When I was not observing it was even warm, yet the temperature was not above 1°C. (...)

[ww]
On 18 August we made quite good progress towards the Sound; it seemed as if we had open water, but at 8 in the evening we had to turn back, since everything was full of ice again.

On the 19th [August, Sunday]   we did not make much progress, the ice had slackened, so we had to stay back; in the evening the ship was laid on the port tack.

[FB/MK]
20th August [Monday]   Yesterday I did not get around to writing to you, since I had too much work to do, observing and calculating. We have still not made any more progress than we had before. Yesterday we were not even as far ahead as on the previous day, and today around noon we had to tack again, because the ice was becoming steadily closer. We have never before risked pushing as deeply into the ice as we did today. It is far from being as close as the ice we had outside. It is mainly very flat, fairly level, large floes. This morning we sailed about 4 n. miles into the ice but finally we were encountering so much ice that we had to turn back again. (...)

I am becoming more worried by the day. Even if we get at least to Kikkerton this week, my hopes are still very close to the zero point. I have to resign myself to the inevitable and am really calculating already whether I shall see you again this fall, dearest. (...)

[WW]
On 21 [August, Tuesday]   it rained all day and at the same time there was quite thick fog; even though it cleared up a little at times, the next moment it would become denser again. At midnight the ship was put on the port tack. There was quite a strong breeze; we tacked a few times and we would have soon run into an iceberg. [Boas made no entry on this date.]

[FB/MK]
22nd August [Wednesday]   Yesterday I was very diligent making calculations on a foggy, horrible day with strong winds; as a result notwithstanding, I now have some fixed points which, however, do not agree at all with the [Admiralty] chart. Today I am writing to you in joyful hope. We are in the process of cruising round Cape Mercy, and I now hope that we will finally be running into the Sound. The ice is very loose but we have a totally foul wind so we have to tack. However, none of the old landmarks have disappeared from sight yet. But there are a large number of new landmarks in sight, lying well up the Sound. Now finally, the sun is breaking through; I have been waiting for it longingly all morning in order to make determinations of our position. I should like to have a few more observations for a control and the sun could not be seen at all. I have just tied a point on the far side of the land to the others here. Today I am really hopeful. (...)

23rd [August, Thursday]   (...) The ice now appears to have become very light, but we cannot definitively know anything certain about it because we are still lying in exactly the same spot. I believe I shall never forget the shapes of this land for my entire life, we have seen them so often and so long. If I had more time I would sketch it for you, but this is not possible and I cannot photograph it from here, because it is still too far away. But my work is still occupying me very much. I am very much afraid that on this approach we will no longer reach {Kingawa} Kikkerton, since it is already so late, but we are hoping for the best. In any case my trip this fall is no longer feasible. I have no hope in this connection any longer. (...)

If only I can get the letters which the Scotsman [the supply ship *Catherine* from Dundee] is bringing me! Yesterday evening we saw a large piece of driftwood floating nearby; we lowered the *Marie* and along with the mate and a seaman we put off to recover it. Then, for once, I was able to see *Germania* under full sail in the open sea, and I was delighted at the pretty appearance of the little vessel. This was my first trip in *Marie*. I should just like to go farther! We really ought to have hoisted the flag, but couldn't because we had left the mast on board ship. This was a great change from the daily monotony of shipboard life, and you can imagine how monotonous it is when I am dwelling so long on this trifle. (...)

There are quite gigantic icebergs clustered here near the land, all carrying quite large rocks on their spines. Today we again had isolated large floes nearby, such as no longer occur here otherwise. They probably came drifting round Cape Mercy, out of a bay to the east. Yesterday I realized that thus far I have been observing the land totally erroneously. One point that I mistook for an island appears to be the outermost outlier of the land, but none of it will agree with the chart at all.

24th August [Friday]   (...) Today I am in a very depressed mood, (...). I want to imbibe new courage and new strength from your gaze and I believe you would say to me: 'Forward, I'm waiting for you.' Therein lies my consolation, my finest hope, which no fate can take from me, which will always hold me up. (...)

25th [August, Saturday]   Finally, finally, we have made some progress. Since this morning we have had quite a light wind, have sailed around Cape Mercy and are now in the Sound. There was still a very great deal of ice at the entrance. But now there is much less. The water is dead calm because the swell cannot penetrate the ice now. For all of us the fact that we finally have made some progress is really a weight off our minds. If we can only continue to have a fair wind now, we will reach Kikkerton in the next few days. What worry the gentlemen at the [German polar] station must already be feeling. They must think that we are no longer coming. Tomorrow we will have been in the ice here for six weeks, but now, finally we hope that we have won the game. Whether *Germania* will be able to get out again this year is very questionable, in my view, since it is already very late. (...)

Everything is dead quiet; only occasionally does one hear a piece of ice break off with a loud crack, then everything is silent again. Just think, yesterday we fished a green twig with quite fresh leaves out of the water. Can you believe that it aroused in me a melancholy longing for leaves and flowers? There are many seals playing around the ship here and it is very amusing, how they watch us inquisitively. Yesterday we saw a small seal which dived as quick as lightning right next to the ship and looked up at us from under water. The water is so transparent here that one can make out everything to a very great depth. (...)

[FB/parents; on board *Germania*]
[**26 August, Sunday**]   (...) I am sending you these lines from Kikkerton to tell you that we are safe and well. I shall not write to you about the progress of our voyage, which you can learn from my reports in the *Berliner Tageblatt*. A longer letter will come back with *Germania*. Unfortunately it was very late before we managed to get into the Sound yesterday, so absolutely nothing will come of my fall trip. I must contain myself in patience and remain at Kikkerton. Unfortunately it is still not sure whether *Germania* will succeed at all in getting home this fall, since conditions between here and Kingawa are very bad. Good though this may be for me, I do not wish it on the crew and for the station at Kingawa. We hope that tomorrow we will encounter the [Scottish] steamer, since it would be really bad if we could not send any news home. Today I will tell you only that we've always been totally cheerful, that Wilhelm and I have become round and fat, and that we are looking to the future with glad hopes. As soon as we reach K.[ikkerton] I shall write to you with my arrangements for the future.

I ask you especially to give the photographic plates which I am sending along, to [J.] Hülsenbeck [photographer in Minden], so that he can copy and improve them. He is not to throw any away, no matter how bad they are, because they all have some value for me. Before he undertakes anything here, he is to wash them all again properly, because we do not have enough pure water here; and where possible he is to expose the plates longer. He is to retouch them only where it is unavoidably necessary, e.g. those plates that have spots.

I would ask you to send copies of the better pictures to the captain and mate, to whom I am indebted in any case, since they have requested them. The addresses are: Capt. A.F.B. Mahlstede, c/o D. Thiedemann, Amagerhafen 35, Bremerhaven; and Mate H. Wenke, Bettingbühren, Amt Elsfleth, Oldenburg. Otherwise you may do with them what you want; but give the plates back to Hülsenbeck, because he still has to coat them with varnish. I would request that you do not open them first, since they can easily be damaged. (...)

[FB/MK]

27th [August, Monday]   Yesterday I had a lot of work to do and when I wanted to start writing to you, my lamp went out. Yesterday we had dense fog again, but still got under way again around noon. Now, on the morning of the 27th we are still in thick fog, with no prospect of it clearing. In addition there is still much more ice in the Sound than we anticipated, so our anxiety level is rising by the day. It is very possible that *Germania* will have to winter here if she cannot get to Kingawa now, and if we encounter the steamer, which will bring you news of us. (...)

We can scarcely speak a word at table any more, we are always all so depressed. Today we have a fresh breeze, but it is so thick that one can scarcely see a hand in front of one's face. Yesterday I used the day to pack away again all my things that I had sorted out for the fall trip; though with a heavy heart, as you can imagine! (...)

More and more masses of fog continue to roll over us; more and more ice masses appear to be pressing into the Sound[,] and we don't have an hour to lose. It is now freezing day and night. The rigging is hanging full of ice; the deck is frozen and it will scarcely be possible to reach Kingawa still. If we can only get to Kikkerton, so that I do not have to head back with *Germania* without having attained anything at all! I am really afraid of writing a word, because it can only be about worries and complaints. It really is a miracle that I have not lost all courage! I can only believe that we have to get to land because we do not have enough water for the return voyage, so I hope that I too will still get ashore. It would be really bad if we could not even reach Kikkerton when it is so close.

Reaching K'exerten, Tinixdjuarbing: Meeting the Whalers and Inuit, August–September 1883

[FB/MK]

28th [August, Tuesday]   The fact that Kikkerton is in sight is the greatest event of the day! It is now just appearing through the fog ahead and we are running with a favourable breeze. This morning at 5 a.m. it began to clear up and we immediately set all sail in order to hurry onwards. We are now off the Middleaktuk [Miliaxdjuin] Islands and hope to be at Kikkerton by noon. I still don't know if we'll run in, but am happy to be as far as we are. Onward, onward, is the cry now. I have been aloft since 5.30 to observe everything, but have not seen much because it is too thick. (...)

[FB/parents]

It appears, dear parents that we are to reach Kikkerten on your wedding day. I hope that in a few hours we will be in the harbour and will be stepping ashore again after 10 weeks. I should like to chat with you for hours, but I have to hurry to conclude these few words. Marie is also to get some. A boat ahead! There appear to be 4 Eskimos and a white man in it; now we'll soon be going ashore and I can get to work. Can you imagine the joy of seeing the first land close by and the first new people, after 10 weeks? (...)

[Notebook/BN]

After a strong southerly wind while it slowly cleared, we sailed northward from Warham's Island [Milixdjuax]. Slowly the Middleaktuk Islands emerged from the fog and around 9 we caught sight of Kikkerton. Before we ran in a boat suddenly appeared. At first we thought it had come from shore, but it was Mr. Alexander Hall (a whaler from the Scottish station) who had come from the area of the Middleaktuk Islands where he had earlier been hunting walrus.

[FB/MK]
... one of the resident Scotsmen who was steering towards us. Soon the boat lay alongside and we greeted him; the captain [A.F.B. Mahlstede] and the mate [Wilhelm Wenke of *Germania*] recognized him as an old friend and I my new countryman.

[Notebook/BN]
We heard from him that our station was in good health. He had last seen it about 6 weeks earlier, and that the steamer from Aberdeen was still not here. Capt. [John] Roach [of the *Lizzie P. Simmons*] had gone out with the ice two months before and had drifted northward with the ice. So far it is not known where he is. In addition, in the boat were Bob, the cook at the [Scottish] station[,] and 6 Eskimos, who were paddling. Hall came on board; as an old friend he was greeted heartily by the captain and the mate. The wind had gradually dropped and since it was absolutely foul as we approached the harbour, Hall's boat towed us. We safely avoided the reef which [extended out] from the entrance to the harbour.

In the Notebook the text breaks off abruptly in mid-sentence and starts up again on 4 September. The original entries had been made by Boas in the Black Notebook, from which the following text is taken from 28 August to 3 September inclusive.

[BN]
(...) Hence Hall's boat towed us forward; we got safely round the reef which stretched out in front of the entrance to the harbour. We arrived just in time to be able to get into the harbour with the flood tide. The American station [of Williams & Co., New London, Connecticut] where Roach's cook [Rasmussen] was watching out, spotted us first and hoisted his flag. Soon we got even farther in and Noble's station hoisted its flag. A boat with women, and steered by an old man, came out to help bring *Germania* into the harbour. The two boats could not move the ship along adequately so we lowered our ship's boat to assist, but then first the towline to the women's boat, then that to Hall's boat broke. An unbelievable howling of dogs rang out from shore; we could now see the tupiks [I. *tupiq* = tent], the houses and the running dogs. Finally at 2.50 we dropped anchor. Mr. Hall was still on board; he had come aboard at 2.00. The Eskimos shouted unbelievably when they saw us coming. Mr. Hall left us at 3.00.

Around 4.30 the captain [Mahlstede] and I went ashore in my little boat [*Marie*]; here we found Hall and Captain Roach's cook on the beach. Farther up [James or Jimmy] Mutch was waiting for us. Innumerable dogs raced around us and tried to snatch at the dead walrus which Hall had brought ashore. Eskimos were rolling barrels over each other; ahead of us we could see the tupiks and houses but we had to stay a while longer down below, since Mutch and Hall had to see that everything was proceeding well. We then walked to the house where they welcomed us with rum. We discussed my affairs and Mutch immediately permitted me to land my things here. Hall showed us a fox that he kept in captivity. In the meantime Mutch and I discussed all my affairs and it would seem that I can arrange things more easily than I thought. Unfortunately there seems to be little prospect of getting away next summer, since they have not taken any [whales]. Nor has Roach.

We also visited many tupiks; they are not as dirty as I thought. We enjoyed a fine dinner with Mutch and Hall, then we returned on board. Immediately after we sat down[,] the women came aboard and they were very remarkable: small, and the old women frightfully ugly! Their fur suits, with the cotton skirts below them were strange! Two older women were still tattooed. Two children were quite pretty. I gave each of them a needle, a pipe and tobacco. They seem to be happy with these. An old woman came back for a second time, laughing. The captain gave one woman a cigar, and the first gesture she made with it clearly signified what she was thinking. The men received a bottle of rum, the women some in a glass. Their clothes are in some cases well made. They (the women) all have bad eyes and worn teeth. On shore I saw the first flowers; how happy I was.

[FB/MK]
(...) The [Scottish] steamer is lying off somewhere and cannot get in. The Scots are looking wistfully at their provisions, since their tobacco and matches are exhausted. (...)

[BN]
29 August [Wednesday]   In the morning I fetched the components of a light breakfast and at 8.30 Mutch came aboard. I met with him, the captain and the mate also being present. We discussed my prospects; it seems that I could travel in winter and could easily reach Lake Kennedy. But I could not detect any agreement on this point in the eyes of Hall and Mutch. In the meantime a start was made at taking things ashore and by

7 p.m. all my boxes had been landed. In the morning a boat was brought inshore, but not close inshore because the tide was too low. At 12.30 p.m. we continued. I went ashore; I am staying with Mutch (Hall was away hunting) and have been discussing my things with him; I saw my things stowed in the porch, and lent a willing hand. I had some rum given to the men. In the evening I returned on board. We have been trying to fish here and caught a massive fish with a very thick head. We were back on board around 7 and were quite tired. In the afternoon Captain Mutch and I had been up on a hill, spying out the situation. We saw a very great deal of ice. A superb view over the harbour, Kikkertassuak [K'exertux-djuax], Haystack [Umanax] and also Niatilik (Naujateling). A strong south wind has started to blow and it is pushing all the ice north.

30th Aug [Thursday]   A very strong south wind, but it is still possible to land things because in the lee of the ice there is {lower} quieter water along the shore. Mr. Hall came aboard in the morning and stayed past noon. We went ashore with him, and some coal, at high tide. I went up to the house to discuss something with Mutch and stayed till around 4, then went back to fetch tobacco [for] the natives, in return for their help in landing the coal. I borrowed some from the captain, then gave him back an ample amount from one of my boxes which I had trouble in finding. We returned aboard at 7. The mate had bought a skin from the natives. The coal is now all ashore and there are only a few boxes left on board.

31 August [Friday]   Got up at 5.30, took my suitcases ashore, then at 8 had some coffee, then stowed the ballast. In the meantime I had been ashore to discuss various things with Mutch. He thinks I should have brought a hut with me, because he does not know where I can leave my things. In the afternoon I went ashore with Wilhelm and the captain to take an observation. I took my compass with me and determined the time on the west side of the island and an azimuth near Mutch's house. By the evening we were pretty tired. Stayed a while longer with Hall and Mutch and went back aboard.

1st September [Saturday]   First I went ashore at 9 a.m. and photographed the ship, then the station. Afterwards I took some things I needed from my boxes, then they were stowed on the floor of the most westerly house [at the American station]. The most essential boxes are generally standing at the front. The boat and the kerosene are lying outside. At 11.45 went over the hill to get a sun altitude. As we walked along

the footpath and downstream, we found that the sun was still behind the
land and had to walk around a wide point, over high rocks, through ice
and seaweed via a very difficult route. When we finally reached the point,
there was an iceberg lying directly below the sun and thus this was practically all in vain. By azimuth the ice is setting strongly northward. It took
us an hour to walk back the distance we had covered in 25 minutes on the
way out. How good the first fresh water on the island tasted. We reached
the beach at 1.30 when a boatload of Eskimos from Kingait [Kingnait]
Fiord came back and one man in his kayak [I. qajaq]; a small boy was sitting in it. Lunch was set aside for us; we were tired by our fast walk and
slept a little. At 4 we went back onshore and took two photographs. Then
the captain and I stayed with Mutch, where we also ate supper. Later the
mate also came ashore. Around 8 we went back on board and slept
marvellously.

2nd Sept. [Sunday]   Sedan [memorial day for the battle of the Franco–
Prussian War of 1870]. To celebrate the day we had a major laundry ses-
sion and put my cabin in some order; I pressed the plants I have collected
so far. Then I developed 3 plates, for which I had good subjects. Then
Hall and Mutch came aboard and stayed past noon. We ate in my cabin.
Afterwards they went ashore and I slept until 6. Then I paid a visit to Mr.
Mutch and Hall on shore. In the evening wrote my journal and letters to
Marie and to home.

3rd September [Monday]   Early in the morning I went ashore with Wilhelm in order to survey the harbour. We took depression angles of the
plan. In the afternoon I determined the height of the mountain by angles
of elevation, and up and down from the highest tidemark to the house
and from there to the top. In the meantime a boat with natives came
ashore from Mr. Roach. Roach is at Kingawa near the upper narrows
where he is fishing for salmon; he is short of supplies and has received
some from our station. Dr. [Wilhelm] Giese [leader of the German Polar
Station] was on board the *Lizzie P. Simmonds* [*Lizzie P. Simmons*] on Thursday 30th, and sent a message via the boat, which had set off on Saturday
1st September, to ask whether the *Germania* is here. He would like to have
a reply from the captain about what he should do, whether the *Germania*
can get there, or whether he should come here with his boats. I offered to
go there with a boat to discuss everything with Dr. Giese, but it is not possible to get a boat today; the Eskimos, who have been travelling since Saturday until today, Monday, don't want to start out before the day after

tomorrow. So I will head back with them the day after tomorrow. In the evening further consultation on this topic in the captain's cabin. The mate is present, but is offended because the captain told him nothing and did not show him the letter, whereas he came up to me on the hill to tell me everything. At the same time I am to check the ice conditions in the upper part of the Sound and report back on them. We think it would be best if the station personnel returned on board *Lizzie Simmonds*, a possibility that Dr. Giese had not foreseen. According to his letter all responsibility would fall on the captain. The box of mail for Dr. Giese is not to be opened, but I will take the letter which the captain has received, and his letters.

A letter had been delivered by Inuit to the captain of the Germania, *A.F.B. Mahlstede, written by the leader of the German Polar Station at K'ingua, Dr Wilhelm Giese, while he was visiting the* Lizzie P. Simmonds *(Captain John Roach), which was beset in the ice and had been at K'ingua since the end of June 1883.*

[BSH:DPK; German Polar Commission, no. 289, station journal]

On board the Lisy P. Simmons

30 8 83

Dear Captain,

Today I went with a boat to the narrows and in so doing encountered the schooner of Capt. Rodge [Roach], who has been prevented thus far from leaving the fiord by the ice. Captain Rodge intends to send his Eskimos to Kikerton tomorrow, and I am taking advantage of this opportunity to send you these lines to Kikerton, especially since the ice conditions in the northern part of the Sound are such that one must seriously contemplate the possibility that the *Germania* might be able to reach Kikerton but not our station!

In that situation I would consider it essential to abandon the station with the personnel of the expedition once all our effects had been well packed and stowed in the house, and to proceed to Kikerton so as to travel home on board *Germania*.

Another, perhaps more probable, situation would be that you will be able to reach our station with the *Germania* this fall, but this would leave us very few days in which to bring the station's effects on board. In this case, it would be of the greatest importance that on your arrival you find everything ready to be loaded. But I cannot proceed with the closing-down of the station and the discontinuing of the observations until I know for sure that the *Germania* has at least reached Kikkerton.

Therefore, may I be permitted to make the following proposal, which I assume you will approve and accept:

As soon as you reach Kikerton, if you are unable to reach the station directly, send us a message via the Eskimos. You should do the same if, for any reason, you think you have to assume that an Eskimo messenger can reach us faster than the *Germania* herself. As soon as this message arrives, I would begin to close down the station; thus, the sooner the message arrives, the sooner the *Germania* can be ready to start for home.

In addition, I beseech you to state specifically in your message whether you

A) believe you can reach the station with *Germania*. In that case, we will wait quietly for you to arrive. If, later, against expectations, it turns out that *Germania* cannot get here, then there would still be time to inform us of this via a second messenger.

B) or whether you consider it impossible for the ship to reach the station and would prefer that we come to join you at Kikerton by boat. In that case, as soon as I receive your message, I would immediately pack and stow our effects, then set off by boat without delay with the entire personnel. It is naturally understood that we would not be able to bring with us in the boat provisions for the voyage back to Europe; I will have to leave it to you to establish ahead of time whether we can obtain sufficient provisions at Kikerton for the crossing (or at least as far as an American port), or to ensure that Mr. Much [Mutch] and Captain Rodge can put enough boats and crews at our disposal that we can bring the necessary supplies with us to Kikerton.

In that I feel sure that you will approve, and thus follow the above proposals, I look forward to the arrival of your message with equanimity. If I do not receive any news, I will assume that *Germania* has not reached Kikerton, and we will occupy the station for another year if no other opportunity arises for returning home.

Yours sincerely and respectfully,

Dr. W. Giese.

[D]

[**4 September, Tuesday**]   In the morning I paid a visit of about 2 hours to a tupik to collect vocabulary. In the afternoon on shore to preserve plants, since they are already withering fast.

Boas recorded his lists of Inuit words first in the Black Notebook and later in other notebooks (see Boas 1894).

[Notebook]

(...) The preparations for the trip are in hand. Mr. Hall and Mutch will lend me a fur outfit. Around 7 p.m. the Eskimos came on board and were persuaded to go with me to Kingawa in return for 1 lb. tobacco and 1 bottle of rum, and a similar gift from Dr. Giese. [D: Ssigna and his boat's crew are prepared to go back to Kingawa again, (...).]

I went to bed early. In the meantime Wilhelm is to help hauling water and cleaning the cabin. My tasks are as follows: 1. [investigating] ice and tides en route, especially in Kingawa Fiord. Locate Capt. Roach and ask him whether he can possibly take the things and the people. Ask about the time of high water in the entrance. Take Dr. Giese's cooking equipment for the station with me. Sulphur matches, kerosene and as much provisions as possible. It would probably be best to go with Roach.

[BN]

Meanwhile best to go [with] Roach, in that he is certainly coming to Kikkerton.

[Notebook]

Captain Mahlstede cannot say anything definite about ice conditions. As long as Roach cannot come down, *Germania* cannot get up there. He must wait until a reply reaches Kikkerton; if Roach hasn't come by the 5th, he wants to go to Kingawa. We could not send any news from here.

Boas resumed his entries in this notebook on 19 September.

[BN]

The captain did not want to open the chest [for the polar station]. In the light of the letters, Cpt. Mahlstede would prefer it if somebody came here, since the instruments for Dr. Giese are perhaps in it. Otherwise the Eskimos have to be paid more for their services. I will have to have supplies with me for 5 days. Dr. Giese himself will have to decide. The captain does not want to go, but cannot say for sure whether he can get back [to Hamburg].

Noble's steamer is still not here. Hall believes that if the instruments are packed and the Eskimos hired, they will be safe for this year [1883–4] (...)

Winding Down the German Polar Station, K'ingua, September 1883

First Boat Trip with Inuit to the North End of Tinixdjuarbing

[D]
[5 September, Wednesday]   The Eskimos came aboard around 6.

[BN]
Set sail at 7.45 [in a whaleboat], after the Eskimos had breakfast on board. Each of them was given a drink [of rum]; then my things were taken ashore, skins from Mutch and Hall were brought back, then we put to sea.

Boas noted Inuktitut words of importance to him next to his entries:

nuna	mainland	[I. *nuna*]
Kikkertak	island	[I. *qikirtaq*]
ikaggan	skerries, reef	[I. *ikkaruq*]

We rowed through the Kikkertens [archipelago]; around 9 a.m. the Eskimos tried shooting a seal but missed; at 10 we got clear of the islands and sailed [D: .. between Kautak [Kautax] and Tuaping [Tuapain].] 2.5 km. Open water near the land; farther out small pieces of ice are waiting for us. At 10.45 heading for the open water; ice to be seen immediately next the coast and offshore. Crew of 6 men. One has brought his young son, a fine little lad, who wanted to row with the rest and tried to copy the movements. At 11.20 much ice to be seen beyond Haystack [Umanax]. 11.35 between Haystack and the land there is still much ice to be seen[,] less at Haystack and Ssedloaping [Sagdliraping], then more ice again.

... At 12 landed at Ssesserchuk [D: Ssesseratok] [Satujanq] and made lunch. The Eskimos gathered heather [lichen] to make a fire to make coffee. I am treating them as commissariat officer. Climbed the hill and saw that there is fairly open water along the coast. Farther out everything is full of ice. Since it is quite far away, it appears very heavy, but I believe it is not very heavy. Since the coast has a major embayment I have determined that we should sail straight across. Set off at 1.15. I let the little lad lick some syrup, which made him very happy. At 2.15 ran into the ice which is lying very close. Once into the ice made good progress, sailing at 2 knots. On Saueralik [Sesseraling] there are two freshwater ponds, which debouch into the sea. Covered by deep peat. At 2.12 3 knots. We have to hug the coast. The ice consists of very grey floes. At 2.37 lay alongside a floe to get water. At 3 the ice is quite broken up, but so close that it is not possible to sail through it. At 3.19 we were rowing again. Off Pagniktu [Pangnirtung] already too much very heavy ice; an iceberg in the fiord.

[D]
Despite the heavy ice we succeeded in getting across Pagnirtu safely, then into a bay called Aupalluktung [Augpalugtung]; more open water and landed there at 9 o'clock to camp.

[BN]
6th September [Thursday]   At 4 woke the Eskimos and made coffee. I went up the hill and could see open water offshore. There is ice lying along the shore. To the north everything is full of ice, but the ice appears to be slacker. Set off at 6.06. Had landed at 8.15 on the evening of the 5th. High water. We pitched the tupik, made coffee and slept. Although the Eskimos did not want to set off before high tide, I insisted on getting under way early in the morning [D: .. at 6]; I said I wanted to be travelling in good time this morning, and keep travelling till we reach the station, no matter how late it is. At 5 a.m. on the 6th the current was setting north. At 6.46 we wanted to reach the open water we had seen in the morning, but became beset in the ice which was moving rapidly offshore. It was touch and go whether the boat would be crushed, the ice was coming from the land ..., so that the boat's sides would be crushed in.

There was a pool of open water near an iceberg, but since it was very close farther on we again had to work our way towards land with great effort, in order to get an overview. Here at 9.30, somewhat below American Harbour [Ussualung] there was ice; we had to stick close inshore beyond here. The entrance to American Harbour was heavily blocked, but then some open water, which we ran into at 10. In the inner harbour there was a great deal of beached ice, large, heavy pieces, so there was scarcely a place to anchor. On the south shore there appeared to be terrace formations of shingle and sand, with steep, vertical cliffs above. In the inner harbour open water and small pieces of ice. On the west coast of Kikkertelluk [K'ekertelung] there was enough room, but to the north everything was full of ice.

Between Kikkertelluk and the mainland falling ice was thundering constantly, like cannon shots, and with a loud echo. The Eskimos at first did not want to go on, for it was already past 12, but I must first get through the passage otherwise we will lose the whole day; moreover it is low water at 3 and it will be dark before we can get any farther. The Esk.[imos] insisted that we could not get through at low water, but I had to give it a fair try and at least get as far as possible. The entire narrows was ice-choked with many stranded floes everywhere. At 1.10 [D: .. off Tinikjuarbing] [Tinitoxajang] everything was completely closed, the ... fiord with very steep side walls. The steep rocks in the fiord are scratched by the ice at the high water mark. At 1.45 we landed. At 4.30 pushed off. At 2.34 low water. Served rum. I climbed to a summit and saw that our route was blocked by a neck of land. Took a height on the land and the variation. When I went back up at 4 far ahead I could see the coast ice free and decided to set off and to drag the boat across. Was wading in water up on the land.

When we were about to set off, one of the Eskimos was missing, but then, after much shouting, he came leaping down from the rocks. It was a wonderful sight as he came down in front of this rock gate. Our shouts developed a multiple echo. Hey!, shouted very loud. The entire fiord is very beautiful. Steep rocks, wide valleys, etc. Some of the cliffs completely striated. The rocks are rounded by ice erosion and thus appear to have rounded shapes, often with very long, very smooth slopes. When one steps on them they usually sound quite hollow. Immediately beyond the narrows the fiord is surrounded by high mountains.

Boas adds to his Inuktitut vocabulary:

ujarak	rock	[I. *ujarak*]
idjua(n)	peat	[I. *itjuq*]
killak	sky	[I. *qilaq*]
zyninnirn(ing)	sun	[I. *siqiniq*]

takirn	moon	[I. *tarqiq*]
udluriak	star	[I. *ulluriaq*]
nu'wuj'a	clouds	[I. *nuvujaq*]
kakkak	mountain	[I. *qarqaq*]
tarriok	sea water	[I. *tariuq*]
imirk	fresh water	[I. *imiq*]
po'adlu'	glove	[I. *pualu*]
ssiko	ice	[I. *siku*]

As the tide rises the water level in the east end of the narrows is higher than at the west end, and therefore a rapid current flows in this direction. As we passed through there was a very strong current race. On the ebb the current is said to run the other way along the north shore. Three large glacier potholes, one of them with three rocks in it, and a second one with a large rock and long, small ones near it. At 6.02 we had safely passed the tide race. 3 men in the boat, the others towing and standing; one man fell into the tide race. Immediately beyond the narrows it suddenly widens out again, a prospect that one sees immediately on rounding the point. At 7 the mainland was glowing the most magnificent {red} purple. At 7.45 we landed on the high shore because of the ice, in order to get a view. It was still very dark and since there was no water to be seen, I decided to stay here. It is a very bad site; very steep and no water; nowhere to make a fire. There is also a lack of fuel. But we have no alternative. High tide at 8.45. The current is running east; slack water from 8.45 until 9.30; then it flows west. Since there is no room to haul the boat up while we wait, and especially since we have to watch the ice movement, I assign Jimmy [Ssigna] and myself to keep watch. I slept from 9.30 to 10.30; Jimmy until 1.00 and I from 1.45, waking in time to set off. At 2.50 the current is in our favour, but the wind is westerly again. In the evening with the flood tide the ice very quickly became thinner, and in the evening with the ebb tide this continued again and thus there were now no pieces of ice to be seen.

[**7 September, Friday**]   At 1.45 a.m. much heavy ice came drifting from the shore, switching to the other side, since here there was none yesterday, whereas it did appear there. Around 3 it was almost rotten but then headed east again with the flood tide. Made coffee around 2.30, but we are short of water, which had to be taken from the sea; also a shortage of fuel so that we have no hot water. But with a SW wind we were making good progress when at 4.13 I realized that it was full of ice ahead.

[D]

Kingawa [K'ingua] (Sirmilling). Set off at 3.45; we soon came to a strait between Kangilieling [Kangidlieling] and Kikkertelluk, which was totally blocked by ice. We waited about half an hour, but since there was no change, we then had to turn back and fighting a strong wind and current round the far side of Kangidliutung [Kangidliuta], through thick ice and freezing water, we reached the north side of the island. There we discovered that Capt. Roach's schooner had left Ssurvsirn [Surossirn]. In about 2 hours we sailed and rowed through the Kangidliuta current, and finally landed around 12 in the East on Kueiinnang [K'uaiirnang]. From there we could see the entrance to Kingawa, as well as Ssarbukduuk [Sarbuxdjuax] and Ssarbukduk [Sarbaxdux] ... quite superb.

[BN]

At about 8 o'clock on Friday morning [7 September] we were in the narrows that lead into Kingawa Fiord, but could not get any farther since we had a foul wind and there was a heavy sea running, along with a strong current. We hoped to encounter the schooner [*Lizzie P. Simmons*] here, but were quite astonished not to see her at her old anchorage. At 10 we put ashore on the island of Kueing [K'uaiirnang] and spied for ice and for the schooner. The entire mouth of Kingawa Fiord was choked with ice. I ordered a short rest and then we rowed onward against a strong current. At 12, as we came through a narrows we saw the schooner lying somewhat farther back. I understood from Jimmy that the station was barely a quarter of an hour from there and we were about to proceed when a boat came from the schooner; I was astonished to hear German being spoken first. It was the mate of the *Lizzie P. Simmons* [Wilhelm Scherden]. We went aboard with him. There we found Cpt. Roach and joined him for lunch.

They were delighted to get news from us. We stayed there until around 12.45, when the captain, mate, harpooner and our boat continued onward. I was in the schooner's boat. At 3 we arrived at the station, which was covered in snow. We were mistaken for natives; also some of the gentlemen were asleep, and I arrived unexpectedly. The captain and mate came with me. I went straight up to Dr. Giese, who didn't recognize anyone, and told him who I was and what I wanted. I told him first what news I had from Germany, and visited the station with Dr. Giese. At the same time we were deliberating about what the station personnel should do. I proposed that he should go with Cpt. Roach. He consulted with [Leopold] Ambronn and decided to do just that. Capt. Roach is prepared to take him without payment. He asked him to bring his Eskimos from the schooner and I gave them to him. In the evening the boat returned; I went to bed around 10 and slept like a log until 7 a.m.

[BN]
[**8 September, Saturday**]   [D: Ssirmilling. German Polar Station.] The house is very smart. German flag; measuring magnetic current using astronometer built at the station. Behind is a tent with the magnetic theodolite. Yesterday's itinerary revised; all sorts of discussions. On board in the afternoon and [Dr. Hermann] Schliephake is now drunk. At lunch a major scandal concerning supplies. It appears that Ambronn is now behaving quietly and respectably. The doctor [H. Schliephake] is very doubtful. Roach has some liquor so the doctor has gone over to his vessel. In the evening they were drinking terribly and it was only by great resoluteness that I got away at 9.30.

[D]
(...) I spent the day at the station, to give the exhausted natives a rest. (...)

[BN]
[**9 September, Sunday**]   Got up at 5.30 today. Wrote letters, a frightful situation. They are still drinking on board! It is a terrible situation here.

Here Boas discontinues the entries in the Black Notebook, but he resumes them in the original from 19 September until 14 October 1883 and then transcribes them for this period, with a few changes, to the Notebook, in which he then continues the entries until 2 February 1884.

On 18 September 1883, Boas wrote the official report of his journey of 5–10 September for the German Polar Commission and Georg von Neumayer, to which he appended the map of his itinerary (see the illustration section, following p. 112), his first cartographic attempt with original geographical names in Inuktitut. Boas sent the report to Hamburg with the Catherine *on 3 October.*

[BSH:DPK, documents 12J; FB/George von Neumayer; 18 September 1883] 9 September. At 10 a.m. we left the station with a very favourable wind and by 11.30 had reached Kueiirnang [K'uaiirnang]. From here I could see that the ice had disappeared from the mouth of the fiord and decided to take the route via Ssarbukduak. The strong north wind barely permitted us to carry any sail, but we reached American Harbour safely; there it suddenly fell calm. At 8 p.m. we landed on a small island near Aupelluktuk [Augpalugtung].

10th Sept. [**Monday**]   We set off at 6, by noon had reached Ssesseradlik and at 7 p.m. safely arrived at the *Germania* in Kikkerten harbour; there we encountered the brig *Catherine* of Peterhead [Scotland], Capt. Abernathy, which had come to resupply the Scottish and American stations.

The Last Days of the German Polar Station

The meeting between Franz Boas and the personnel of the German polar station and the winding down of the station are presented from the viewpoint of Dr Wilhelm Giese through his entries in the official journal that he was required to keep. The personnel consisted of seven scientists, Dr Wilhelm Giese (physicist, leader, and commander), Leopold Ambronn (astronomer, deputy leader), Albrecht Mühleisen (navigator), Heinrich Abbes (mathematician), Carl Wilhelm Boecklen or Böcklen (engineer and geodesist), Carl F.W. Seemann (mechanical engineer), and Dr Hermann Schliephake (medical doctor), as well as four workmen who, as soldiers, answered to Dr Giese, their military commander; they were Albert Jantzen (carpenter), Paul Hevicke (sailmaker), C.E. Albert Hellmich (cook), and Richard Weise (carpenter). There was also the Inuk Ocheitu, who with his family had been hired by the Germans and had settled in front of the station buildings during the station's existence between September 1882 and September 1883.

The station journal, although written in a rather terse official tone, reveals considerable social tensions among the crew as of April 1883, towards the end of their stay. These tensions were partly related to the separation of scientific staff and workers, which was expressed in the assignment of accommodation: for the leader, single bunk; for the staff, double bunks; and for the workers, group quarters. The allotment of provisions, especially alcohol, which was available in great abundance and great variety, created further dissatisfaction and led to protests, brawls, threats, and excessive binges. Dr Hermann Schliephake seems to have been a troublemaker and an unpredictable companion right from the start, having requested special treatment even before the trip began by asking to be accompanied by his sixteen-year-old boy servant, which Neumayer did not allow. It can be surmised, since some veiled references can be found in the journal and correspondence, that this minute male society displayed homosexual tendencies and relations. The tensions were reined in only by the severe punishments that Dr Giese could impose on the workers and soldiers. He was powerless with regard to his professional colleagues, with whom he could only appeal to their code of honour. It is perhaps indicative that Neumayer did not allow the crew members to publish anything after their stay in the Arctic unless is was cleared by the German Polar Commission.

[BSH:DPK, no. 289, station journal, Dr Wilhelm Giese; 7–16 September]
Friday, 7 9 1883   All the preparations for Mr. Mühleisen's departure had been made, and between 3 and 4 p.m. Capt. Roach's boat appeared; to our amazement it was followed by a second boat, in which, as it approached closer, we could distinguish only Eskimos. Once the boats came ashore I walked down to greet the captain; but to his left another man, unknown to me, pushed forward. Outwardly he was dressed in native costume but by his walk he was immediately recognizable as a European. While still at a distance he shouted to me: 'Greetings from *Germania.*' It was Dr. Boas. So *Germania* was at Kikerton! It was therefore decided that tomorrow we would start packing up. After further discussion with Mr. Boas, who is now familiar with the ice conditions between here and Kikerton (on the basis of my letter, he had come to us with Capt. Roach's Eskimos, since no other Eskimos were available at Kikerton), I have decided to entrust ourselves and our effects to Capt. Roach's schooner for the trip to Kik. because, given present conditions, it seems very questionable whether or when *Germania* can get through to us and even more questionable whether she can make the return trip. It all thus becomes a matter of seizing the right opportunity at the right time, and we can do this best by using the *Simmons.* Here I am in agreement with Capt. Mahlstede, whose views, however, I know only from Dr. Boas's report; our captain has put nothing in writing. I am greatly relieved by the decision to implement our retreat by this unusual and complicated procedure, in the precise form in which the letter from the president [Georg Neumayer] of the P.C. [Polar Commission], brought by Mr. Boas, stressed that it was my duty to return in good time. This evening was the occasion for a celebration, during which we chatted with our countryman. Tomorrow we set to work; I still have two days to take variation observations. In the meantime, we will move coal and provisions on board and otherwise pack whatever is possible. Then on Monday we can discontinue everything.

[Saturday to Monday] 8, 9, 10 Sept. 83   As I write this the station is already actually closed down; the bulk of the instruments, all our provisions, etc., are already on board and tomorrow [11 September] we ourselves can go aboard during the course of the morning if the captain wishes. I myself would hardly have believed it possible that we could have everything ready in three days. The entire cable had to be taken up; apart from variation observations, I still had determinations to make on the 8th and 9th, and these were possible only after discontinuation of the hourly observations (Herr Abbes assisted me); Herr Ambronn also had to take angles with the universal instrument on the far side of the fiord; Mr. Böcklen still had to survey the north arm of the cable trigonometrically, and yet (except for Mr. Böcklen) we got everything finished and, in addition, have packed up the station's effects. I can write a testimonial to the effect that they all lent a hand efficiently; only Mr. Schl.[iephake] opted instead to go aboard on Saturday and indulge in a heavy drinking bout with the captain and mate, which lasted until Sunday morning and was glorified by a serious brawl, in which the ship's cook dislocated an elbow. It was not until early this morning that Mr. Schl. returned to the station; we did not miss him during his absence.

The speed with which we have closed down the station would not have been feasible if we had not had 10 Eskimos at our disposal during the entire period. Naturally, we had prepared for closing down in every respect.

Tuesday, 11 Sept. 83 We have not yet gone on board today because, after the last of the station's effects were taken out in two last boatloads, there was still too much to be done on board for the ship to get under way. In the evening, after they had finished everything, the captain and mate came ashore once more, and we agreed that if the wind was fair, the station personnel would go on board early tomorrow morning with their bedding and personal baggage; but if it was not possible to set sail, we wanted to stay another day on shore in our house.

Today, in the evening, our rooms looked very bare; there was nothing more to do; we played a last game of skat by the light of a candle stuck in a bottle, then went to bed early when a NNW wind arose.

Wednesday, 12 9 83 At 6 o'clock we were wakened by the announcement, 'Fair wind!' Immediately after we had had breakfast, I ordered all the luggage still in the house to be moved out; then, after I had checked that nothing important had been left, I let the Eskimos and their wives salvage any little items lying in the rooms and then sweep them out. In this fashion I hoped to have taken the best possible measures for preserving the house, since the Eskimos now knew from their own experience that nothing in any way useful to them was left inside. I then had the carpenter nail up all the doors and windows. In the meantime, the bulk of the personal baggage had been moved on board, and I went on board in our boat with the entire expedition personnel and the observation results. At 10.15 the crew began to weigh anchor; shortly after 11 we made sail and by 4, with a light but fair breeze, we were out in the Sound; at the time of writing, we have already passed American Harbour.

Unfortunately, the behaviour of the crew today was bad. While clearing out the house, the men had found wine and spirits in various places and had started drinking; fortunately, I came on the scene just as they were clearing out the remnants from the wine cupboard and ordered the bottles smashed. Even so, the carpenter [Weise] was no longer sober when we came on board; the cook [Hellmich] was in no better shape. I drew Mr. Abbes's attention to the situation and instructed him to take precautions in future; thereupon, he gave each man a bottle of wine, with the result that after lunch the cook was impertinent to Mr. Abbes and the carpenter to Mr. Schl. But I was able to restore order again.

Thursday, 13 9 83   For us on board the *Simmons* last night, naturally it could scarcely have been more comfortable; we slept in chairs and on the cabin floor; whenever the captain, mate, etc., were on watch, they gave up their bunks for us. Since it was only late at night that I found an opportunity to get some rest, I slept without interruption until breakfast (7.30), at which time I was wakened by the news that we were off Kikerton. Indeed, the *Germania* and a brig (but no steamer) were lying in the harbour; the latter had brought supplies for the Scottish and American stations. Capt. Roach first let his men have breakfast, then ran into the harbour. Before we reached it, a boat appeared bringing the *Germania*'s mate, our old acquaintance; he had been sent by Capt. Mahlstede to discover why the *Simmons* was lying off the harbour. After breakfast the schooner anchored alongside the *Germania*; we began transferring our effects immediately. I used this period of relative quiet to quickly distribute the incoming mail; I found time to read my own mail only during the noon break. Hevicke and Mr. Seemann have received bad news from home; the former's father and the latter's mother have died.

By around 4 transhipment of the cargo was complete, but we still had a lot to do organizing things on board the *Germania*; there could be no thought of being finished before evening, especially as many cases had to be opened to satisfy Dr. Boas's wishes [see the list of effects that Boas received]. When I went to bed late in the evening, it took me about another half hour before I managed to clear enough space in my bunk, which I could just squeeze into.

Friday, 14 9 83 It is Capt. Mahlstede's intention to set sail tomorrow; everything has been stowed in the hold as well as possible, and we have taken on water, etc. Today, above all, I had to make our arrangements with Capt. Roach, and we finally agreed that I would pay 300 m[arks] for the crew, and I made a gift of 800 m for Scherden [the mate] and the captain (£15 and £40). This occurred after an earlier detailed discussion with Mr. Mühleisen and Capt. Mahlstede. Capt. Roach declined to ask for anything but was easily persuaded to accept a 'gift' for himself and Scherden. In addition, I had to negotiate with Mr. Mu[t]ch about taking over our station buildings, but accomplished nothing; Mr. Much declared that he could do nothing there. By contrast, we can only hope that at least during the upcoming year Dr. Boas, to some degree, will be in a position to make use of the houses. [Boas did not visit the station again during his stay.] In the evening I also went to see Capt. [Abernathy] on board the *Catherine* to give him copies of our mail for delivery to the German consul in Aberdeen.

The need to exchange personal gifts turned out to be a very irksome additional task on top of all these other items of business, one for which none of us was at all prepared.

Saturday, 15 9 83 It turned out to be impossible to set sail today; the wind was foul and there was also still much to do on board.

The exchange of gifts continued all day and gave us no peace. It ended with us being in debt and with us deciding as a group to give Capt. Roach a hunting rifle.

Tomorrow morning our captain wants to get out of the harbour; and the two other captains, as well as the mate [Wilhelm] Cherden [Scherden], Mr. [Alexander] Hall, and Mu[t]ch, will escort us out.

Sunday, 16 9 83 This morning, as we were departing from Kikerton, Mr. Abbes could not refrain from creating a scene; it came to a good end only because the champagne ran out; he had again given the men too much, so once again there was a scandalous scene. The cook refused to cook, and I finally made short work of him. I appointed Jantzen as cook with the cook's salary, and as punishment for the time of his strike, I withheld Hellmich's wages except for 55 reichsmarks per month. I have neglected to keep a special record in the journal, since Hellmich so far has always avoided being present when they are announced; making him aware of his punishment in front of witnesses must suffice here. Jantzen was installed as cook, at a cook's wages, in the presence of Messrs. Abbes and

Seemann, while Hellmich was informed of his punishment in the presence of Messrs Seemann and Jantzen.

Soon after our escort left us, the *Germania* found herself in a quite abominable short sea, and we were almost all victims to seasickness; only Mr. Mühleisen escaped.

Thus, the eleven-man German party left the Arctic after a sojourn of a year; and after a four-week crossing of the North Atlantic, the group reached Hamburg in the early morning hours of 17 October 1883. Its members then scattered to every corner of the German Reich.

The scientific results appeared in the pertinent literature for polar research in the closing years of the nineteenth century: Abbes 1884a, 1884b, 1890; 1992; Ambronn 1883; Neumayer and Börgen 1886; Neumayer 1890, 1891; see also Barr 1983, 1985, 1992; Barr and Tolley 1982.

At the Scottish Whaling Station at K'exerten and **Germania**'s Departure

[ww]
Tuesday, 11 September   Last night the ice drove more strongly into the harbour, so at 1 a.m. they dropped the port anchor again. During the day there was a fairly strong wind and dull weather. We have not left the ship. Was selecting plants. In the afternoon I did some laundry [,] and after writing letters and doing a general clean-up, I put on clean linen and washed naked.

Wednesday, 12 September   There was a strong north wind so the ice was still driving into the harbour; by evening we were totally beset. I did not go ashore during the day, and tonight was the last night that I slept aboard *Germania*.

[FB/parents, sisters; Boas sent the letters written before 16 September back to Germany on the *Germania*; written on 12 September]
(...) I am all straightened away with Dr. Giese and have received *everything* I want, so am now very well equipped. As soon as everything was arranged there I returned with my boat and arrived safely back here on Monday evening [10 September]. I have slept only about 10 hours during this entire week! (...)

When I arrived here, I found the ship from Aberdeen with your letters. [According to Weike, the *Catherine* had arrived on 7 September.] Can you believe me when I say that I was delighted? (...)

I still have to report on my trip to the *Tageblatt* and write to Neumayer, since during this time to a certain degree I have put myself in the service of the Polar Commission. You can be sure that never again will I travel as fast as [I did] this time, about 50 German nautical miles in 4 days of travelling! My people were all deathly tired when we arrived here. I would have taken Wilhelm with me if we had not had to travel fast and since we could not take anything superfluous with us.

My plan is now to stay in the vicinity of the island [K'exerten] and then pursue my topographic studies in particular. When the travelling season begins I want to go to Lake Kennedy and see what can be done there. It is possible to get there in 4 days from here. Whether I can get any farther than that is very doubtful, because I want to be back here by July to watch for ships. In any case I hope to be home by next fall [1884]. If I do not succeed in this, you should not be unduly worried. I am outfitting myself with provisions for 2 years in order to avoid possibly starving later, but I firmly believe that I will see you next October in Scotland or America. When I was still at home I had imagined everything here to be better than it is.

Almost all the Eskimos understand English and I can manage very well with them. They are willing to work and are good-natured; they just want to be treated well. On this first trip I heard no grumbling, although I had to tax the men severely. But I always lent a hand myself and ate exactly what they ate so that I could always say that I had it no better than they! The helmsman [Ssigna] in particular is a marvellous man whom I am seriously contemplating engaging. Thus he told me in the evening that if I would not keep the rum with me, it might perhaps occur to somebody to set about it. For this I have also given him a knife. I had lost my watch chain in the boat; today he came to give it me. (...)

The brig [*Catherine*] from Aberdeen will be staying here about another two weeks. I plan to send you further news via her. (...)

13th [September, Thursday]   7.30 a.m. The schooner [*Lizzie P. Simmons*] is now in sight! She is just coming round the corner of the harbour and we hope she will run straight in. But now to add the last greetings to your letter. Farewell, dearest ones, I send you thousands upon thousands of greetings. Always love me as I love you and don't be unduly worried. (...)

[WW]

(...) This morning as we came on deck Captain Rosch's [Roach's] ship was in sight. Now there was much to do and we had to move out as soon as possible, so our last things went ashore, because we will be receiving more things from the company [German Polar Commission]. It was a pleasure for the gentlemen [of the polar station] to come on board our ship again. During the night more ice had moved into the harbour, so it was difficult to get aboard through the ice; all day long there were all sorts of different people in the boat, sometimes Americans, sometimes British, and sometimes Americans again; it was great fun. The best time was in the evening; then there were boats from all three ships on shore and we gathered at the American station, where a concert was held in the evening; the company's carpenter [Jantzen or Weise] played a harmonica, and we sang both German and English songs. It was late when we broke up; we first visited all the *tubik* [I. *tupiq* = tent], then I headed for bed; I had to sleep on the floor in the room where I had spread a mattress and a blanket.

From 13 September 1883 until 6 May 1884, Boas and Weike used the Scottish whaling station as their base and living quarters, though with numerous interruptions.

14 September, [Friday]   I had quite a fine night sleeping on the bare floor. I did not get much sleep; it was 6 a.m. when I got up and had coffee at the station. At noon I went aboard the *Germania*; in the afternoon we were still going from shore to ship; finally we hoisted our flag using our boat-hook as a flagstaff.

15 September [Saturday]   There was still a lot to be done today, so the ferrying from ship to shore continued because we had brought all our things to the American station. One incident occurred in the evening; we had been ashore and had brought a case of rum aboard; a gentleman on the ship was supposed to take it. Dr. Boas wanted to pass the case from the boat to the ship, but the other gentleman couldn't agree and so the boat was pushed off and heeled, and Dr. Boas fell into the water, the rum along with him and myself after that. In this emergency I grabbed the boat with one hand and then stayed in the boat. Dr. Boas swam to the ship; I had to fish the case out and then went aboard too and stayed on board for the night.

As had been agreed at the end of May in Hamburg, before the Germania *sailed*

Boas provided Dr Giese and the German Polar Commission with receipts, having inherited from the polar station a number of useful instruments and other material which would ensure his and Wilhelm Weike's sojourn and which Boas committed himself to return or to make good to the German Reich.

[BSH:DPK, Act 12J, 15 September 1883, extract]
A centre-fire rifle and accessories
A Mauser rifle
1500 Mauser shells
20 lbs. powder
3 bags shot
2 harpoons

An assortment of fishing tackle

A standard thermometer
3 thermometers
A mercury barometer
An aneroid barometer

Tent
Sledge

6 cases of bread @ 144 lbs.
10 lb. unroasted coffee
2 cases of flour @ 100 lbs.
1 barrel of pulses
$\frac{3}{4}$ barrel of peas
1 case of alcohol
6 packets of matches
Pressed vegetables
A case of butter and pork lard
40 bottles rum
2 bottles kerosene
[also cooking utensils, hand tools, paints, wicker chairs and other items]

[WW]
16 September [**Sunday**]   Things began early; in the morning anything went: red wine, champagne and everything mixed up together. Around 10 *Germania* put to sea; this was not so pleasant, since first the friends

whom I had made on board ship, and then the acquaintances whom I had made on board and on shore. When the *Germania* departed those were almost the last Germans we would see; there were just two Germans left on board the American ship [Fred Grobschmidt/Sherman and Wilhelm Scherden]; we stayed on board the ship for the afternoon and got pretty drunk again. As the *Germania* departed I hoisted our boat's flag three times, which made me feel good. We were in good hands at Captain Rosch's; when we arrived we got a meal immediately, so we remained on board until evening; afterwards we went to the station and went to bed early because next day we planned to be travelling.

[FB/parents, sisters]
(...) You can be sure I shall come home healthy and happy. Wilhelm and I are well thus far, and, trust me, I am careful and will return to you in good health. Farewell; think of me, as I will of you. (...)

Late Fall Boat Trips in the Sound, September–October 1883

K'exerten

[WW]

17 September [**Monday**] Nothing came of our plans for departing, because we had a foul wind and therefore stayed at the station. In the morning Dr. B. took observations and we went so early that we still had time to cook something. I got everything ready, but we had to eat at Mr. Mosch's [Mutch's] so our meal was left lying. In the afternoon we built a cairn on the hill, and afterwards we filled shells. There was still a strong wind, to the extent that the sand was flying markedly; we are delighted that we have got this far. I had not slept particularly well the past few nights.

18 September [**Tuesday**] There was still a very strong wind, so we could still not get away and we had to stick around the station; at noon, at low tide we went looking for mussels and sea creatures and preserved them in alcohol. Around 4 p.m. we went in our boat to the other side of the harbour and built another cairn. There we found a couple of seals and two rabbits, but we didn't have a gun.

Boas sent the letters written before 3 October with the Catherine *via Scotland to Germany. They reached his family in Minden i. W. on 11 November 1883, and copies were then forwarded to relatives and friends.*

[FB/parents, sisters]

Kikkerton, **19th September** [**Wednesday**] Now just a few words more. Until today I could not get around to writing to you because there were too many things to be done here. I now want to go on a second trip that will last from today, Wednesday, until Saturday. The weather is clearing up and I want to take the opportunity because the boating season will soon be over. I am quite at home here now; I have been made welcome in a *very* friendly fashion and hope to be able to complete, if not everything I intended, then at least a good part of it. I hope to be able to return to Scotland or America quite definitely, or I can even say definitely, if no unforeseen obstacles arise. My provisions are in good order. I have hired an Eskimo [Ssigna], who understands English well and is very reliable, for the entire winter, and now have no further worries. So don't you worry either. Believe me, I shall return to you healthy and happy, and just take care that I find you all healthy.

[Notebook/BN]
(...) In the evening Capt. Abernathy and Roach were visiting Mutch. We talked about everything possible. Roach has again promised to let me have Ssigna. Later the boat's crew, including the second mate from the brig, came to fetch the captain. The mate told me that a great many Inuit lived at Merchants Bay [no Inuktitut name indicated] and Pond's Bay [Inlet; Torsuxateng], as well as in Admiralty Inlet [Tununirusirn]; he had once counted 130 tupiks in Admiralty Inlet. Blood feuds still prevailed there. If there was no sign of the killing ending, the ultimate measure was to lash the latest culprit to the mast. He thinks there are about 2000 natives in this region. The Scottish whalers usually call at Pond's Bay and Button Point [no Inuktitut name given]. They went back to their ship around 10.30. I said goodbye to Abernathy.

Journey to Kingnait Fiord

20th [September, Thursday]   Got up at 5.30 a.m.; Mutch and Hall were rolling barrels to the brig. I said goodbye to them and around 7 we launched Jimmy's [Ssigna's] boat. First we laid alongside the *Lizzie Simmonds* where Jimmy picked up some powder and a boat's anchor. By about 9 we were off the outermost point of Kikkerton. I took observations, but a thick fog rolled in during this process, though it disappeared again after about an hour. We sailed with a fair wind to past Kikkertalik [K'ekertaping], where it fell calm. We then rowed for a long distance to the back side of Tellirrua [Talirua], where there is a small bay. Above it there was some masonry; Capt. Roach's station had once stood here, and he had spent a winter here [1875–6]. After our noon coffee [BN: .. high tide at 2] Wilhelm and I climbed the hill on Tellirrua. To our right was a very steep cliff from which parts were breaking away almost constantly. Very high. A powerful stream flows through large boggy meadows between this and Tellirrua. On a terrace on the slope of Tellirrua facing inward towards Kingnait (...) lies a pond. Tellirrua means flipper [I. *taliruaq* = whale or walrus flipper]. Immediately beneath the summit there lies a deep pond. From up there there are superb distant views over Middleaktuk, Kikkerton, the south shore of the Sound and into the inner part of Kingnait. Whereas on the ascent we had climbed up the slope of the mountain, we returned via the valley between Tellirrua and Kikker-taktuak [K'exertuxdjuax]. En route we drank some water, and at this point I lost my field journal, but found it again next morning. We then sailed across the fiord (for about 45 minutes)[;] there I took my angles and since there was a heavy swell and no safe place for the boat to land we returned immediately. At first there was a strong wind blowing up the fiord, then a calm with a high sea. We wanted next to proceed to Kignait Harbour [Tornait] with a south wind, but since it grew dark and fell calm we could not make any progress. So we pitched our tent and spent the night.

21st [September, Friday]   At 5.30 a.m. I woke the others. We made coffee then returned to the spot where I had lost my book. The steep slope of Kikkertalik is almost devoid of vegetation, like anywhere where there is constant soil subsidence and where steps and terraces are thus forming. Initially it was calm, but then a good wind; we fired unsuccessfully at seals. A thick fog developed, yet the weather remained fairly favourable. By 12 noon we were at Kingnait Harbour (Tungnirn [Tornait]). I obtained a noon altitude. Made coffee at noon and immediately thereafter went inland with Wilhelm while Ssigna remained with the boat.

[BN]
(...) We climbed a steep hill and reached a large pond, while water poured down to the rocks in torrential streams. Magnificent view from the hill. Down below there was a raging stream flowing in a narrow valley with numerous meanders, without waterfalls at the harbour and the foot of the pond. Caribou tracks and dung. Later we stopped at the waterfalls. Here there was a glacial pothole about 5′ wide and 18″ deep; there was also a small rock in it. Many sandy islands. Wilhelm fell into a rapids on the return trip. ... Very deep and with sand and mud. It was impossible to

get across there because the water was everywhere too deep. Right across rapids in a narrow rock canyon. Finally stopped there for a rest, then back over the hill. The entire valley represents a floodplain, evidently with an abundance of tributaries from the mountains. The pond (see above) lies barely above sea level. The stream coming from the pond becomes a small river at its mouth; the rocks all around are washed smooth. Jimmy had {made supper} pitched the tent, and fetched water. So we were able to cook immediately. Jimmy towed the boat to a safe spot and at 8 we went to bed. (...)

[Notebook]

22nd [September, Saturday]   After a cold night it cleared up in the morning. Snow. Got up at 4.45; got under way at 8. We are retracing the route by which we came back yesterday. At 10.15 we stopped at a fine waterfall on the west side. It is difficult walking uphill and downhill across boggy ground with many rocks. We took with us only bread, butter and liver sausage. So far we have seen nothing worth shooting. The sun is starting to break through. (...)

We stopped at 11.05 and had lunch, consisting of water and ship's biscuits with liver sausage. Then we climbed up a hill a little to spy for caribou. We spotted only a rabbit on the other side. Jimmy clambered farther up but I did not follow him. Wilhelm and I went back to wait for Jimmy, but he did not come. We continued and Jimmy caught up with us at the waterfalls, where the route to Pagniktun [Pangnirtung] runs. He had misunderstood and had gone back over the mountains. Finally we arrived back at Tungnirn at 7 p.m.

23rd [September, Sunday]   We pushed off at high tide at 8.30 a.m. At first there was a strong breeze out of Kignait [Kingnait] and farther up the fiord there was a very rough sea. But the farther out we went the less wind. We had to row and finally landed at Jaboon Pt. [Jawbone Point; K'arsax]. There I took observations and we had lunch. We had to row all day, since it was a flat calm. We were unable to land on Kikkertuktuak, because there was an excessively high sea running out of Kignait. Finally at 10 the wind was slightly more favourable and at 11 we reached Kikkerton, very tired. We had eaten in the boat during the evening. The Eskimos helped me haul the boat up. Slept late next morning.

[FB/MK]

Kraksak [K'arsax; Jawbone Point], 23rd September. Every day I have to record another movingly beautiful name at the top of my letter. Yesterday was a very strenuous day for us. We hiked with full load, i.e. rifle and provisions, for 8 hours, but not on a level route; it was uphill and downhill through bogs and water, over rocks and stones. Moreover we are now wearing genuine native Eskimo boots, cummings [I. *kamik*], which do not have a firm sole, so our feet are still sore today. We are now on the homeward leg and are waiting longingly for our noon coffee to be ready. Yesterday it was our legs that were tired; today it is our arms. We have been rowing for 3 hours already. We are still in Kignait Fiord and are terribly hungry, so goodbye for now. 5 p.m. We are heading back to Kikkerton. After we had rowed for another 2 hours, a wind got up with which we could make use of the sail. So I am making use of the time to write you some more. (...)

My Eskimo, Ssigna or Jimmy, as the Scots call him, is a good soul; he does what he is told unquestioningly and does not drink. (...)

[BN]

24th [September, Monday]   [K'exerten]. Sketch of Tugnirn [Tornait] somewhat closer to completion and my itinerary complete. Cleaned my rifles and wrote home. In the evening Capt. Abernathy was here and invited me to go to Warham Island. I accepted with pleasure and have postponed my plan to sound the harbour or to visit the Kikkertons. Ssigna [BN: Jimmy] came to see me in the evening and I came to terms with him. He gets the Mauser rifle. I believe I should do this because I have nothing else left. In addition he will receive a weekly ration of bread, molasses and tobacco.

25th [September, Tuesday]   Have finished my letters and my reports to the [*Berliner*] *Tageblatt* [Müller-Wille 1984:119–20] and the Geographical Society [Boas 1883d]. Then packed my things and by 2 p.m. was ready to leave. Wilhelm will stay here; he has to take care of the house. Capt. Roach will be leaving in the next few days to land his things at Neiatlik [Naujateling].

[FB/parents, sisters]

Kikkerton, 25th September. Dear parents and sisters, The brig is now in the process of leaving the harbour and I can send greetings to you again. The night before last I returned safely from my trip to Kignait and yesterday I rested. I had already told you that Ssigna, Wilhelm and I travelled in a whaleboat. We had 4 tough days and unfortunately it was always so foggy that the results are relatively limited. In the interior of Kignait Fiord we encountered superb weather, and I took advantage of that day for a trip into the interior. There are magnificent landscapes here. You can't imagine the beauty of the waterfalls, the massive, snowy mountains and the precipitous, bare cliff faces.

On the 23rd we came back and that day we had to row for 12 hours; you can just imagine how tired I was. I can't write in great detail at this last minute, because I am obliged to produce an article for the [Berliner] Tageblatt and I have some other things to write. But let me just tell you again I am always thinking of you all in sincerest love and friendship. Be assured, as I am, that I shall return to your arms healthy and well. You will hear from Herr Mühleisen [a member of the German Polar Station] that conditions here are not at all as bad as I and you expected. Mr. Mutch is obliging in *every* way; the difficulties of travelling are not great; or at least not as great as I had thought. I now want to use the open water season and to survey as much of the Sound as possible.

Today Mr. Mutch and I are going about 30 English miles south with the Scottish brig, commanded by Capt. Abernathy of Peterhead, which is leaving the harbour today; there the ship, which is the same one that brought your letters, has to take on another 42 barrels of oil. Then we will come back in a whaleboat with Mr. Mutch and his crew (6 Eskimos). Wilhelm will have to stay here and look after the house.

As regards my plans, I cannot say much about them yet because everything depends on the snow, wind and weather. The Sound usually stays open until the end of October, then I'll have to stay here on the Kikkertons [I. qikirtait = island group] until Christmas. In January the Eskimos begin travelling again and then Mr. Mutch wants to take me with his sledge and dogs to Ananatu [Anarnitung] where an Eskimo he knows lives, who wants to go to Lake Kennedy with me. What and how much I can do there depends on what supplies Biräs [Piera] has (this is the man's name). Ssigna and his wife will accompany me for the whole trip. During this past four days he has again proved himself thoroughly. He is more reliable than many other Eskimos, and even than good white servants. Above all he does not drink and does not eat much. That is all I can say so far.

Capt. Roach will be going to Niautilic [Naujateling] on the west side of the Sound, where perhaps I can find him on my return journey. He has placed a sledge and one of his dog teams entirely at my disposal. I am also indebted to him for providing Ssigna's services, in that he has made him available. I am very sorry that I cannot write to you in more detail from here. But the demands on my time are too great. So once again, all my loved ones, farewell; give my regards to relatives and friends. You can't imagine how much pleasure all your news gave me. Marie wrote so lovingly. I hope she is now with you, and no doubt you often talk about your 'polar bear.' I can give you the consolation that there are no wild animals here; no bears and very few wolves. I have been on the mainland for days and have seen nothing but mice [voles, lemmings] and rabbits and the tracks of caribou. I shall be careful and will keep my spirits up! (...)

Please send the letter to the Geographical Society [in Berlin] one day later than the one to the [*Berliner*] *Tageblatt*, and remember to send the *Tageblatt* to Lindeman [in Bremen].

On Board the Catherine: *The First Voyage to Naujateling and Milixdjuax*

26th [September, Wednesday]   Once again I am writing to you from on board a ship, the *Catherine*; we are just off Warham's Island [Milixdjuax] and with luck will soon be landing. We are now a good distance from the Kikkertons, although they are still in sight. Perhaps these are the last greetings that I will be sending you. May I ask just one last thing of you, dear Toni, namely to write to Mr. David Bruce, manager of the Old Dundee Whaling Company in Dundee next spring (February) to ask him to tell his captain to possibly pick me up. It is very probable that I shall be returning with one of these ships. And now, dear ones, farewell once again. Keep your spirits up as I shall. It will not be so long before I am back with you.

[Notebook]
Since there is too much of a sea running, we have to cruise off Warham's Island. Overcast and snow.

[BN]
12 noon, 23°16', Warham's Island. Capt. David Abernethy, Peterhead, 7 James St., Scotland. The ship's chronometer aboard *Catherine*, compared with that of the [German] expedition on 15th September, was losing 0.5 s per day.

[Notebook]
27th [September, Thursday]   Very high seas; squally; soon there was a very strong gale and I was seasick. In the evening I asked the second mate

about the different conditions on the west shore of Davis Strait. C.[ape] Kater [= Cape Raper, Niaxongnang] always steam = Naikerneiak[?] [I. *niaquunjaq* = headlike]. Last night we encountered a piece of ice, since with this strong south wind the ice in the Gulf [BN: Sound] is beginning to drift; the captain has resolved to run into Neiantalik.

28th [September, Friday]   The wind is gradually slackening and the barometer rising. At 11 the west shore emerges through the fog and we sight Bear Island [unidentified; K'aluviang?]; by 2 we are at Blacklead [Umanaxtuax] and at 3 we anchored in Neiantilik Harb[our]. Unfortunately it is quite overcast and snowy so I cannot go ashore.

29th [September, Saturday]. Last night slept on the bench. Went ashore with David Smith, one of the brig's people and took observations. Obtained a sun altitude. Since the snow is deep I had to abandon my intention of climbing the mountain. It cleared up and at 1 the opposite shore of the Sound appeared. At 12 I had to run to get back in time to take the noon altitude. Earlier I had tried in vain to find an old mica mine, since we were constantly sinking knee-deep in the snow and could not see the holes in the ground. By 1 we were back on board to find that everyone had finished lunch. Latitude 64°55'. Earlier there was a mica mine here and a tramway was built for bringing the rock down in summer [the mica mine of an American mining concern, established in Philadelphia in 1873, probably set up and worked by the crews of the *Tigress* or *Polaris* in 1877–8; see Boas 1885:38; Goldring et al. 1984].

We heard an Eskimo dog howling on Niaktalik Island. On Norris Island [Inukdjuax] there are the graves of many Scots. The harbour is very good, protected from all winds, and open only to the south wind a little. Coarse bottom, sand and mussel shells; clay in places; bottom at only 20 fathoms. Very spacious. Probably the best harbour here. Jenimi [Ssigna?] tells me that at Harrison's Point [on K'ekertelung] there is a deep hole with 3 large stones in it, apparently a giant pothole [BN: glacier pothole], presumably formed by a strong tidal current. The tide rises very high here. But I am unable to make any observations. In the afternoon there is again a strong south wind. Unfortunately I cannot get any observations towards Warham's I. In the afternoon, with the captain, I compiled a plan of the harbour.

[FB/parents, sisters]
Neiantilik, 29th September. I am very glad that I can still send you news

so late in the year. We are still on our way to Warham's Island. When we were quite close to it, we were struck by a severe gale, which drove us back west. Since at the same time the ice began to drive out of Davis Strait into the Sound, Captain Abernethy sought a harbour, and we are now on the west shore of the Sound, about 70 miles from Kikkerton. Although I am delighted to get to know a new part of the Sound, I do not enjoy leaving Wilhelm alone for so long at Kikkerton. The American schooner [*Lizzie P. Simmons*, Capt. Roach] has left now too, and he is the only white among the Eskimos. He has to distribute their daily rations and look after them in every way. This would not be so bad if he understood English, but as it is I am rather anxious. I had hoped to be back by today, but unfortunately the weather has been very bad.

Today it is better and I hope we can get away tomorrow. I cannot do much here, either, because as a guest of the captain I cannot make many demands. I hope that you did not wonder why my letter via the *Germania* was so much thicker than yours, but one can always write only on one side of this sort of paper with copying pencil, hence the bulk. In about a year from now I shall be on board a ship on my way back to civilized people – I really should not say that since people here are very civilized. Mr. Mutch – this will set your minds at rest in many respects – is a teetotaller, and prays before every meal. My Eskimo [Ssigna] is a very fine fellow, better than very many whites I know. For example when I went to Kingawa, he told me that I should be concerned about my rum, because somebody might make free with it. In Kingnait where I went on a trip from Kikkerten recently, I went into the interior with Wilhelm. In the meantime he pitched our tent, without my having asked him to do so. Cold coffee, etc.

Moreover Wilhelm has told Mathilde [Nolting; Weike's fiancée and later his wife] and Lina [WW: Linna; surname not given, a servant in the Boas's home] (to whom you must extend numerous greetings from me too) that he has never been given so much coffee in his life before, as here. We get coffee morning, noon and evening. You will certainly wonder at the irregular form of this, my last news before I myself return, but I cannot help this because I am extremely glad to find an opportunity to write. I wish I were back at Kikkerten, because I am too dependent here. Also I do not like to take advantage of the captain's hospitality for so long and I do not like to leave Wilhelm alone for so long.

When I get back to Kikkerten, I want to set off again immediately to explore the fiords in the vicinity. Overland travel has temporarily come to an end here, because the last storm contributed much snow. This morning I tried to climb the hill here, but had to turn back after one and a half-hour of struggling, for I was constantly sinking to well above the knee in the snow without being able to make any progress. Unfortunately I was not able to get any good sketches of the harbour. I do not need to take my leave of you with these lines, dear ones. I think that I will be granted another 2 days here before I return to Kikkerten. Do you think of me often? (...)

[Notebook]

30th [September] Sunday   The captain wants to leave tomorrow possibly since his lay-days are over. I shall go with an Eskimo boat to Neiatilik where I shall observe the tides and the lie of the land towards Warham's Island. Jenimi has been telling me [BN: the various] place names and is carrying rocks for me. Later calculated the tide. In the afternoon Hall and both mates and I went first to Neiatilik and Arilik Island [Irselling], [BN: .. we found] a grave on the latter. Skulls were lying in a box beneath a large rock; nearby I first scratched two flags on a {large} piece of wood; [BN: .. which probably belonged to the grave; by it there was some dog hair and canvas. The corpse in a box, but no skull with it, wrapped in a blue cloth.] also some dog skin, which I did not think was an Eskimo addition to the grave. The corpse was wrapped in a blue cloth. Clearly very old. On the return journey shot a nauja [I. *nauja* = gull]. At noon Mutch was boasting that he had given permission for the boat with which I went to Kingwa [BN: .. to go to Kingwa], although they were Roach's people! Tomorrow we'll make another attack on the oil, if the wind permits.

[FB/parents, sisters]

(...) We are still at Neiantilik, but tomorrow morning will probably try again to visit Warham's Island. I hope that we will return to Kikkerten soon afterwards because I want [to see] Wilhelm very much. Thus perhaps I will have to send you my last greetings tomorrow. Then perhaps still another year and I will be on board a ship and return to you. I am now counting the days till my letter via *Germania* will be in your hands. I hope you will at least receive news from the Pentland Firth that *Germania* is back while Marie is in Germany. In 28 days she should have got that far. And what should I say to you as my last farewell this year? I won't make it a final farewell but will wish only that 'I will see you again, safe and happy in a year's time.' I shall come home healthy and cheerful; don't worry unnecessarily and make sure that I find you all well. I am constantly thinking of all your love and loyalty; I thank you for all the last hours I experienced with you; and I think of how often you are probably thinking of me. Yes, it is only when one is separated from *all* one's loves, only then does one feel truly how intimately and deeply one is bound up with them all! Tomorrow it will be six months since I last saw Marie; when will I see her again? It is now almost like departing from Germany, as I again send you fresh greetings. But probably tomorrow will be the last day on which I can write to you.

I have obtained good observations here and am pleased to have fixed the point firmly now. I have now progressed so far that I can concentrate on *my* major work, investigations of the {Innuit} Eskimos. At Kikkerten I now want to get organized with my mapping, then I shall start on it. The days are very short here. The land lies deep under snow and it is now impossible to travel across it. Yesterday I tried to climb a hill, but was constantly sinking knee-deep or deeper into the snow and had to give up. It is now freezing day and night and now ... it will probably start freezing. (...)

I have just been rereading everything I have written, to see that I have forgotten nothing. You know my plans; I should like just to describe the house [the whaling station] somewhat for you. Herr Ambronn received a photograph from me; he may well send you a copy. The plan of the place is as follows. In the room there are two sets of beds, one on top of the other; my table lies between them. The room is spacious and nicely papered, etc. In short it is quite comfortable inside the house. In the storeroom we keep only things that are in daily use; everything else is in special huts. I am now very completely equipped and can face the future confidently. (...)

[Notebook]
1st Octb. [Monday]   A sw wind in the morning. I got up at 6 to write home; afterwards I took some angles. [BN: Shake a Head Pt [Iliximisarbing], n.[orth] of Warham Island, seen from Niantilik.] It is not very comfortable lying on the narrow bench in [Alexander] Hall's room, so I prefer to take my fur pants off. I hope we can get away today. Hall[,] who went with me early this morning to fetch water, brought me good specimens of mica. [BN: My artificial horizon (molasses) has been eaten by the Eskimos again.] 30th Sept., low water at 23.42. Written in the afternoon.

[FB/parents, sisters]
(...) I had completely forgotten that I wanted to tell you a story that will certainly amuse you too. When I arrived at Kingawa, there was naturally great excitement on board the American ship and at our station, and I

was welcomed joyfully everywhere as the bringer of the latest news. On the last day [9 September] as I was heading back by boat, I went aboard the schooner *Lizzie P. Simmonds* [*Simmons*] once again to ask if there were any messages for Kikkerton, and to say goodbye to her people. As I was shaking their hands, one of them rushed up to me with the words (in English): 'You are a Jew, are you not?' At first I did not understand him, but soon grasped what he meant. His entire face beamed with happiness at having found a tribesman here, and he hoped that he would see me again often, which has not been granted him yet. Yes, indeed. One finds Germans and Jews everywhere, even at the Arctic Circle.

The crew of the *Lizzie Simmonds* is certainly a mixed company! Capt. Roach, a tall, lean man with a grey beard and only one arm (he lost the other while whaling) has been here for 22 years [since 1861]. He is a native of Montreal, and has an Eskimo wife here, with whom he has lived for years. A son by her is being educated in America. He is the personification of kindness.

His words were: Doctor, I think in this country everybody must help everybody. I'll do for you whatever I can do. If you come near my schooner, come to me, you'll find your bed and everything comfortable for you.

So I shall certainly visit him here during the winter. His mate is a German from Memel, who has lived in America since 1869. He is so Americanized that he can barely speak German any more; a sample of his German would be : *If Sie kommen zu uns, und sehen den Schoner, dann Sie werden finden Jedermann bereit, zu helfen Ihnen u.s.w.* [instead of: *Wenn Sie zu uns kommen und den Schooner sehen, dann werden Sie jedermann bereit finden, Ihnen zu helfen, u.s.w.* (If you come to us and see the schooner, you will find everyone ready to help you, etc.)]. He was previously (from birth) named [Fred] Grobschmidt [but uses the name Sherman].

The second mate, Wilhelm [Scherden] is also German, the son of a New York doctor. He is a truly fine person, certainly the best of the ship's crew. Moreover he knows Uncle [Abraham] Jacobi by sight and by name.

The crew are mainly Americans but among them, as I have said there are a Jew and a mulatto, whose African ancestors also never suspected that one of their offspring would one day be freezing in the polar ice.

I am now writing to you shortly before 6 o'clock. At first it was so dark that I had to write by lamplight. Unfortunately there is still a S wind today, which will not let us leave the harbour. I wish we were able to get out. I wish I could think of something I could give the capt. in return for his hospitality. He clearly considers it a special pleasure to have a scientific man on board and later will often talk about it. He asked me to name some location after his ship [Boas did so with Farewell Catherine, the southern tip of Miliaxdjuin, included in his 1885 map]. I don't like to do this, but I will have no choice. My collection of Eskimo place names is making very rapid progress. I hope that I will bring home a good haul, in every respect.

My English will be delightful when I come home. Here one would say (spoken as written): 'Khvi khvere out in our boat catching khvales, khvenn khve khvent on {land} shore khve picked up several stienes {stones} in the afternien' [E. = We went in our boat to catch whales; when we went on shore in the afternoon we picked up several stones]. And when operating in a foreign language it is difficult to avoid such pronunciations. Mutch speaks English not so badly, but uses so many Scottish words and sayings or expressions that I often have no end of trouble understanding him. But I get along quite well with my English; at least they understand *me* quite well.

A conversation with the Eskimos goes something in the following vein. I would say: 'Jimmy; take *umiak*, catch *ugjuk* for me, good eating for dinner,' i.e. 'Jimmy, take the boat and catch a bearded seal for dinner.' Then Jimmy would reply: 'Yes, Sir, can't get boat in water, no *Innuit* here, to help me. Me thinks, much *appuu* today,' i.e. 'I can't get the boat into the water since there are no Inuit here to help me. I also think it will snow too much today.' We understand each other very well in this sort of language. When we are travelling and I am sitting aft in the boat, I can give orders to the Eskimos in their language very well: *Ipputit!* i.e. watch your oars; there is ice or rocks near the boat. And in the morning, to get them up I shout: *Akalerit!* i.e. get up. In short I am getting along really well here. They always look happiest when I say '*Koffilirputit*' i.e. make coffee!

Do you know that it is six months today since I was last in Stuttgart [visiting the Krackowizers on 1 April]. I think Marie should be with you now and now it is 11.45 with you, while we are drinking coffee here; at 8 you will be at lunch and perhaps will be speaking about your 'polar bear' over here. I am always thinking of you, my loved ones, of how you are waiting longingly for my return, and of how you probably think of me sometimes with anxiety. But believe me there is no need for anxiety! I am healthy and strong, and Wilhelm is just as reliable; I am always thinking of all those whom I have left at home and am heading quite determinedly towards my goal, but despite this am careful and prudent. Since I am totally adequately provisioned you do not need to worry further. As I was making my first trip with Wilhelm recently, he kept saying: 'What would they say at home if they could see us here?' This was especially so one time when we were eating lunch, consisting of bread and water. You just do not know how good that tastes when one is tired and hungry! But now I will be happy when I can sleep in a bed at Kikkerten for the first time again, since here I sleep on a narrow bench. Fortunately my fur clothes keep me warm enough.

You know, if you read of too much discomfort in this letter, you will certainly be saying: 'The poor lad!' But you have no cause to do so, since we are enjoying ourselves royally under all these strange conditions. And if it occasionally becomes a bit too much, one curses inwardly, but after a soft sleep one very quickly forgets the strenuous efforts. It is good that we are being prepared so gradually for the strenuous aspects. I do not know if I wrote to you already that I ate my first seal and my first local birds with relish. They tasted superb. Naturally you must not believe the old fable about blubber. No Eskimo eats blubber. The fat is carefully cut off in order (in the case of the Eskimos) to keep the fire burning, while they eat only the meat. I have not tried walrus meat yet.

From this month on I shall begin counting down the year that I must spend in this inhospitable region. I believe the ship that brings me back to you will leave here in mid-October. But as I have said, if I do not come, you should not be unnecessarily concerned. *I hope* this will not be the case; but in terms of provisions I have planned for 2 years so that I shall be covered in any eventuality.

But I have to wonder whether we will get out of the harbour today. I hope so very much, since I have no further work to do here. If I had my boat with me, I would have plenty of work, but as it stands I cannot always be asking the captain for his. You cannot conceive what a dreary impression this snow-covered land makes; only the steepest parts project bare and barren out of the snow! And how deep the snow lies after only the first snowfall. Yesterday I again tried, in vain, to climb a hill but the snow defeated me. Later in the year when more snow has fallen and the wind has been blasting across it, it becomes hard and one can travel across it easily, which is now impossible.

The harbour here is very good. Earlier, when there were still many whales here 12 ships might winter here at the same time. So every little feature has an English name. On Norris Island[,] a small island in the harbour[,] there are numerous graves of seamen from the whalers who died here. There are also two shipwrecks here. One of them was set on fire by the captain because it was unseaworthy; the other was beached intentionally [probably the American ships *Antelope* (1866) and *Oxford* (1869) or *S.B. Howes* (1873); Goldring et al. 1984].

There are usually natives here too, but so far we have seen nothing but some dogs which they leave on the islands in summer, a few tent sites and graves. I hope I can get back here again in winter in order to see more of the surrounding area then. I will then make Capt. Roach's schooner my base and will travel around the area by sledge. I'll perhaps do this in January, then go back to Kikkerten[,] then travel west to Lake Kennedy and Foxe Channel. I hope you will not be angry at this scratched-together letter. But I am using every available scrap of paper to write on. I am very glad that my last news will arrive so unexpectedly well; the remaining time will appear shorter as a result. (...)

Mr. Alexander Hall, from the local station, who is now going home[,] has shown me very many kindnesses and, among other things, has given me two complete fur suits. He does not want to take any payment at all for them, and I cannot give him anything here, because I have nothing. I would be very glad, dear Papa, if you would send him a gift in my name, via *Mr. Crawford Noble, Fountain Hall Road, Aberdeen, Scotland.* He would like a hunting rifle after the model of the Mauser rifle. You can easily get one at Dreyse's in Berlin, about at the corner of Mohrenstrasse and Markgrafenstrasse. Select the smallest possible calibre (9 mm, I think) and do not forget to order the accessories, i.e. bullet mould. The whole thing will cost about 60 M. But I cannot avoid it. I will also have to give something to Mutch when I leave here, but do not know what. (...)

You might send a note to the *B.T.* [*Berliner Tageblatt*] on my behalf to the effect that I have not had time to report to them in detail! I have written everything important for them and they can put it into the proper form for the newspaper. (...)

[Notebook]
2nd Oct [Tuesday]   Calm in the morning; at 8.30 the Eskimos towed the ship out of the harbour; afterwards there was a good northerly breeze. Overcast; east shore clear. Soon afterwards we had a very strong north wind and high seas which probably make it impossible to pick up the oil; very cold.

[FB/MK]
(...) Listen Marie, if you want to be proud of me about it [his research] because the people in Hamburg praised me as I was leaving, you have no real cause to be. It was quite natural that they should flatter me ostenta-

tiously on the last day. Don't be afraid, I know what such talk signifies, so I remain your sensible Franz. And even after what I later read about myself in the newspaper, [which was more laudatory] than I would prefer, I shall still be writing sensibly; I know too that the *Berliner Tageblatt* will be tooting its own horn. The only yardstick of what one does is the acknowledgment that one has done one's duty, whether the success is great or small. Believe me, no idle gossip will ever turn my head. I have my eye firmly on my goal and know what I have to do and what work is worthwhile. You know, I don't even think much of the fine expressions about devotion to science. Anyone who goes out to investigate something has his own good personal reasons, whether it be the pure desire for knowledge, the desire for adventure, or whatever. And you know what it was in my case: the desire to establish an independent existence – even before I knew that my beloved loves me again – and scientific interest. I do not know what would have been more difficult for me, to go or to stay. (...)

[FB/parents, sisters]

3rd October [Wednesday]   And now, dear parents and sisters, I shall say goodbye to you for really the last time this year! (...) We are now about 15 miles from Kikkerten; because of the persistent stormy weather the captain has been unable to reach Warham's Island and is now taking us back to Kikkerten. So I must conclude this letter.

I now feel, as I send you my last words for this year, almost as if I was going through the entire process of taking my leave again; but with luck I will be with you again a year after you have read these lines, and I can tell you that the Eskimos are far from being uncivilized people. (...)

Boas sent the letters written to his parents and sisters between 16 September and 3 October with the Catherine, *via Dundee to Minden i. W., where they arrived on 11 November 1883. After having been copied, they were relayed to family members and friends. The letters addressed to his fiancée, Marie Krackowizer, were sent via Dundee to New York, where she was living in 1883–4.*

[Notebook]

(...) Since the weather is no better, and since there is no prospect of a change in the weather, the captain has decided to take us to Middleaktuk, and then to return home. If it is better on the morning of the 4th he wants to take the oil with him. In the morning I finished my letters; I could see only extensive, heavy ice masses to the north, lying immediately

west of Middleaktuk I. An ice field about 15–20′ high; we are passing a
piece that has broken off. Three last cheers and the final parting from
Europe for this year.

We are sailing towards the Middleaktuks. Since the sea is too high, we
are spending the night here in a very tidy tupik. I climbed the southerly
hill and from there could see the brig again (5 o'clock). A fine panorama
including Kignait Fiord, Salmon Fiord [Exaluaxdjuin] and Kikkerten. A
footpath leads along the plain between the two hills. This is the best vege-
tated plain that I have seen. There are many rabbit tracks everywhere.
Many old tent rings. Eskimos lived here earlier, but now only in spring
when the ice leaves this coast. There are 3 rocks lying on the ground, with
which the old Eskimos are said to have tried their strength by carrying
them on their shoulders. I can barely lift them myself. I found a worked
bone. Chiselled with coarse-grained granite. The island is seamed with
massive veins of feldspar, which give it a red-veined appearance. A deep
crack runs across it from SSW to NNE; it is heavily weathered and filled
with talus. There are also other deep cracks with veined walls. Much mica
interspersed with the feldspar. At one spot in the north of Middlis Bay
[Miliaxdjuin] there is a layer about 20 cm thick of very fine-grained granite with brown weathering nodules. On the rocks there are said to be
some graves of old Eskimos, who are said to have had unusually long
thighs.

[BN: listing of the Inuit place names collected by Boas for the southeastern archipelago in Tinixdjuarbing]

Ukádliujánga	Northern part	[Ukadliujang]
Middliáktuik	the plain	[Miliaxdjuin]
U-miuják	south hill	[Umiujang]
Ku'mü(r)pá-	southwest island	[K'umirpan]
Tirlá-tirlá	NW	[Teratirax]
Kadliro-schili-k	N	[K'alirosiling]
Ka-jué-	SE	[K'aijuin]
Ssegdliá-ping	small NW island	[Sagdliraping]

[Notebook]
4th Oct [Thursday]   In the morning took some angles on the Middluk-
tuk. On the evening of the 3rd the Esk.[imos] tried the rocks, ... then we
sailed to Kikkerton, landed on the east side and walked overland to the
house. Found everything in good order. Cpt. Roach sailed away two days

ago taking his best dogs and Eskimos with him. 2 boats with Eskimos have returned from caribou hunting. Wilhelm is in good health; he has erected a cairn and has shot a rabbit and 2 ptarmigan. We have been taking provisions from the chest and are preparing for another trip to the mainland.

5th [October, Friday]   [K'exerten] Ssigna has gone seal hunting while I still have things to do in the house. Gradually some light is appearing in the darkness of disorder, but there are still lots of things lying around. I obtained a time-difference and a difference in longitude between Neiatilik and Kikkerten. 5m 50s difference in longitude, and the latitude. In the morning I cleaned my rifles. In the evening Mutch told off the Eskimos for their summer employment. It is like Christmas for them. Shouting, running, racing and yelling. My provisions are stowed in the little room beside my bunk. In the evening Ssigna came with his rifle to have me show him how to clean it. Mutch wanted to have a pipe of Wilhelm's and to give him a rum for it. ... W.[ilhelm] is cooking for one of the Eskimos. Today I bought skins for our clothing. A boat came from Kingawa today. While we were away two boats arrived, one from Kingawa, from which I received Dr. Schliephake's rifle. Fortunately 16-calibre shells fit it.

Boas now begins the letters that he wrote sporadically for his parents and sisters as well as the much more regularly written letters and letter-journals for his fiancée; he would not be able to send them to the addressees (or even deliver them himself) until September 1884.

[FB/MK]
(...) Arrived here at Kikkerten safely at noon where I found Wilhelm in good health. I am *very* happy with his performance during this period; he has carried out all his tasks, looked after the Eskimos and the house properly; nor has he been extravagant with the food and has employed them well. (...)

[FB/parents, sisters]
(...) Now the brig has left and we are quite alone here in the Sound, left to our own resources. No word of love and no greeting will reach us for a long time; nor can we send any greetings, no matter how much we long to chat with all those whom I love! But courage, beloved ones, I will struggle forward, work forward, in order to see you again soon. Oh, I can see in the future that only the greatest happiness awaits us. Don't

Franz Boas as a student, wearing the sash of the *Alemannia* Student Association, in Kiel, c. 1880–1. (Photo: Schmidt & Wegener, Kiel [American Philosophical Society, Print Collection: Franz Boas, B:B61, no. 1g])

Franz Boas and Marie Krackowizer as a young married couple in New York, c. March 1887. (Photo: Naegeli, New York [American Philosophical Society, Print Collection: Franz Boas, B:B61, no. 21])

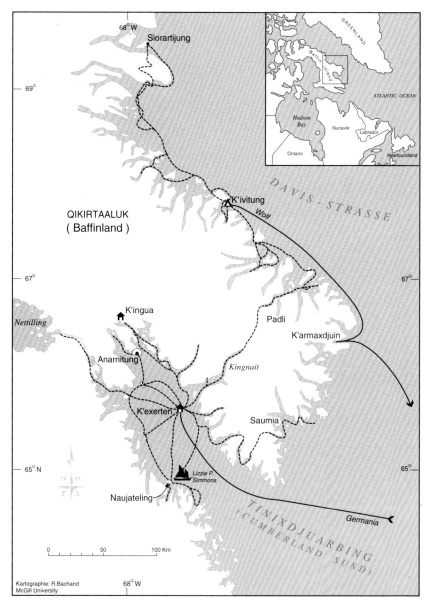

Travel routes of Franz Boas and Wilhelm Weike on Baffin Island, July 1883 until September 1884. (Source: Boas 1885: Plate 1; design: Ludger Müller-Wille; cartography: Richard Bachand)

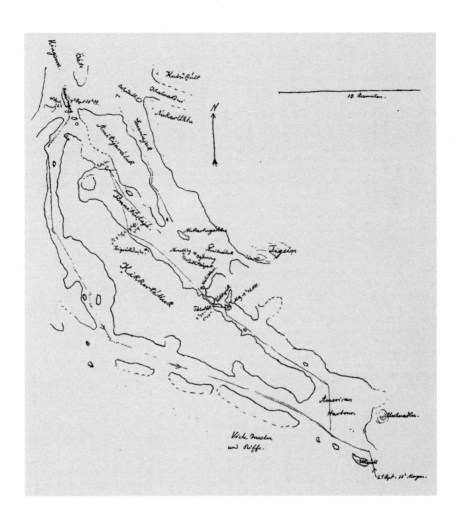

First boat trip from K'exerten to the German Polar Station at K'ingua, 5–10
September 1883; a map prepared by Franz Boas for the German Polar Commission, with Inuit place names. (BSH:DPK, Acta I.2.J.; 18 September 1883)

Franz Boas (right) and one of the seamen on board the *Germania*, 6 August 1883.
(Photo: Wilhelm Weike [American Philosophical Society, Print Collection: Franz
Boas, B:B61, no. 71])

Franz Boas's cabin on the *Germania*; boat and sledge pennant with insignia *Marie*,
July 1883. (Photo: Franz Boas [American Philosophical Society, Print Collection:
Franz Boas, B:B61, no. 7e])

Drifting iceberg off Cumberland Sound, early August 1883. (Photo: Franz Boas [American Philosophical Society, Print Collection: Franz Boas B:B61, no. 31a])

Iceberg sketched by Franz Boas, 28 July 1883. (American Philosophical Society, Print Collection: Franz Boas, B:B61, no. 30g)

Franz Boas's Baffin Island journals in the reading room of the American Philosophical Society, Philadelphia. (Photo: Ludger Müller-Wille, August 1983)

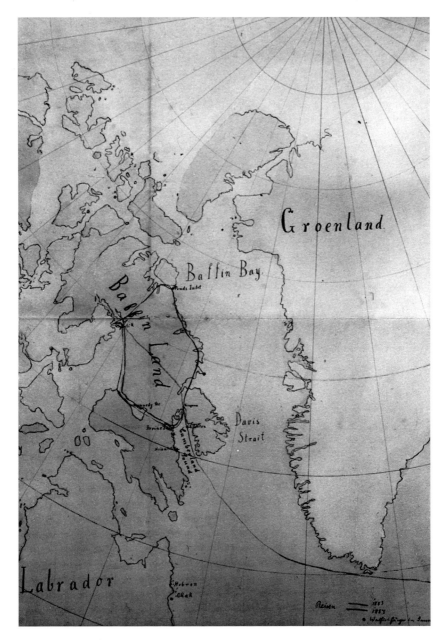

Map of Boas's planned travel route in Baffin Island, which he drafted for Marie Krackowizer on 27 April 1883 in Minden i. W. (American Philosophical Society, Print Collection: Franz Boas, B:B61, no. 30a)

View northwards to the Scottish whaling station at K'exerten (left) and K'exerten harbour with (left to right) the *Catherine*, the *Germania*, and the *Lizzie P. Simmons*, the latter being the American whaling schooner that had evacuated the German Polar Station, c. 13–15 September 1883. (Photo: Franz Boas [American Philosophical Society, Print Collection: Franz Boas, B:B61, no. 7c])

Modern-day K'exerten harbour, taken from the same viewpoint as in the preceding photo. (Photo: Ludger Müller-Wille, August 1984; 84/178)

Representation of hunting seals at a breathing hole in the ice of Cumberland
Sound: Franz Boas standing in Inuit winter clothing with his harpoon ready to
strike and snow knife (right) in a photographic studio in Minden i. W. in the fall
of 1885. (Photo: J. Hülsenbeck, Minden i. W. [American Philosophical Society,
Print Collection: Franz Boas, B:B61, no. 7d]; also Boas 1888:476)

Wilhelm Weike in Inuit winter clothing with dog whip in a photographic studio in Minden i. W. in late 1884 or early 1885. (Photo: M. Sweers, Minden i. W. [American Philosophical Society, Print Collection: Franz Boas, B:B61, no. 7g])

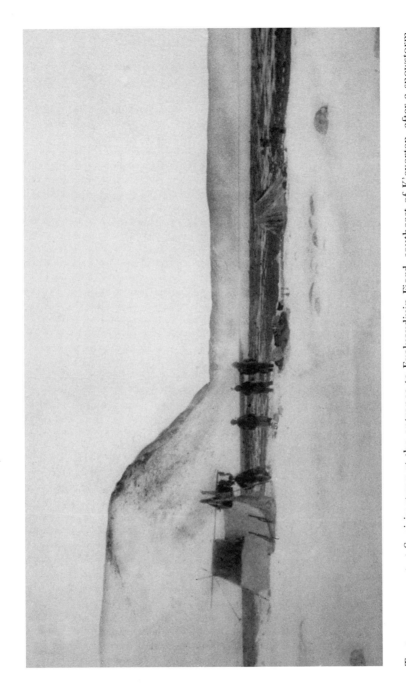

Tent encampment at Supivisortung at the entrance to Exaluaxdjuin Fiord, southeast of K'exerten, after a snowstorm between 20 and 22 October 1883; Wilhelm Weike (left) with Nachojaschi, Ssigna, and Utütiak. (Photo: Franz Boas [American Philosophical Society, Print Collection: Franz Boas, B:B61, no. 3li])

Landing the *Marie* through ice floes on the eastern shore of Cumberland Sound, c. 16–22 October 1883. (Photo: Franz Boas [American Philosophical Society, Print Collection: Franz Boas, B:B61, no. 31j])

The German Polar Station at K'ingua, Cumberland Sound, early September 1883. (Neumayer and Börgen 1886, vol. 1:xx)

Noon break at Ujarasugdjuling in Kangertloaping Bay during the final autumn boat trip along the eastern shore of Cumberland Sound, 16 October 1883; Wilhelm Weike (left) and the Inuit Nachojaschi, Ssigna (Jimmy), and Ututiak (Yankee) enjoy a cup of coffee. (Photo: Franz Boas [American Philosophical Society, Print Collection: Franz Boas, B:B61, no. 31k])

K'exertalukdjuax Fiord on the west coast of Davis Strait, early June 1884. (Sketch: Franz Boas [American Philosophical Society, Print Collection: Franz Boas, B:B61, no. 30s])

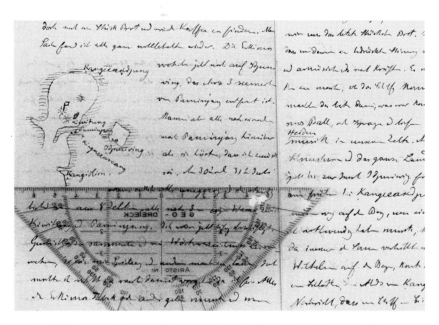

Map of K'ivitung and a sample of writing from Franz Boas's letter to his parents, 20 September 1884. (American Philosophical Society, Franz Boas family papers, B:B61p)

you all love me? Don't I have my Marie? I hope that through this voyage I shall succeed in laying the foundation of an assured life in the near future. Now I must get to work afresh without looking back; the goal lies ahead.

On the 3rd when there was still a storm blowing we travelled with the brig over to Middliakdjuin where we, i.e. Mutch and his 7 Eskimos[,] climbed into our boat and sailed northward, while the brig turned and headed for home. I certainly had a heavy heart when I heard the last three cheers, but I joined in loudly in the Eskimos' shouts and thought of the time when I shall turn my back on this country. (...)

Trip to Pangnirtung Fiord

[Notebook]
6th October [Saturday] When all the preparations had successfully been made, Wilhelm and I, with Ssigna, Yankee [Utütiak] and Nachojaschi set off in Jimmy's [Mutch's] boat at 10 o'clock. [BN: Initially a fair wind (N) with fog and snow; at 12 we finally landed on T.] We landed on Tuangnirn [Tuapain] where I made observations. It is now quickly clearing up. The summit of Kikkertuktuak [K'exertuxdjuax] is coming into view. Yankee hauls on the ropes with his teeth, in which he has great strength. Last night the cooper [Rasmussen] visited us. Since there is no water at this spot we have to use ice for cooking. Mutch has lent me his sleeping bag. We are missing one tent pole, since it is still standing up on the mountain. I took two sun altitudes. Later there was more snow and thick weather. Ssigna was rowing while I steered. We are hunting seals. Yankee got a netsirn [I. *natsiq* = seal]. At 5 pm we obtained water on Ssessirnadlik [Sesseraling] and at 6 we found a campsite on the mainland behind Innuksululik [Inugsuling]. Pitched the tent, using my tent as groundsheet and Mutch's bearskin as the door. I am writing by lamplight in my sleeping bag. Took the altitude of the pole star. Around 8 it was high tide and we hauled the boat up. There is quite a lot of snow lying on the land.

7th October [Sunday] Set off around 8. Calm; very fine weather; clear. Yankee buried his seal under rocks. We are making only slow progress, because they are constantly hunting seals, but we ran into Pagnirktu. Ssigna has never been in this fiord so cannot give me any names. Nachojaschi does not understand me. At noon we made for a small island which I mistook for the mainland and I got another sun altitude. We next headed across the fiord to stop for lunch. Afterwards I went up on the hill and saw 3 rabbits; I ran after them, but didn't get any. Yankee, who walked to the next point, saw only a fox. The land on the south side is covered with snow, whereas the north side is snow free. On the north side rises the steep, conical mountain of Angiukvangin [Angiuxax; in BN: no place name given], showing the same cone shape as when seen from Kikkerten. It forms the core of the great mountain system between Pagnirktu and Kigned [Kingnait]. Here two routes lead upstream to Tungnirn [Tornait], apparently across the level foot of the mountain. Beyond, up Pagnirktu, the mountains are very jagged and steep; the only place where I observed this. Ssigna shot a seal. On the north shore there is a high terrace, and a causeway of large rocks along the edge of the deep water. All the rivers have formed large talus cones that extend out from the coast. There is young ice in the bay on the north shore. In the evening I first tried raw seal liver and some roast seal meat for supper [BN: !]. It tastes not bad, but I have to overcome a certain repugnance. On the site of our overnight camp there are 6 old dwellings made of rocks and whale bones. We hauled the boat ashore and pitched 2 tupiks, mine and the sail. Wilhelm, Ssigna and I are in mine. At noon I made a sketch of Pagnirktu. It was overcast in the evening so I was unable to get a shot at the pole star. Nachojaschi was here all summer. Pagnirtu means pagnir [I. *pangniq* = adult caribou bull] a large animal similar to the reindeer, with massive antlers, which no longer lives here (Elen?) [G. *Elen* = archaic for deer or moose] [.] From the head of Pagnirktu [Pangnirtung] a route leads overland to another Pagnirktu [Pangnirtung] on Davis Strait in 2 sleeps and from there about 4 days to Padli. Nobody has travelled this route. [BN: From here another route leads overland to Padli in 2 days?]

8th October [Monday]   7 a.m.; 763 mm; −3.4°. Set off at 7.45. The fiord appears to be entirely closed by a low headland projecting from the north shore. Here it swings round to the north; when one travels around this point, one can see once more the exit again. Very high, jagged land here. Fine-grained granite. Small glaciers in the upper parts of the side valleys; on the north shore a distinct terrace, which gradually rises and can be traced to the head of the fiord; its edge is formed of coarse boulders, with gravel below, usually broken through by streams. Lateral moraine? The innermost part of the fiord is very shallow. Clay and sand bottom, which dries out to about 3 miles out. Much young ice with many seals in it; since we are hunting we are making only slow progress. Made a halt at the head of the fiord at 4. Found some water only with great effort. The glacier snout here is about 200′ high.

9th Oct. [Tuesday]   Set off with Wilhelm to a route inland this morning. We reached the level floodplain of the river that debouches here via the mountain slopes. One can see large glaciers in the background. We can see the frozen river, though it still contains open water in many places. The bottom is sand and small pebbles. We walk for about 6′ [six miles]. First a glacier extends its snout far out into the plain from the east side; opposite it is a small one that comes halfway down the mountain then breaks off on the steep slope. On the lower one, which has been formed from two parts, there are fine medial moraines. The end moraine displays large boulders and looks as if it were an earth hill. A powerful stream flows away from it. About 2 km farther there is an even larger, widely spreading end moraine. Immediately beyond this one is a third upper-end moraine. Finally on the west side lies a moraine whose lower parts are pushed well out into the plain.

A glacier, which descends only halfway[,] breaks away at its snout and an avalanche thunders down from it into the valley. In the background rapids on the river are steaming heavily. Very fine, magnificent summer ice. Distinct terraces on the west shore. Beyond the three glaciers on the east shore is an ice hill, from which water flows from a cave. It now stands quite isolated, a sign of an old end moraine. In the middle of the valley, broken through by the river, lies a low terrace, with just the same appearance as those at American Hrb. [Ussualung] and Kingawa [Sirmilling; German Polar Station 1882–3]; hence I consider these too to be glacial phenomena. The flat areas at the head of the fiord are clearly alluvial products from the glaciers. They are all blue with deep longitudinal and transverse {valleys} crevasses. Firn extends as far as the steeply dropping edges of the fiord.

Unfortunately we cannot go any farther. On the return journey saw many ravens and a fox. Got back tired. Ssigna and the others were out seal hunting; I shouted and they came back. We had lunch here but had to hurry to get away because the water was dropping fast. Next high tide is at 10.45 [in BN: 11.45] so we would be left stranded. Got away at 13.30. Set off with a fair wind, but as we hoisted the sail a rope broke and as a result we lost a lot of time. Around 17.00 we reached our campsite of the day before yesterday and camped there again. Could not haul the boat up, since the water was too low[;] had to wait until 8 o'clock.

10th October [Wednesday]   8 a.m.; −3°; 767.5 mm. Set off with a fair [BN: strong] breeze and made rapid progress. ... At the last bend at the exit from Pagnirktu the wind dropped. Made a main boom from 2 tent poles. Initially 2 reefs, then calm. Emerged from the fiord at 12, so I was just able to take a noon sun altitude. Then landed at the flat terrace north of Alikun. I went ashore and found traces of rabbits and three graves, which were very old. In two there were skulls overgrown with moss and lichens. Rectangular rock structures, 4′ long and 2′ wide, much too small for an extended corpse, onto which rocks had been rolled. The entire structure was an oval heap of rocks. Here there are high terraces, which have been cut through by the descending streams. Unfortunately I cannot take away the skulls that were in the two graves, because of my Eskimos.

From here on a strengthening north wind. We are between Aupatluktun and the mainland and I intend to go to American Hrb. In the evening shot 2 nauja. Stopped on a narrow headland opposite Niu'ktuk [Niurtung].

We had scarcely landed when another sail appeared; it soon rounded the point and made for us. Eskimos coming from Lake Kennedy. Immediately behind them was another boat, Takun and Mitu. They pitched their tupiks near us, at a site where there were already tent rings. 6 tents in total; 4 Eskimo tents and my 2. 12 Eskimos arrived; they have many caribou skins. [BN: I would like 12 skins for clothing and sleeping bags. One of them showed me the connections to Lake Kennedy.] I gave them all some tobacco, visited them in their tents with Ssigna, and ordered the caribou skins. They are going back to Kikkerten, but if it is calm, they want to go seal hunting for another day.

In the evening many of them visited me in my tent. I gave them rum and tobacco. A cooney [whalers' expression for an Inuk, an aboriginal woman] is drying my stockings and kommings. I took the evening measurements and the angle of the pole star. Very fine evening. Illumination from evening glow and behind it a bright moon and in the middle [BN: .. the glow and the snowy landscape] the landscape of firn, ice and snow. I have bought caribou meat for tomorrow.

[FB/MK; written on 11 October]
(...) Yesterday was an eventful day for us. When I stopped writing, I was soon back at work again and by mistake I began to write a part of my coastal survey on the back of my journal. We rowed north along the coast; my intention was to go as far as American Harbour, if possible, thus com-

pleting the coast from Kikkerton to Kingawa. At noon we rested on a well-vegetated terrace. While lunch was cooking I climbed up and found three well-preserved old graves there. I would have very much liked to take the moss- and lichen-grown skulls with me, but did not dare because of the Eskimos, since this would have greatly insulted them. So I had to row on without saying anything about my find and around 5.30 p.m. we ran in safely to our overnight quarters. It was a small rocky headland, off which lay large, elongated islands.

I had slept earlier on one of these Aupelluktuk [9–10 September] when I was on my way to Kingawa. We were busy unloading our things when we suddenly spotted a sail that was heading towards the same spot. Soon my people recognized the Eskimos in it; one of them, Yankee[,] spotted his brother; they then quickly ran down to help them unload. You cannot imagine the loads in these Eskimo boats. They are high-sided whaleboats, 30 feet long, full of men, women and children. Fore and aft they were piled high with skins, the product of the summer's hunting. In the middle lie the dogs which from time to time raise a dreadful music; astern tows a small kayak[,] the landing boat of the Eskimos.

They too quickly pitched their tupiks (tents) (there were 2 families) and began cooking their meal. Immediately after them another boat arrived, which had been travelling with the first one, and now we were an entire village on the small headland where previously there had been nobody. 4 Eskimo tents and myself with 2 tents!

First I visited the natives and gave them tobacco which they accepted with delight, since during their summer hunting trips they had run out of tobacco. At the same time I bought 12 caribou skins from them for winter clothing; now that I have them a weight has truly been taken off my mind, because for a long time I had been unable to buy any caribou skins, without which it is impossible to travel in winter. One of them brought a rock from Lake Kennedy which I also bought. These people had spent the entire summer on Lake Kennedy which I had sought so long; so I could already have been there for a long time! Now I must be content, since this fall I have surveyed the major part of the coast of this sound.

Afterwards the Eskimos in turn came to visit me; they made themselves comfortable in my tent which probably had never seen so many visitors before. Everyone received another half piece of tobacco and a glass of rum. I had visitors, men and 1 woman until 18.00. I am quite glad that they came because the woman is making me skin boots and stockings, a real essential in these cold regions. I do not know what I should do without skin boots. Last night it was –8°; you can imagine that it is not pleasant to be sleeping in the open. This morning [11 October] I bought another caribou leg and now we are all heading back in 3 boats. (...)

[FB/parents, sisters; written on 14 October]
(...) On the evening of the 11th [October] [probably the 10th is intended] I had the noble intention to keep on writing despite a temperature of −11°. But just as we had pitched our tent and were about to cook our supper (and lunch), we saw 2 boats full of Eskimos approaching, who had been at Lake Kennedy for the summer. They pitched their tupiks near us and naturally there was so much commotion and visiting that we had no peace to do anything. They stayed visiting till late at night. You should have seen how delighted they were at the tobacco I gave them, and when in the morning every woman received a cup of coffee, their joy knew no bounds.

Next day I simply cooked, since I wanted to buy caribou skins for winter clothing from the Eskimos. We arrived here [at K'exerten] in the afternoon [11 October] with a very strong wind. The Eskimos, who could not travel with their heavily laden boats, did not arrive until next day [12 October]. I have been lucky to acquire 11 caribou skins; Mutch will buy the outstanding 7 and thus tomorrow I can be off again. Everything is prepared, and I hope to be able to travel to Salmon Fiord south of Kikkerten early tomorrow [15 October].

I wish you could see how cheerfully and comfortably I am sitting here in my room. Jimmy Mutch is lying in his corner reading; I am sitting at my table writing and in here it is beautifully warm. (...)

I did not want to write to you saying that next year I want to go to Davis Strait to meet a ship there, because there is really little prospect of seeing one here, whereas there are always many steamers calling there. Why should I alarm you with that long, difficult journey? Who knows whether I shall see you again in a year or not? But everything still lies ahead of me! I do not lack for will, but fortune is certainly not favouring me! (...)

[Notebook]
11th October [**Thursday**]   When I got up the other Eskimos were already striking their tents, yet we sailed off almost at the same time. When we had been under way for an hour, Yankee realized that he had forgotten his shells and powder. He borrowed one of the kayaks from the second boat and went back in it. As a result, we wasted a good 90 minutes. Later there was a stiff breeze out of the N; we crossed Pagniktu and by noon were at Brown's Hrb. [NW of Pitiuxsin]. Yankee cannot find the seal

he buried. By 2 o'clock we were off A[rctic] I[sland] and see the two boats astern of us put in to shore. A heavy sea running. Yankee has to hold the kayak above water the whole time so that it does not fill. When we got into quiet water behind Tueinong [Tuapain; Arctic Island], he tried to tow it astern again[,] but it overturned as he let it out astern and filled with water. We finally reached Kikkerten ... at 5 o'clock. Mutch immediately served us a good supper, of which we were in real need. I went to bed early in the evening.

12th [October, Friday] [K'exerten] In the morning unpacked and repacked, in order to get some space, and transcribed my observations. Capt. Roach arrived last night; he had been at Neiatalik where he had arrived at 4 p.m. on the same day as we had left it in the morning [2 October]. As we were leaving[,] Eskimos from Lake Kennedy (Nettilik) had arrived right after us, bringing many caribou skins. I bought a 200 lb barrel of blubber from them for my winter travels. The two boats have not yet arrived. But 4 other boats with about 50 Eskimos arrived, then 3 from Kingawa. In the afternoon the other two also arrived. Today I got 9 caribou skins. Mitu and Takun are the two boat steerers; Takun is going with C. Roach to Neiatilik. I gave Wilhelm [Scherden], Roach's second mate, a concertina; he has promised to take wind observations for me. Fred [Grobschmidt], the first mate, got some German books.

13th [October, Saturday] Capt. Roach has left. Ssigna's boat is not yet ready, so I continue packing my things and I have other things to do. Pouring bullets etc. I bought a bird skin and a bear skull as well as rocks from Lake Kennedy. In the evening Pakkak and Mitu were here, teaching me numbers.

14th [October,] Sunday Ssigna has gone to hunt seals. I want to rest for one day. I compared the chronometers, took some tide measurements and did some writing. I have finished copying my journal. If the wind permits I want to go to Salmon Fiord tomorrow. Pakkak was showing me how to make the route with string figures.

[FB/MK]
(...) I have now been back here at Kikkerton for 2 days. When I came back[,] Mr. Mutch had set up my table and hung my lamp so that everything was in order. I have now purchased my skins and largely unpacked the remainder of my things. I now own 11 caribou skins, but must have

another 7, which Mutch will buy for me. I would like to set off from here again, but I am afraid that it is too late, since we already have constant frosts (−8° this morning), so the harbour will probably soon freeze over. Capt. Roach came back the day after me, intending to take natives and dogs with him from here. He stayed only one day and is now off again to Neiatilik. This last trip was by far the most interesting one I have made so far, since I saw many new things, the high, jagged mountains of Pangnirktu and their long glaciers. (...)

[Notebook]
15th [October, Monday]   Since there was too much wind in the morning, I postponed setting off, especially since with the heavy swell Ssigna could take the boat over the reef into the water only at great risk. Instead I packed to be ready and fetched the last of the supplies. The Eskimos have generally abandoned their summer tupiks now and are living in large tupiks, several families together. I traded for another 3 caribous skins so I am short of only 4. I have made all my preparations to set off tomorrow.

Trip to Ujarasugdjuling and Exaluaxdjuin

16th [October, Tuesday]   Left Kikkerten at 8. Mutch set off shortly before me to go whaling. We rowed westward out of the harbour, then sailed with a fair wind directly for the south point of Kignait [D: for Alibi Head] [Akuliaxting]. From here we headed into the narrow, little fiord. Here I shot a fox on shore from the boat; it could not escape and had hidden behind a rock. [FB/MK: Here I shot a beautiful white fox today. I wonder who will wear it one day?] We saw 2 more.

Stopped at noon on a flat point [D: Ujarakschukdjubing] [Ujarasugdjuling]. Took two photos. Tent sites here. Farther in[,] everything is full of young ice [BN: so I headed back. At first there was a heavy swell, then a strong west wind, but one that still allows us to carry sail], so I abandoned the attempt to reach the head of the fiord, still about $\frac{3}{4}$ of a mile away, and headed for Salmon Fiord. At the head of the little fiord there is a level area, which leads over to Jaboon Pt. [Jawbone Point; K'arsax]. As we headed out there was a heavy swell at first, then a strong west wind, though it still just allowed us to carry sail. Squally. We ran into Salmon Fiord. Here the rocks are brown; the land looks very crumbling and chopped up. At the entrance to the little fiord there is a vein of heavy, dark rock (Kau-tak) [I. *kautaq* = hammer][,] which is about 20′ thick. According to Mutch it definitely runs from Kikkertuktuak to here and I have followed it as far as Kognuk [K'ognung] in Salmon Fiord. It stands almost vertically.

In the evening we camped on the delta of a river on the north shore: Schupüvisuktung [Supivisortung; BN: no place name given; D: Tschupüvisuktung]. The river is frozen over, but there is still plenty of water flowing under the ice. Yankee and I go to get water and I chop a hole in the ice. At our campsite on the west of the river there is a very old tent ring and a kayak rest, designed to protect the kayak from the dogs. There is an elongated heap of rocks, perhaps an old passageway but with no visible purpose, clearly artificially piled up on top. Crawled into the tent at 7 o'clock; –8°.

[D]

1 kagmang here [I. *qarmaq* = a sod house with rocks and whale bones]. Pitched the tupik and made coffee.

[FB/MK]

(...) I am sitting in my tent; (...) next to me Ssigna has just crawled into his sleeping bag and Wilhelm is almost snoring already behind us in the corner. In the next tent I can hear Nachojaschi and Utütiak [Yankee], my two other Eskimos, chatting, while the sea roars below. (...)

[Notebook]

17th [October, Wednesday]   Set off at 8 a.m. There is a strong current in the narrow passage in the fiord, especially on the south side. We tried unsuccessfully to hunt seals and *naujas*. Stopped for lunch by a steep torrent on the north shore. Still able to get water from the river. *Carne pura* [trade name for dried pea's meal in sausage form] pea soup, which the Eskimos really love. Here there is very nicely layered gneiss. Continued on to the head of the fiord, where it is already full of ice. It is frozen solidly to the bottom, i.e. to the sandy tidal flats at the head of the fiord (Kingawa), so that as the tide rises it remains on the bottom. Pieces frequently break off and rip up sand and rocks from the bottom. Kingawa is the name for these level fiord heads [I. *kingua* = bayhead or fiordhead]; only one fiord to the north is *called* Kingawa. The north end is formed by a flat-topped terrace, which is bordered by a beach, just as at Kingawa and Uschualuk [Ussualung; American Harbour]. The upper end of Rocky

Fiord [Kangertlukdjuax] is said to be barely 6 miles away. Here there are three old earth houses, just as at Pagnirktu, but much less well preserved. They contain neither whale bones nor rocks; only turf forming the sides. Smooth stones have been used only for roofing the entrance tunnel and for a surrounding wall. At 7 p.m. −11°. We discover that the tea tin contains starch.

[D]
(...) We are sailing along with a fairly strong wind. At the Kognung narrows there is a very strong ebb current, against which we can barely make any headway. Previously we were passing the time by shooting at gulls. Eventually we began to make fairly rapid progress. At our campsite there were some kagmangs made of earth; the large river reaches this far. There is a lot of young ice on the beach, which is now all being driven in by the wind. Got a latitude in the evening, but not a very good one, since it was cold and windy. (...)

[FB/MK]
(...) Like yesterday I am in my tent again. Ssigna until just now has been showing me Eskimo games and I must watch him more attentively; because I have to write down and learn everything! (...) Today was a very unfriendly day, with fog, snow and wind in this narrow fiord. But fortunately I managed to obtain an observation this evening. Just think, it is −11° here now with a wind; so you can understand that one's hands don't want to function properly. The ice is cracking beneath our feet; then the wind has been driving all the young ice out again. (...)

[Notebook]
18th [October, Thursday]   [FB/MK: Today is a lost day. At about 8 we set off from our last campsite with a strong wind.] In the morning we set off with a strong breeze, but soon a fierce gale arose with powerful gusts. At first we reduced sail to a minimum; but then had to take it in completely and finally had to unstep the mast. The snow squalls were whipping the crests completely off the waves and coating everything with ice and snow. We went ashore at 10 in the lee of the first convenient point on the S side where we could find some shelter. Since it appeared that around 13.45 the force of the wind had slackened somewhat, we crossed the fiord to get back to our campsite of the day before yesterday. But we were scarcely out in the fiord when the storm broke with renewed violence [BN: force] and we were happy to reach a small harbour. We were unable to haul the boat up.

By noon we had become totally soaked and had pitched the tupik in the lee of a rock in order to dry out somewhat; Wilhelm in particular had been completely overwhelmed by a wave. It was scarcely possible to make any headway, rowing into the wind. On one occasion the wind snatched Wilhelm's oar out of his hands and hurled it over Yankee and Nachojaschi into the water; Yankee lost his oar at the same time. The boat came very close to capsizing. We weighted down the tupik thoroughly for the night to prevent it from blowing away. I lost another 2 oars in the violent gale. A great deal of snow fell. The Eskimos stayed in the boat until 10 p.m., when they hauled it ashore and slept till 5, when they refloated the boat. At low water there is a shelving beach, but at high water a steep coast. Later the wind swung around.

[FB/MK]
(...) Well, one has to put up with days like this, too! (...)

[Notebook]
19th [October, Friday]   [FB/MK: And another lost day!] Set off at 6.30 a.m. A strong wind against us. We reached only the spot where we spent the night recently, and dried our things somewhat, cleaned our rifles, etc. By noon it was clearing up; in the afternoon a little snow and dull. It began to blow down the fiord again. We pitched the tent and began to dry our things somewhat. We were able to haul the boat up safely across the ice-crusted rocks in the river mouth. Our firewood is running low, so we can cook only another 1 or 2 meals. The *carne pura* keeps very well. Since there is too much snow lying outside now, we are eating in the tent. As soon as the lid comes off the pot it begins to snow, and it is only when the pot lid is replaced that we can look around us. The meat is frozen hard on the inside.

20th [October, Saturday]   Last night the gale rose again. The tent was almost blown over. We have been lying in the tent almost the entire day because it is snowing and blowing. In the evening we were singing. Ssigna sang the Nettiling [Nettilling] song and the bad weather song.

[FB/MK]
(...) Today, once again, my hopes of returning to Kikkerton have been dashed. Last night it began blowing and snowing terribly, to such an extent that I was constantly afraid that the tent might blow down. This morning it was blowing so fiercely that it was impossible to light a fire and

we had to content ourselves with eating a piece of dry biscuit. I am really concerned about how we can get back to Kikkerton. The bad weather is persisting so long and there is no way of knowing how suddenly it may turn cold again. Today it is only –5°, and this morning even just –0.5°. Fortunately the barometer is starting to rise, so I have at least some hope of a change for the better. Given this persistent storm we naturally have caught nothing and our firewood is also running low since there is no more to be found because of the snow on the land.

You can imagine that I am rather worried about the next few days. Today we have nothing to do but sit miserably in the tent, going out only occasionally when it is a little calmer in order to get some exercise. The wind has now blown the snow completely away again; only the holes and hollows are filled with snow, so that occasionally one sinks hip-deep. It is frustrating that I am losing a few more days during the open-water season. Time is valuable. It was my intention to go farther south, but naturally that has been thwarted by the loss of 3 days. I believe I shall retain pleasant memories of this fine spot, Schupüvisuktung! (...)

[Notebook]
21st [October, Sunday]   Somewhat better. We all went out to find firewood and brought back enough to cook several meals. So we can brew coffee again. I am rather worried because I have enough bread left for only 3 days, and there is no sign of better weather. Ututiak, Wilhelm and I have been trying to shoot something, but found nothing. We have repitched the tent which the wind almost blew down on the 20th.

[FB/MK]
(...) Today, too, my hopes of getting away, have been dashed. However, the weather is somewhat better, but there is still a lot of wind and a high sea running. Tonight the storm was still raging furiously with drifting snow, etc, so that I was completely covered with snow because I was the last one to cover over my place. It has grown cold again now; –8° this morning. You can just imagine how I have to blow on my fingers frequently to be able to write. We are now in the process of cooking lunch. We were all outside all morning looking for some more firewood under the deep snow. Fortunately we found enough to make a fire. Hey! Won't the pea-sausage taste good!

This morning we had to repitch the tent entirely, because the wind had reduced it to total disarray. The roof lay on the ground and everything was full of ice and snow. For 3 days we unfortunates have had no dry gloves left, so this morning I hit on the bright idea of using stockings as gloves; this works quite magnificently. (...)

Due to the shortage of firewood I have had to reduce our meals to one, at noon, when we have coffee and bread with frozen meat, or soup, bread and butter. In the morning and evening there is only bread and meat. We had been working all morning to be able to have lunch and now the hot soup pot has appeared in our tent, and with it all the Eskimos, each with his tin cup in hand. Then the cook, who today is Nachojaschi, opens the pot and immediately we are all enveloped in a thick fog. It begins to snow inside the tent, and it is only when the pot lid is replaced that it becomes possible to see each other again. Not a word was spoken during this meal; because everyone is striving to drink the warm soup as fast as possible. Now we have been out again. Ssigna and Nachojaschi to fetch firewood; Utütiak, Wilhelm and I to try to shoot something. But we did not get anything. The weather is now fairly good, but the wind is utterly foul. Moreover it is still blowing fairly strongly (...)

[Notebook]

22nd [October, Monday]   In the morning a light southerly wind. We set off around 7 and rowed out through pancake ice. [Also] more wind and heavy snow. Next we ran ashore again to assess whether it might blow too much, since the barometer had dropped rapidly. But the weather held. We set off with one reef, but soon were able to shake it out. The wind swung round into the SW and we lost our course. Around 1.00 it cleared up a bit; we mistook the Kikkertens for the Middlis [Miliaxdjuin] and began steering a wrong course, but we soon realized our mistake. At about 4.30 we rowed into Kikkerten against a steady S{W} wind. Eskimos helped us unload and carry things to the house. Mutch had again cooked supper and we really enjoyed it. In the evening the cooper [Rasmussen] came to visit and played some music.

Investigations at K'exerten,
October–December 1883

Science and Epidemics:
Between the Environment and People

[Notebook]

23rd October [**Tuesday**]   I began to work out my observations. After long contemplation the barometer was mounted near the table. I gave Nachojaschi and Yankee bread, powder and tobacco; I also gave N.[achojaschi] another knife since he had lost his. In the afternoon they asked me to go and see a sick woman. She had pneumonia and was very sick, with a high fever. I wanted to put warm, wet poultices on her chest, but realized that it was impossible, because she was continually sitting with her chest and abdomen bare, catching the full draught from the door. So I could do nothing but give her some opium for her cough and quinine for her fever.

24 [**October, Wednesday**]   I have had Wilhelm make a box for the thermometer. I am continuing to work up my data from Pagnirtu. My things are gradually getting finished; thus my stockings, *curletang* [I. *qulittaq* = outer coat] and pants are ready. Mutch's kuni [Inuk woman] is complaining of a sore ear. The sick woman appears to be slightly better, but I prefer not to give her anything more, since I still cannot help her.

25th [**October, Thursday**]   There is still a lot of wind, so we cannot get away, but I am getting W.[ilhelm] to prepare everything for the trip. I have finished Pagnirktu. I visited the sick woman again and wrapped her in my shawl in order to at least protect her somewhat. As we were sitting working in the evening, the Eskimos announced that she had died. When

I went there next day they were engaged in laying out the corpse. A woman sat in the background, with her back turned, singing and talking and clapping her hands incessantly. Today it was the same again. During the day I had Ssigna fetch the barrel of blubber from the American station. It would almost appear that ice was trying to form in the northern entrance to the harbour.

26th [October, Friday]   In the morning Mutch made a coffin for the dead woman, who has not yet been buried. Itu did not come to make coffee for Mutch this morning, because his son was very scared over the woman's death. The occupants of the hut have abandoned her. One woman immediately tore her skin pants off and ran outside when she realized that she was dead. She had died unnoticed by anyone. Yesterday afternoon ice had already appeared between Akkudliruk [Akugdliruk] and Kikkerten. Today there is only a narrow passage open there; this morning the harbour is covered with ice as far as the smithy, though farther out it is still open. By evening, despite the strong wind, it was covered with thin ice up to in front of the house. The wind has now been blowing very strongly and without interruption for almost one and a half weeks. At noon Pakkak came to see me and I had him describe Pagnirktu for me. He sketched the coast from Warham's Island as far as American Hrb. But he can no longer come for the lesson in the morning. In the afternoon he brought me a drawing which he had made in the interim. He is always greatly amused when I pronounce the local names for points. I had him show me the sites for summer camps for caribou hunting. In the evening I pottered at things and wrote to Marie.

[FB/MK]
(...) Last time I wrote to you I was really worried. We had been away from Kikkerton for 7 days and had had continual bad weather. My supplies were starting to run low so I was very glad to get back here again. That was the only day we had a chance to come back, because the wind has been blowing strongly ever since. I am now completely recovered from the stress of the journey and wish very much that I could get away again, but I am afraid that travelling is over for this year. It has continually been very cold for some days now and the harbour is covered with ice.

[FB/parents, sisters]
(...) When you get these letters from me, you will certainly rebuke me endlessly for being lazy, but you would be wrong. It is so abominably cold

outside that I am delighted when I can crawl into my sleeping bag; there, after I have finished my notes, I prefer to write letters. The day before yesterday we had just returned, tired and famished, from the abominable trip we had just made, and this means that travelling is probably finished for the fall, because today the harbour is half full of ice, and by the day after tomorrow may be completely frozen over. Since we had utterly foul weather when we were travelling, we had plenty of time to think of home and to dream of the past and future; and I am doing that very happily again here. I can picture all of you at your daily work; see you sitting at the coffee table in the morning, picture you at noon and in the evening. Oh!, I could have been doing that too, instead of freezing in a tupik at −10°; I could be lolling in an armchair, with my feet on a stool! I wonder whether Marie has reached New York yet? I must break myself of the habit of posing such questions since I cannot get an answer. (...)

Now, fortunately, I have finished setting up my meteorological instruments and hope to be able to get a decent run of readings, at least until I leave Kikkerten. On the day after I arrived here, I was called to see a sick woman, who probably had pneumonia. I was expected to help the poor woman but could do nothing. They sat there the whole day and 'ankuted' [I. *anguqtuq* = exorcized, anglicized], while the woman sat, her body uncovered, in a cold tupik and the wind and weather blew in her face. I wanted to ensure that she at least wrapped herself up, but there could be no thought of that, since her belief in the 'angekoks' [I. *angakkuq* = shaman] is stronger than anything else. She died yesterday evening, and I feel really miserable that I was unable to help. As soon as they noticed that she was dead all the occupants of the tupik raced outside, shouting (her death had gone quite unnoticed), tore their clothes off, and ran to other tupiks; only the husband and the children stayed. The Eskimos are very afraid of dealing with the dead, since they believe that their spirits would kill them. Today Jimmy Mutch made a coffin for the woman and now she is already buried, i.e. she was carried up the hill and placed there.

Evening. Now there is ice in the northern entrance to the harbour, so there can be no thought of setting sail again. The harbour will now freeze over terribly quickly, so that in a few days the Eskimos will probably be walking on the ice. I wish you could see how congenially I am sitting here now. My table is installed and now I am sitting on one side, Jimmy Mutch on the other side of the room, reading, while Wilhelm sits on another chair when he is not cooking or visiting Capt. Roach's cooper [Rasmussen]. I think we will get on well together this winter. (...)

[Notebook]

27th [October, Saturday]   Since the weather is very fine, with little wind, I went with Ssigna up the hill to Cairn V [one of the cairns erected by Boas and Weike around the station for surveying], to take observations from there. I obtained the entire round of angles from Warham's Island to Kikkertuktuak; but eventually it became very cold so I was unable to write down everything. In part the going is not too bad across the soft snow. The ice extends now to beyond the American station. In the Sound it extends for about 4 miles outside the harbour; to the east the Kikkertens are entirely icebound, whereas it is fairly open to the south. Despite the constant north wind this ice is forming and quickly expanding in area. From up on the hill Ssigna went hunting with the rifle while I took my observations, packed up the theodolite and left him up there. By 1 o'clock I was back at the station[,] where they had held the meal for me. In the afternoon I transcribed my observations. The dead woman's husband and mother are still in the tupik, mourning, but the others have moved out. In the evening the cooper visited us and was again playing his music. Along with Wilhelm I took some star altitudes. In the afternoon Mr. Mutch was out with the boats in order to tow them out of the harbour again. But the task turned out to be very difficult and he must have been glad simply to get back ashore again.

Geographical Names and Maps: Comprehending the Area

28th [October] Sunday   In the morning we had breakfast contentedly, then got Tom to draw maps. He showed himself to be very skilled and soon produced a very good map of the entire Sound as far as Frobisher Str[ait] [no Inuktitut name given]. There is a new patient, Kanaka, who has a severe inflammation of the throat. Kokutscha has a small abscess in his ear. The Eskimos are going out on the ice to hunt seals for the first time. They got one.

Monday 29th [October]   In the morning I went out with the winding drum and surveyed the harbour from the American station to the northeastern headland, and took angles from Cairns IV and III; walking across the northeast headland was very difficult, because of large boulders with deep snow between them. I returned across the ice and reached the station at 1 o'clock. In the afternoon Kanaka drew a map for me, but it is not yet finished. I did not do much else, because I became very tired. The Eskimos got 12 seals.

30th [**October, Tuesday**]   Yesterday Wilhelm built my bed out of boards, and yesterday afternoon I made it up. Today I am restowing my trunk in order to set out a few more things, since I now have enough room in the bed. Thus the entire morning was spent in packing. In the afternoon I studied the map with Kanaka; in the evening Jimmy came over to give me some news. His speciality is Frobisher Bay [Tinixdjuarbiusirn]. At first I thought he was very stupid, but he turned out to be very experienced. He had been with Tyson in Greenland [see Hall 1865]. I also learned from him and Pakkak the names for Cumberland Sound, Davis Strait [no Inuktitut name given], Frobisher Bay, etc. Wilhelm and Mutch are now cleaning the stove. 4 seals.

This morning Jiminie's child, who also had pneumonia, died. I saw him carry the box away, while his wife carried the dead child in her arms, sinking to her knees every few steps. Another woman accompanied her. Yesterday Mutch found her standing outside the house [and weeping] that her piccaninny would die. Later another woman fell sick with diphtheria! This is bad. The ice now extends to far outside the harbour; a small strip of water is visible very close to the entrance.

31st [**October, Wednesday**]   This morning the thermometer screen is at last finished; in the afternoon a frame around Marie's picture. In the evening I drew a little. Itu and Pakkak brought their maps. Itu's are very poor. Today they covered their tupiks with heather and pulled another skin over it. They said they really should not have done so yet, because the woman had been dead for too short a time. 2 seals taken.

[FB/parents, sisters]
(...) I should so much like to write to you daily, but despite the best will I find it quite impossible. I must now sit calmly here in the house, because there is always something here to disturb me. Specifically I am now trying to collect information from the Eskimos about the country, and I spent the entire day drawing one or other of these maps. The language is quite abominably difficult! When the weather is tolerable I go out to survey the islands, but this does not achieve very much, since walking in the deep, soft snow is very bad. It is terrible what devastation diphtheria and pneumonia are wreaking among the poor Eskimos now. One person or another is sick in almost every tent. Since the woman died recently another 2 children have died and a third is very sick! And they always come to me for help, yet I can do nothing. Then they take the sick children to a small snow house and the mother looks after the poor crea-

tures! I feel really wretched that I cannot help these poor people. They come so trustingly to the Doctoraluk [I. -*aluk* = big, mighty], as I am called here, yet I can do nothing.

They are now all beginning to move into their winter houses; 2 or 3 families move into a tent together, cover it with heather [moss], then pull a new skin cover over it. These huts are very warm and comfortable for Eskimo conditions. Naturally the caribou hunters are all long since returned; yet I still have not been able to buy enough skins for my winter clothing. I hope the women will soon start working so that I will get a complete new suit. They only begin when the ice has become firm, and they may not work for 3 days after somebody has died; so there is now no prospect of getting winter clothing custom-made.

I wish you knew how comfortably we live here. My room is so pleasantly warm. Jimmy Mutch is as peaceful and obliging as possible[,] and since we are pooling our supplies we can prepare excellent meals. Wilhelm is improving as a cook day by day! It is remarkable that the Scotsman [James Mutch] and the American [Rasmussen, a Dane] have scarcely any contact with each other. Capt. Roach's cooper lives at the American station, but we see him only on Saturdays. He comes up here on Saturday evenings to play cards and play his concertina. I want to move out to the ice with my tent in a few days in order to take tidal observations.

I wonder what you are doing now and how you imagine me? How I would like to take a look around your home and know what you are doing and making. The Krackowizers are certainly in America already. Are you still corresponding with Marie? I must break myself of the habit of asking these questions, because it is pointless. When I see how little I have been writing to you, I am quite depressed, however, but then I think that I will then have all the more to tell you later. Now another month is over. Another year and I will be back with you again! What a delight that will be. Naturally I am keeping my diary regularly; I will then read out to you from it what I cannot write now. I would like to describe for you all the minutiae of life so that you can form a picture of it; there would be no end to it. But the main purpose of my letters is to let you know what I am doing; you must save the details for later.

Back home I thought I would have plenty of time in winter for all possible activities, but that seems to have been a fine mistake, since my time is always fully occupied, whether with cartographic or ethnographic work. And I have already realized that I must restrict myself to these two areas if I want to achieve anything at all, since the available time (a year) is too short! *I hope* that it is no longer; for although there is no prospect of a ship coming here, I shall make every attempt to get home. I shall travel [across] to one of the [Cumberland] Sound fiords near Davis Strait and then north from there in order to meet the Scottish whalers there. Perhaps I shall also see the only American ship [*Wolf*, actually out of St John's] which calls there! In any case I have still not lost hope of being back next year. (...)

[Notebook]

Thursday 1 Nov.   In the morning Mutch brought down a stove for the tupik; however it needed to be cleaned and repaired. I have been doing further calculations and have obtained enough observations to complete a tolerable map of the surroundings of Kikkerten. 7 seals taken. The Eskimos are to continue drawing again after my observations. In the evening Ssigna came by; he had taken a seal. I showed him pictures from [Charles Francis] Hall's first book [1865], which portrayed Kanaka's mother, who acted as pilot for Hall. I showed the picture to Kanaka, who was enormously amused at the picture of himself in his mother's hood, and showed it to everyone. Ssigna is to draw me a map of Nettiling.

Joe came in the morning to pour out the fact that his wife was sick and had stomach pains. I consider this to be pleurisy and *at his request* went with him to his tent. The fever which she had evidently had, had abated, and she seemed already to be improving. I gave her some rhubarb and turpentine liniment, as well as some quinine liqueur. In the evening she felt slightly better, especially after she had emptied her bowels. The tupik in which the woman died has been torn down practically on the spot.

2nd November [Friday]   Visited the woman in the morning again. Finished the map. Shummi brought a sketch, but I did not learn very much new from it. In the afternoon I climbed the hill with Mutch to look around. There is a very heavy swell from the s which is breaking up the ice. As far as the entrance to the harbour the ice is all adrift. Yankee had drifted away with the ice and had lost his harpoon so he could not get back. I therefore lent the Eskimos my boat and around 8 they brought him back safely. The woman is recovering significantly. The Eskimos always want to give me something for my help and cannot understand that I don't expect anything. This applied to both Kanaka and this woman. Subsequently, in the afternoon, I unpacked my entire photographic box; it now becomes a *carne pura* box. In the evening we played a game of chess. Wilhelm began to remodel the tupik. Ssigna was cooking blubber. Nachojaschi and Wilhelm were helping me pack.

3rd Nov [Saturday]   I got up early this morning. The tent is fairly dry again and I have had ears [ventilators] and stockings [an entrance] sewn onto it. Mr. Mutch went out in the boats in the morning, but was unable to get far because of the bad weather and returned at 12. In the meantime Wilhelm was baking bread, but it was a total disaster because due to a misunderstanding I gave him only tartaric acid for baking. In the morning I sent the sick woman some cocoa, and at noon I sent some bread and meat because they have nothing to eat. In the morning I was stowing bottles in my bed, but had not quite finished when Mr. Mutch arrived. In the afternoon I wrote a little to Marie and then began transcribing the names from all the maps. While I was still writing Ssigna came with his map. I obtained from him valuable information about Lake Nettiling and the boatloads of Eskimos who went over there; as well as about the people who have quite recently seen Eskimos over there. (see ethnogr.[aphic] book). [Boas kept this notebook with detailed information on individuals, censuses, etc; in APS:FBFP; cf. Boas 1888:426.]

In the meantime Joe arrived; his wife[,] [my patient[,] had lived there for a long time and knew about Amarok, who has travelled from here to Iglulik. The news came back from Home Bay [no Inuktitut name given] that one of these Eskimos is still alive. The sketch maps are always valuable. The table is opened out and a large quantity of paper laid out on it. We and Mutch lie on the table and then the conversation proceeds, seven-eighths in Eskimo and one-eighth in English. In the morning Pakkak and his kuni were here, mapping Kignait and Padli for me. Since I am giving the natives tobacco for their maps, they are arriving with them of their own accord; thus in the evening Bob arrived with a grey blotter showing the Davis Strait coast from Padli to far to the north.

[FB/MK]

(...) I must now stay here in Kikkerton for a long time. We were already completely frozen in. But today the ice broke up again with a strong, warm SE wind (−7°) and drifted away from the islands. The Sound is totally covered with ice and the view from up above is truly desperately desolate. (...)

During the next week I hope to be able to start my tidal observations. For this purpose I shall move out to the ice with my tent and shall stay there for about a month. I want to survey the Kikkertons at the same time. I hope that in the meantime enough ice has formed that I can think of further travels. (...)

After mature reflection I have decided to leave Cumberland Sound next spring, since it is certain that I would have to stay here 2 years. Thus

I shall travel across to Davis Strait in May and attempt to find a ship there as early as possible; unfortunately it is almost exclusively Scottish ships that frequent that coast. I knew this when I was on board the *Catherine*, but did not want to tell you, so as not to worry you needlessly. Now I am pinning my hopes on a St. John's steamer [from Newfoundland] which I may encounter there. I hope to be able to move to Capt. Roach's at Neiantalik early next year in order to familiarize myself with this coast; perhaps I will then be able to push south and continue south directly overland, but I still know nothing about that. (...)

[Notebook]
4th [November, Sunday]   In the morning I went to see the kuni [Bob's wife]. Bob came back with his map and we had great fun for 2 hours. I ate early. Cooper here in the morning. I took sun altitudes on time and azimuths to the cairns. Wilhelm went out in the afternoon; I stayed here because Bob was coming back. His wife is not better yet. In the evening played chess and wrote. In the morning I want to go out on the ice to start drawing.

5th [November, Monday]   I got up late; Joe is also still sick! I went out with Ssigna on the ice quite early to find a site for the tupik. However, travelling across the drifting floes below the American station is not pleasant, though it is better there than in the small harbour, where the floes are very small. I therefore selected a site between the reefs and the American station. Jimmy [Mutch] has been sewing the tupik, which is now so altered that the poles stand vertically. In the afternoon Mr. Mutch sent about 10 men down to fetch flat pieces of ice and lay them around the tupik. This morning and over noon Ssigna and I were knocking old boxes apart to obtain boards for the floor of the tupik. Thus the foundation was laid today. Today I called Eisik in and pumped him about the surrounding area and especially about the famous 3 boats. I obtained information from him about another route to Nettiling, which is no longer known today and leads via a lake, Imerarktuang [Imeraxdjuak] near Kingawa. Since I could not understand the situation from his description, I gave him some paper. In the evening I transcribed some of the information about the land.

[FB/MK]
(...) The amiable Eskimos are constantly coming and going here. Almost the whole of Kikkerton is engaged in drawing maps for me, from which I hope to get on the track of my questions. I have already achieved a good part of what I need to know, but you can't imagine how much an effort is

involved to drag all this out of these people. Today I really wanted to pitch my tent out on the ice, but the weather is so foul that I have given up until it gets better; it is warm (−4°) however, though there is a storm blowing and it is snowing with full force. But can you imagine how comfortable I am sitting here in the house! (...)

[Notebook]
6th [November, Tuesday]   In the morning Ssigna spread snow on the ice under the tupik. Jimmy (Mutch) continues sewing the tupik. We have erected the tupik up here in order to test the door. In the afternoon I cut up the lines for tidal measurements and for sounding, which took about 2 hours. Then Eisik arrived with his map. I called Nuktukarlin in and I tried to get information from him too, but he appears to be very reluctant. The glance he gave me when Eisik left the room was quite crazy; he thought he was meant to leave too, without receiving any tobacco. He has had 5 wives.

It is better to question the Eskimos individually than several of them together, because it seems that they are shy in front of each other. One can never get as much out of them when there are several together as from one of them alone. Finally we summoned Shangin [Shanguja][,] a young man who has migrated here from Tudnunirn [Tununirn/Eclipse Sound, North Baffin]. From him I finally heard the name Iglulik for the first time! I gave him some paper so that he could draw a map. He knows Xpeastin [place and name not identified on any map by Boas] a location on the coast of Foxe Channel [no Inuktitut name given]. How excited I am at his news. He can make nothing of the map from Hall's book (1865) drawn by Oong-er-luk (Pond's Bay and Foxe Channel). In the evening I played chess with Wilhelm.

[FB/parents, sisters]
(...) Tomorrow I shall at last move down onto the ice; the tent and everything else are ready. The Eskimos have made a good floor for the tupik and I want to start my tidal observations. The ice is quite good now[,] so one can get up and down dry-shod. (...)

Tidal Observations in the Harbour at K'exerten

[Notebook]
7th [November, Wednesday]   Joe and his wife are still sick. I have started pitching the tupik. At first Ssigna began bringing the boards down, then

Wilhelm and I followed with the tupik and the poles. By 12 it was pitched. We ate up here, and spent the afternoon getting organized. The tide gauge was quickly set up and thus I was able to start my observations at 5 o'clock. Today I was content with half-hourly readings, simply to determine the time of high water. I had the watch until 8 p.m.

8th [November, Thursday]   We were taking observations all night; it was very cold in the tupik. Next morning I had the watch from 8 until 2. It emerges from the observations that the tide gauge is not working well enough yet. I have now lowered a stone on a cord. The cord was twisted yesterday. But for one thing the cord has shrunk badly and secondly it is elastic, so an error factor of 2–3 cm results. So at 1 p.m. I abandoned the observations and went up to the house. I am also thinking of using a steel tape measure, but Mutch offered me a 25′ boat's mast, which I sank in the afternoon, with the help of Wilhelm and Ssigna, weighting it with rocks. It works very well. During the day a good wind arose out of Salmon Fiord and by 8.30 a.m. it had driven the ice out of the harbour. Ssigna had gone out, but he noticed the crack soon enough and was not drifted away. We sat waiting all day to see whether the ice would start moving, but despite the strong wind there was still no sign of movement by the time of the night-time high tide. During the day an [ice]berg was driven out of Akkudluk [Akugdliruk] Bay and at 11.30 p.m. I noticed, since I had the watch, that our mast had lost its measuring strip, and that in half an hour the ice had moved out about 2′. Since[,] moreover, I was observing a swell of 3 cm amplitude, I considered it advisable to go ashore and take everything important with me. So I closed up the tupik, and at midnight headed home with some effort, against the raging storm. On land there was a violent blizzard; in places the snow lay so deep that we had to slide forward on our knees; when we reached the shore I fell down an ice crack. Wilhelm was able to get dressed quickly and come [to my rescue]. I was then very tired, since last night I slept only 4 hours. So I slept until ..

.. 9th [November, Friday]   8.30 a.m., but even when I have fallen asleep rather late, I seldom go back to bed again and sleep through till noon. After noon I developed 4 photographs. Afterwards Shangin arrived with his map. Previously (yesterday evening) he had already told Mr. Mutch all kinds of things[,] but I learned most of it today, for I was questioning him systematically. His knowledge extends to the north coast of North Devon [Tudjan] and perhaps farther. These inquiries are very valuable to me. In the afternoon Wilhelm hurried down to the tupik and put everything in order again, and brought the superfluous material up to this path. Yesterday we had great difficulty bringing the boards up across the drifting floe ice. Mr Mutch is making their tupik ready and has promised to lend it to me so that I can pitch it around mine.

10th [November, Saturday]   We began observing again on the evening of the 10th. In the morning there was still plenty of work to do. I developed the rest of the photographs and obtained a total of 7 plates. After lunch Wilhelm went down and began the observations. I soon followed and thus we obtained a good series until 12 a.m. The weather is fine. During the night, when I had a watch of 8 hours, I read three books. We are standing 4–hour watches, and 8–hour watches during the day.

The Inuit's Fall Festival: The Sedna Ritual

11th [November, Sunday]   Wilhelm had the watch this morning. Today is a major festival for the Inuit which they celebrate every fall. Last year they omitted it since there had been two deaths shortly beforehand. Around 9 o'clock the men (mainly) assembled down below amidst a lot of noise, then ran around the entire settlement. They all have their best pants on, and some are wearing the voluminous woman's coat as their coat; all were wearing bird decorations: duck feathers on their backs, or skins and wings of ptarmigan on their hoods. They are now running from house to house shouting *trü*!

In the evening the women came out and threw bread or meat high in the air for them. They even came to visit Mutch and the cooper. Then they assembled down below, and took a circular loop of rope; those born in summer ['the ducks'] stood on one side and those in winter ['the ptarmigan'] on the other. Next they pulled as strongly as possible on each side in order to see whether summer or winter would win. Then the rope was laid down. A large tin pot was placed in the middle and the women brought some water from every house in pannikins.

In the evening the oldest mother went out first and stated where she was born, then old Nuktukarlin, then all the rest, whereupon they next pointed out the direction. Then a snowman with coal for eyes was built down below, and the men shot at it. In the meantime the two torngasuck [I. *tuurngasuq* = like the protective spirit (*tuurngaq*)] were dressed ready and made their appearance. Masks made of ugiuk skin [I. *ujjuq* = bearded seal], tattooed as the women are now. Wearing women's inner coats. The backside stuffed with bulky bags. In their hands an old seal harpoon with walrus [ivory] point, and on their backs an inflated nettirn which is closed with an ivory stopper. A harpoon line over the right shoulder. Their legs heavily padded and tied with sealskin lines into 4 and 3 sections, which are almost as large as elephants' feet.

They first called individuals in and seemed to tell their fortune. (Prior to this the women came out of the individual huts and threw strips of ugiuk meat, berries, pannikins and plates among the crowd.) I threw out ... and beads. There was a fine struggle for the beads! Afterwards men and women arranged themselves in separate lines and the spirits led the men to the women, who took them into their tupiks. Apparently, however, they did nothing with them. Then they took the harpoons away from the spirits and stabbed them dead from behind and cut up their limbs with their hands. They then remained lying and the seal was opened up and half squeezed out. The hollow was filled with water, which everyone brought in a mug. Individuals then came to inquire about their fate.

The shaman takes their mug and drinks from it. He never speaks but often emits strange throat noises, which I had sometimes heard earlier to my amazement. Finally they summoned fair winds, seals, etc. In the evening, before it grew dark they enthusiastically chased a round lid through the whole of Kikkerten. [This fall festival was described in detail by Boas in *Berliner Tageblatt*, 16 November 1884, and in Boas 1888:604–6.]

Discontinuation of the Tidal Observations

12th [**November, Monday**]   Last night the tide rose so high that the mast disappeared; moreover it also drifted out a little and the ice moved; a long crack appeared across the entire harbour. Since I was afraid of losing the mast, I had to take it out again and thus had to abandon the half-hourly observations. Now for a while I shall observe the times of high and low tide. In the afternoon, with Ssigna and Wilhelm I rowed across the harbour from the American station to Cairn II. A high tide observation at 4. I have now sunk the steel tape measure.

13th [**November, Tuesday**] During the night observation the rock dropped off the steel tape measure so I again lost the height of the high tide. In addition it appears that the steel tape is badly corroded and will soon be eaten through by rust. So I must begin again and will take the full moon as my starting point. On the morning of the 13th I went down to the water to take some measurements; I surveyed the low water mark from Akkudliruk to the passage to Kignait, went back through the valley between two hills and returned to Kikkerton at 1. After lunch Wilhelm and I measured a 300 m baseline on the ice in order to determine the distance to the cairns. In the evening Shangin came back and gave me more information [on place names]. Kikker often served as interpreter. He gave me samples of the Iglulik dialect. The view from the valley at Akkudliruk is superb! In bed by 10.

14th [November, Wednesday]   In the morning I went down to the water to check the tide gauge. I tried a new line. In the morning I transcribed information. At noon Ssigna arrived and I transcribed a song. He gave me another old koudschuguk [I. *qaudjaqdjuq* (FB) = song], as did Kikker. In the evening they taught me to make string games. Tom gave me some information on Armarkjua [Amaxdjuax]; he told me that his mother-in-law had been there. (...)

In the afternoon I played a little with the children, who call me Doctoraluk (see October 31).

15th [November, Thursday]   In the morning went down with Ssigna and chopped holes for sounding. On this occasion I froze my nose. In the afternoon was sounding with Ssigna. W.[ilhelm] pulled the sledge while I sounded and hauled the line in while Ssigna rolled it up. In the evening I was doing calculations, but I was exhausted so not very motivated. I will have to interrupt my tidal observations again because I cannot get onto the ice at high tide. I am still having to feed Joe and his wife.

16th [November, Friday]   Today I stayed at home in order finally to transcribe my observations. I am getting everything more or less ready. In the evening we called in Nuktukarlin's kuni[,] who I had been told knows Armarkdjua and the surrounding area. I heard a new song from Kakodscha and his son, Atteina (the sick boy). In the evening Kikker showed me how to make some string figures.

17th [November, Saturday]   Another boy is very sick with diphtheria? In the morning I went down to the ice with Ssigna to dismantle the tupik. The dogs have attacked my sleeping bag. I finished dismantling the tupik. Then I remodelled the small winding drum and the compass in order to be able to use them by securing them to the camera tripod. On Monday I want to start at the Kikkertons.

Sickness and Death among the Inuit

18th [November,] Sunday   In the morning I was called from bed to see
the sick boy, who is dying. I tried to get him a little air by means of hot
poultices; he regained some colour, but died under my hands at noon.
Nuvukulu [I. *nuvuk* = point, *kulu* = small, lovable; personal name] started
crying and called the mother; he refused to be comforted. The boy was
buried immediately. They had built a small snow house for him yesterday
to allow him to die there. Joe was quite depressed today, since he was
thinking of his little lad who died in the spring. In the evening I was visiting Ssigna and saw my little friend Kokutscha, with whom I always play.
Once again I tried sampling raw seal meat there. Tomorrow I want to go
to Akkudliruk and Angiuk [Angiux].

[FB/MK]
(...) Many days have passed now since I (...) last wrote to you. You should
not be angry with me since the tidal observations and my conversations
with the Eskimos consume a great deal of my time. I am still at Kikkerton,
busy with interviewing the natives, who give me information on this or
that part of their home areas. (...)

It is not yet 3 p.m. but it is already quite dark. It is very cold here now;
according to your thermometer −10° [Fahrenheit]; according to ours
−24° [Celsius]; the house is now surrounded by snow walls and well protected against the cold. (...)

This is the second deathbed I have attended here! And I have another
patient, a woman, who had pneumonia but fortunately recovered,
though for 3 or 4 days I was afraid she would die. These poor people,
man and wife, lay sick together, and although the other Eskimos supplied
them with meat, they would have been in a bad way if I had not brought
them food and drink. I keep telling myself that I was not to blame for the
child's death yet it weighs upon me like a reproach that I was unable to
help. (...)

[FB/parents]
(...) You should not be angry that I have not written to you for so long.
However, I could not help it since my disastrous tidal observations
demanded so much of my time. I have now been living in the house again
for some time, but my numerous conversations with the Eskimos don't
allow me to rest. Today, once again, I was standing beside a sad deathbed. I was called to see an Eskimo boy to assist him and found him and

his mother in a small igloo [I. *illu*] (snow house). The mother looked at me fearfully, hoping to read some comfort in my eyes, but I could only feel the small body becoming colder and colder and soon he was quite dead.

You can't imagine how the awareness that I cannot help these poor people weighs heavily on me, yet what is the point, I cannot do anything. Yet they are so confident that the 'ankuting of the Doctorádluk,' as they call me, will be of benefit that I do not have the heart to destroy their faith. Sometimes I can help a little but usually, when they call me, things are already so far gone that a doctor can scarcely help. This is already the second deathbed I have attended here! (...)

Hikes across the Ice: Surveying the K'exerten Archipelago

[Notebook]
19th [November, Monday]   In the morning I went out with Ssigna and Wilhelm to begin our surveys. I have been measuring the heights of the surrounding hills from the 300 m baseline, and the distance to the reef that extends from Akkudliruk to Kikkerten. From here I measured right and left as far as the entrance to Union Passage [no Inuktitut name given] and the spine of the reef. Measurements taken with the theodolite. We were back by 3.45. In the evening Kidla came to tell me a story. Afterwards Pakkak arrived and gave me some extraordinarily interesting information about old stories, as well as a list of words which they use when ankuting.

20th [November, Tuesday]   Went out with Wilhelm and having established yesterday's baseline, surveyed around Akkudilruk. In the evening I was too tired to do anything. We did not get back until after dark.

[FB/MK]
(...) Today we hiked about 3.5 German miles [26.4 km] across the ice. (...)

[FB/parents, sisters]
(...) Yesterday and today I hiked so far that I am really tired. I am now surveying the Kikkertens [archipelago] and thus have to hike far and wide across the ice. Your flags, dear sisters, are now constantly in use. At every station a 'Vorwärts' or 'Marie' stands out [embroidered by Marie and his

sisters as emblems on the flags.] I am using them as markers for my observations. I shall be going out again tomorrow, north towards {Kautak} [Kautax], in order to survey another island. The day after tomorrow, approximately, I plan to make my first sledge trip. Please be content with these few words today; I am too tired!

[Notebook]
21st [November, Wednesday]   In the morning I wrote my journal, then I set off with Wilhelm and Ssigna. We are heading for Adams Island [Mitiluarbing] and around Union Island [Angiux]. I wrote a little in the evening.

22nd [November, Thursday]   A rest day. I have been taking all kinds of things out of the house and have been transcribing stories. Today Atteina was telling me stories of the mouse [lemming; Boas 1888:649] and the fox [p. 655] and the crow [raven; p. 655] and the seal [p. 650]. In return I also told a few stories. It is really fine to observe how they listen and concentrate. In the evening Shangin told me stories about Köolu, the lightning [and thunder] maker [I. *kallu* = thunder] and about sisters [story of the three sisters; Boas, 1888:600; see also Rink 1885].

23rd [November, Friday]   Went out again today. At 7.30 a.m. there was a remarkable swell; the snow appeared a purplish-red. Afterwards walked around Kikkerten; we walked around the north point until we came south of the churchyard [whalers' cemetery]. In the evening Shangin was here again, telling stories about the tudnik [I. *tuniit* = legendary ancestors of the Inuit; Boas 1888:634–6, 654]. They ascribe the old stone dwellings which they find here to the tudnik. –18°C. at 10 p.m. I am also concerned about some tudnik songs.

24th [November, Saturday]   We travelled around the south end of Kikkerten; this involved a lot of effort because of the difficult ice that has been heaved up everywhere. There is a lot of water not very far from the coast. In the afternoon I was doing calculations and writing.

Sunday [25 November]   Writing and lazing about all day.

[FB/MK]
(...) Throughout this period, when I came home I was so tired in the evening that I scarcely wanted to stir, and in the evening my good friends

would come to tell me some stories or sing for me[,] and then, like it or not, I had to write down what they said. (...)

[FB/Parents, sisters]
(...) You really must not be angry, dearest ones, if I write so little now, but my time is completely occupied by my survey of the Kikkertons [archipelago] and conversations with the Eskimos, so I hardly have any time for anything else. I can scarcely even keep my journal properly. Unfortunately I am very much in arrears with transcribing, etc. You certainly must be wondering about these 'polar letters'; which appear to contain nothing, as if I had just taken a quick break from my books to send you greetings!

This evening I played dominoes with Wilhelm and I found a scrap of paper among the dominoes with a violet painted on it. At first I was quite sure that you, dear Hete [Hedwig] had put it there. But now I am quite uncertain, since under the violet is written: Think often of your distant friend Hedwig, dear Anna.' And also the violet is painted in oils and on the cross around which it is twined there are some Hebrew letters. Now I am quite uncertain whether it is you since, in the first place my name is not Anna, then you cannot paint in oils, and finally you certainly would not have painted a foreign cross. This scrap of paper gave us food for thought for an entire evening! The day after tomorrow is Wilhelm's birthday. Then I shall formally hand him your letters; and in 4 weeks it is Christmas! I wonder whether I shall have been away again before that?

It is just too silly that I cannot get my caribou clothing made. Their beliefs forbid the Eskimo women to work at it before this moon is past, so it will be another 3 weeks before I can be properly outfitted. Yesterday and the day before I was surveying Kikkerten. We are constantly running at an acceptable speed across the ice and are always thoroughly tired and hungry when we get home. Now a fine, strong wind has arisen; perhaps it will prevent me from going out tomorrow. I am not exactly praying for it because I have plenty to do! (...)

With this letter Boas interrupts his reports to his parents and sisters. He did not write another letter to them until 30 April 1884, before he left K'exerten to travel across to Davis Strait.

[Notebook]
Monday [26 November]   There was a cold wind this morning[,] −23.8° with fog, so that one could not see the flags. So I stayed at home, and sim-

ply surveyed the missing portion of Akkudliruk at noon, then was drafting in the afternoon. Joe is much sicker. In the evening Pakkak came to visit and I obtained valuable information on the beliefs of the Eskimos, as well as another old song.

27th [November, Tuesday]   Overnight a severe southerly storm had arisen, and it persisted with violent snow-drifting all day. +18°F [−8°C]. The snow has been blown off the hills; Bob's {tupik} snow house, which was erected only yesterday, has been blown completely away by the wind. Today Joe has come out in a rash; I don't know what to make of him. I again gave him some bread, for he is very hungry. I was transcribing stories all day. In the evening Kikker was here and gave me a new song that was linked to a story. (...) [Inuit names:] Betty − [also called] Akuschiakschu. Kamelischu. Kaschodluajung.

28th [November, Wednesday]   Wilhelm's birthday [he is 24 years old]. I have letters from home for him, which also enclose some notes for me. I gave him the Don Quixote. All day long I was copying maps and stories and am now finished with it. I am still missing the names of the places that I must transcribe. I want to go back to Angiuk tomorrow. The women are now working on caribou skins, since it is now a new moon and seals are being caught beneath the ice. Yesterday the men saw an ugjuk's [bearded seal's] breathing hole; if they catch it they can no longer work[,] so I am having this work accelerated as much as possible.

[Temperature data in Celsius]
29th.   7 a.m. −23.8°   1 p.m. −23.6°   7 p.m.−27.8°
30th.   7 a.m. −27.8°

29th [November, Thursday]   In the morning went to Angiuk with Wilhelm and Ssigna. I went over the point at Akkudliruk in order to measure magnetic directions there. Then we travelled around Angiuk. At the point where the ice had broken away with the violent southerly wind of the day before yesterday, the going was very bad, since the new ice crust was still not safe in many places. Wilhelm went ashore and I lost him. After about an hour I found him again. We had headed in different directions. Back home around 5. Pakkak and Shangin met us with their sledge and we travelled home with them.

Kikker came in the evening to give me some new songs. I obtained the melody for Takuninga unga [I. *Takuvunga una* = I see it!] and 2 new sto-

ries [song not included in Boas 1888]. In the afternoon Eisik's granddaughter and Kokutscha's daughter here because of the songs. Eisik's
granddaughter is called: Audlacheak, Secheelling, Paudle, Nivijuktauja,
Iijuktua, Ugnung, Shegmung.
[Temperature data]
[29 November]   1 p.m. –25°   7 p.m. –26.4° (...)

30th [November, Friday]   In the morning I went with Wilhelm to Akük-
serbing [Axbirsiarbing]. It was very cold and we often froze our noses and
cheeks in the sharp north wind. As we were coming back in the afternoon, we were met by Itu and Tom with their sledge, with which we travelled part way back. In the afternoon I was very tired yet I worked until
12. Kikker gave me another part of a song.

1 December [Saturday]   (...) Stayed home today in order to work some
things up. In the afternoon Arne came to give me the words to one song.
Ursuk showed me how they play the kilauju (I. *qilaut* = drum]; they strike
the edge of the drum with the hand while rocking on their feet. Then
Madla's kuni sang a song, which she rarely does. The women arranged
themselves in a circle and sang with a wonderful throat sound. One could
clearly see their throats moving. They produced a strong rhythm, in time
to the drum, involving sounds similar to snoring or sobbing, but in the
throat. When the young boy died some time ago, all the Eskimos were
forbidden to empty their piss pots before sunrise. If a walrus is taken in
winter, the women can no longer work on caribou skins. In the evening
the cooper was here (Rasmussen is his name). (...)
[Temperatures at 7.00 (8.00), 13.00, and 19.00]
[1 December]   8 –26.8°   1 –24.2°   7 –23.3°
[2 December]   7 –22.0°   1 –22.2°   7 –16.8°
[3 December]   7 –8.5°

2nd [December] Sunday   In the morning I did a little writing then took
a walk over Akkudliruk in a biting wind and a temperature of –22°. In so
doing I became as warm in my caribou pants as at the height of summer. I
have finished drafting Angiuk, Akkudliruk and Kikkerten. Later Koketschu was here, and I played with him a little. He is now very trusting and
always comes running to me when I want him to. In the evening I discussed my further travel plans with Mutch. So many dogs have died now
that it would be difficult to acquire a team. So I am proposing to travel on
foot. We have agreed that as soon as all my clothing is ready Mutch will

take me to Aupelluktu [Augpalugtung], from where I shall go to Ssurvisik [Surossirn], and from there he will fetch me again.
[Temperature data]
3rd [December]   1 p.m. –9°
4th [December]   7 p.m. –23.6°

[FB/MK]
(...) I was interrupted at this point because a woman arrived who has been making fur stockings for me and wanted to be paid; then another woman came with her youngest child in her hood and leading the other by the hand. The latter, a little lad called Koketschu, is a good friend. As soon as he sees me he shouts 'Doctoráluk, hopp, hopp! Doctoráluk' (my name here means the big doctor) and now and then I let him ride on my knee. He always talks a lot, telling me things, but unfortunately I can't understand a word, or at best very little, since the language is very difficult to learn. I am on very friendly terms with most of the children, because I often play with them. Now and then we also sing and play together, wherein I have a hidden motive, that of getting to know their games.

I wish you could only see me here among the Eskimos, and realize that it is not so bad as you probably think. I feel as cosily warm in my skin clothing as I could possibly want. Thus today I took a walk for about 2 hours purely for pleasure, and despite the glorious wind and a temperature of –23° was as warm as I ever was at home. How I look forward to being able to show you on the photographs where all I have been! I have just been wandering around the Kikkertons to take these photos[,] and in the evening I have been having important conversations with the Eskimos about their customs, songs, religion, etc. Mr. Mutch is very obliging as an interpreter and gives me an enormous amount of information on every possible subject. Now all my caribou clothing is under way, and I hope it will be ready this week. Then I can think of travelling again, and can hope to go north. During the next month I am thinking of establishing a depot of provisions on the shores of Davis Strait, and then of going to Lake Kennedy. (...)

[Notebook]
3rd [December, Monday]   I set off by dogsled to Manituk [Manitung] Island and surveyed it. When I came back it was already 5 p.m. We had lunch, and then I worked in the evening and read until 1. My caribou pants are ready, as well as the boots which Betty [Ssigna's wife] has been adjusting.

By Dogsled across the Pack Ice

4th [**December, Tuesday**]   Last night a little snow fell; since it was blowing out of the SW in the morning and the light snow was drifting badly, I
had to stay here. I wrote for a while then went to Akkudliruk in order to
tie it in finally with Kikkerten. In the afternoon I played a little with
Koketschu, who is now a close friend. In the evening Mikidschu first gave
me a song, then Chummi and Mitu arrived; the latter sold me some skins
and they gave me some information.
[Temperature data]
7 a.m. –23.1°   [noon] –20.8°   7 p.m. –20.4°
Drifting snow.

[FB/MK]
(...) Travelling by dogsled is great fun. Just imagine a small, low[,] hand
sledge, such as is used at home for pulling loads but lighter, with 12 dogs
harnessed to it, all pulling continually. Ssigna, Wilhelm and I were sitting
wrapped in our furs on this low sledge Ssigna driving the dogs with his
20′ whip. He constantly has to yell and shout at them to keep them moving[,] and then they run and jump over and under each other, occasionally bite each other, so that in less than half an hour the traces are in
such a tangle that one has to stop. I hope that a week from now I can get
away from here to begin my trip to the north. Now Ssigna is harnessing
the team again, because we want to travel to the most northerly [islands]
of the Kikkertons [= the archipelago]. This is about 7 English miles from
here. (...)

The English that I'm learning here is worse than atrocious. I'm afraid
it is more Scottish than English. Everything one sees here, whether it be a
table, a chair, the sky, the earth or whatever is always *he* or *she*[,] and the
chwales (whales), even though they no longer come here, form a major
topic of conversation.

However it would be unfair of me to say anything against Jimmy
Mutch[,] my host here. He is in every way obliging towards me and helps
me with his better knowledge of the Eskimo language wherever he can, so
I am greatly indebted to him for increasing my knowledge in this regard.
Also he has been lending me his dogs for excursions; in short I must be
grateful to him in every way. He is a very devout man, who allows no work
in his house on Sundays. But I do not allow myself to be prevented from
working at whatever I want; I simply avoid all noisy work such as carpentry
or repairs etc. Back home I had thought I would have much free time in

winter, but in this I was greatly mistaken since I have scarcely a moment to myself. (...)

[Notebook]
5th [December, Wednesday]   In the morning we headed out in foul weather with drifting snow; we went to Manituk Island and despite the wind we reached Kautak safely. There we turned back and got back here half frozen. I was very tired; I slept a little then called Pakkak in; he told me some old stories for a while. Kikker also came in with a sketch. (...)
[Temperature data]

6th [December]	7 –22.0°	1 –23.6°	7 –24.3°
7th	7 –27.0°	1 –28.6°	7 –30.0°
8th	7 –30.8°	1 –29.2°	7 –28.0°
9th	8 –32.4°	1 –32.4°	

[ww]
6 December [Thursday]   Due to a blizzard we had to stay at home today and went out of the house as little as possible. I got my things ready to be washed and since the natives were not out hunting seals, Kikker was here doing laundry for J.M. [James Mutch]; the two of us sat side by side with our laundry.

7 December [Friday]   Today we stayed at home again, since we had to unpack things; it was 8.30 when we had coffee. When I had washed up, Herr Doctor and I went to the provisions hut and unpacked the cases and got thoroughly frozen; we were glad when we were finished. Then I had to make a start with the noon meal. Dinner at 2.30; we had to light a lamp for the meal; this evening we had a temperature of –20°.

8 December [Saturday]   There was no particular weather today. The Dr. went out; I had to melt ice for water all day. When I saw the Dr. coming back, I prepared the meal. In the afternoon I washed out the woollen clothing once more. In the evening the cooper [Rasmussen] came over and we played cards; this was the first time we had done so on land.

[Notebook]
6th, 7th and 8th stayed home, because the caribou skin clothing means a lot of work and the women have to be supervised. My inner curletang, stockings, pants and cammings are now finished. I hope I get the rest soon so that I can travel. I was collecting songs and was working up the

map of the Kikkertens. On Saturday the 8th the cooper [Rasmussen] was
here in the evening; we played cards for the first time. (...)
[Temperature data]
[9 December]   1 –30.8°   7 –31.4°
10th   1 –36.0°
11   7 –35.3°

9th December [Sunday]   Today we had visitors for the first time. Padloaping and Shorty, 2 Eskimos from Tininirdjua [Tininixdjuax] arrived here
yesterday evening with wife and child in 2 sleds around 10 o'clock. Unfortunately another 2 children died today from a diphtherialike illness. One
belonged to Ssegdloaping and Nachojaschi[,] the other to Bob. This
again results in an inconvenient disruption in the making of my caribou
clothing, because the women will now not be working for another 3 days.
At the end of this period, which is not quite firmly fixed, they will ask the
mourning woman whether she has any objection to them working.

[**10 December, Monday**]   In the morning I questioned Padloaping and
Shorty about Nettilling. I obtained fairly valuable information from them.
Padloaping had seen traces of an eagle near Tudnirn [Tunirn: position
unclear]. They were cut off just at the points. He thought the bird was
walking on the bearskin. The footprints were slightly turned inwards.

Monday [actually **Tuesday**] **11th** [**December**]   Padloaping and Shorty
have completed their map of Nettilling. They wanted to go back in the
evening, because they had not achieved their aim, namely borrowing
dogs in order to bring their furs down from Kangia (head of Tininirdjua). There are few dogs in Kikkerten since illness has been raging
fiercely since last fall. Now there are few cases. I am getting everything
ready for leaving. I was finished by about 11 p.m.
   Luckily the women have been working on my birdskin slippers,
although I was afraid that they would not make these either. However,
they are prohibited only from working on sealskins and caribou skins in
making new clothes. They can patch old clothes, and can also work on
birdskins and European material. They do not all know these rules precisely; Nuktukarlin replied to my questions as usual; Eisik or Koukodloap-
ing are also aware of these rules.

Inuit, Igloos, and Dogs:
Journeys on the Ice of Tinixdjuarbing,
December 1883 – May 1884

First Trip to Anarnitung and K'ingua

[Notebook]
Tuesday [actually **Wednesday**] **12th** [**December**]   Got up at 6 a.m. and by
8 were ready to leave. Around 10, as we were passing Kautak it struck us
that I had forgotten my lamps so have nothing to cook with. Itu and Tom
have their Eskimo lamps, however. Padloaping and Shorty are still here.
In the evening the dogs were very tired. Near Browns Harbour [NW from
Pitiuxsin] we see Utütiak, who is retrieving his seal from the trip to Pagnirtu [7 October]. Mr. Mutch sends Itu and Tom to procure seals from
the water holes. I want to go to Anarnitun [Anarnitung] if possible.
Around 9 p.m. we are at the spot where we once met Mitu [on 10 October, at Niurtung]. Here Itu and Tom were engaged in building an igloo.
We hauled everything up the vertical ice-foot face with cords. Soon Pad-
loaping arrived and we all crowded into the same igloo (8 occupants).
Shorty has his own small igloo nearby.

13th [**December**] Wednesday [actually **Thursday**]   Igloo 1. (Mainland
near Niuktung). In the morning I went down to Pagnirtu with Wilhelm
and surveyed the coast around Aupaluktung [Augpalugtung]. Walking
through the soft snow is very tiring. The Eskimos went to the water holes
to hunt. The igloo is built too close to the water so at high tide last night
some water penetrated into the igloo. Wilhelm and I went north early in
the day and made the coast at Niuktung. Near the igloo the ice-foot face
is very high and steep so we managed to get our things down it only with
difficulty. The fog greatly obstructed my surveys, so I made only slow
progress. Itu and Tom have taken 3 seals. Itu is going back to Kikkerten

tomorrow. I gave him a letter for Mutch, to ask him for the things which I have forgotten. In the igloo in the evening we again played dominoes with the Eskimos.

From 13 December onward, Boas wrote his letters to Marie equally as journal or diary, from which he transcribed passages until 2 February 1884 to the Notebook, and from 1 January 1884 also to the Diary and Diary 2.

[FB/MK]
(...) Today I have already begun my work in bad weather and have been running around diligently. Although the temperature is −35°, one does not feel cold while walking; on the contrary I found my caribou suit too warm. I had almost gone alone with Ssigna because Wilhelm's suit was not finished, but Mr. Mutch took pity on me and lent him his outfit. (...)

Do you know, I once believed that I myself did not have a heart, because there were many things that I did not feel very intensely, or so I thought; but now I know better. You, Marie[,] have taught me that I can still feel. How happy we are going to be. But I am getting sidetracked from my trip to Aupelluktung. (You once wrote to me that I should not apply a logical measure to your letter; don't you do so here either.) So I thank you [for making me aware] that one can only feel truly happy as a member of humankind if one knows that according to one's powers, one is working towards a great goal with a large group, and that one will naturally have to bear one's share of joy and sorrow. I believe that if one always felt so, one would cope with difficulties more easily and accept every joy more gratefully. (...)

Wilhelm and I will go north tomorrow morning to survey the coast further. We are coming to the water holes, which are kept open by the current and prevent us from going farther. As we were leaving the 3 Eskimos brought our sledge and dogs down the steep ice-foot face. At low tide the face drops steeply about 15′, so everything has to be let down on lines.

The fog hinders us greatly, but we advanced about 4 miles northward. When we came back Ssigna was busy chopping up food for the dogs, i.e. sawing up frozen seal meat, then chopping it into smaller pieces with an axe. Today it is −40° with a strong N wind. Itu and Tom were at the most northerly polynya and brought back 3 seals, whereas Ssigna has none. (...)

You see, Marie, here I am writing the same things on the pages of my journal and to you, since this is the only possibility of getting some information about my daily life to you. The igloo is too cold, so I do not write more than is absolutely necessary and if I wait a few days you will not learn what I am actually doing. So please accept these brief notes with the occasional words addressed specifically to you.

Now, when we have been in the igloo for about 4 hours, it is warm enough to write something, though it is still not up to the freezing point, yet I feel quite comfortable. Feelings of what is pleasant and unpleasant are really quite relative. At home we would be infinitely sorry for somebody in our situation, yet here we are cheerful and in good spirits. I hope that by then I shall be at Ananatu [Anarnitung], a camp near here, and to hurry back to Kikkerton by sledge from there. (...)

A Bitterly Cold March to K'ingua

[Notebook]
14th [December, Friday]   Ssegnirun [Sednirun]. 2nd igloo. At the same time as Itu and Tom set off for Kikkerten, we began sledging northward. As we were bringing the sledges down [from the ice foot] I was trying to steady Wilhelm and fell into the water at a temperature of −45°. At first we were following Itu's sledge tracks but then switched ... ahead.

[FB/MK]
(...) We are at the same time heading farther north, and arrived here around 2 after it got dark. As we were getting under way, we had great difficulty in getting down from the ice foot; my sea bag tore and I fell into the water up to my knees, though I did not get wet inside; −38°. At first we were following Itu's sledge tracks of yesterday, then went from Keirvun [Kaivun] over to Ssegdnirun [Sednirun]. Ssigna built an igloo and fortunately our meal was ready in 4½ hours. The going is very heavy because we have a heavy load and the snow is too soft. The most unpleasant thing is that everything becomes wet from sweat and then is frozen solid next morning. We could not reach Opperdinirvik [Operdniving] because we got under way too late owing to various accidents in loading the sledges. It is a beautiful evening today. The landscape rather resembles Tinichuta-jan [Tinitoxajang], since the strait is very narrow and the islands are steep. One can still see the jagged Pyryruikten [Piroirtung] to the south, all glowing red in the protracted evening glow and then, in this beautiful landscape I think of whom? (...)

[Notebook]
15th [December, Saturday]   Snowy and warm. Wilhelm and I are head-

ing north to survey Ssednirun and part of the mainland coast. Because of today's snowfall the snow has become so deep that we can no longer haul our things. So I will have to leave a good part of them here. I hope we will reach Opperdniving tomorrow; Mutch's sledge is supposed to be coming there.

[FB/MK]
(...) This morning we found it astonishingly warm, since snowy weather had set in. This hindered my observations greatly, yet I succeeded in reaching the entrance to American Harbour. Often we could see barely 100 paces. Well offshore it is clearer and the snow is better. Ssigna reports that the snow is soft here year-round. We are tormented most by thirst and we were very glad when we got back here to the igloo at 4 o'clock. Ssigna was here already with a small seal. We made coffee then cooked some seal meat. Tomorrow we want to set off for Opperdniving, but will have to leave some of our things here because they are too heavy to haul in this soft snow. This poor snow is hindering us greatly. I hope it will be better tomorrow.

You see, although such a trip is quite simple in theory, its execution involves major difficulties. But today I feel quite comfortable since it is relatively warm so we are not freezing even in the igloo. I do not know if we will reach our goal tomorrow but I hope so, because I really am in a hurry. Then I will have the remainder of the things fetched by dog team, either Mutch's or one from Anarnatu. At this speed we will probably be spending Christmas outside. Everything would be gimy [Scottish dialect *gimy* = neat, brisk] today if only the snow were better.

[Notebook]
Sunday, 16th [December]   Igloo 3, north of Pamiujang. Last night more snow fell so we can make progress only with great effort. When we stopped for the night we were utterly exhausted though we had covered only 4 miles. In the evening we devised an alcohol lamp, since the blubber is exhausted and we must have heat.

[FB/MK]
(...) When we got up at 6 a.m. it looked so dark and threatening that I initially thought we could not possibly set off. During the night probably 9″ of snow had fallen and it was quite soft. So we could make progress only with great effort and by the time we reached here at noon today we were utterly exhausted. We are not 3 miles from our last igloo and still not at

American Harbour, which I had hoped to reach much sooner. If only the snow were hard this would not be such terrible effort, but as it is every step costs an infinite amount of effort and work. I left a good part of my things at the last igloo because we were scarcely in a position to haul what we have here, namely just sleeping bags and something to eat.

This morning, as we sat inside the igloo, Wilhelm and I together devised an alcohol lamp, for this was our greatest need. For this purpose we took just an old butter can[,] in the lid of which we cut three holes. In addition we made a pot from an old tin can. Now, fortunately we have 2 lamps and can make coffee quickly and keep the igloo much warmer. Ssigna was quite in despair at the heavy work today, but it truly is excessively strenuous.

I want to stay here tomorrow and make a survey. In some incomprehensible fashion my thermometer has been left at the last igloo. The only thing that is troubling me now is that the sledge from Kikkerton may miss us, for if it continues to snow, it will not find our tracks. But today at noon it cleared up and we hope that we will have good weather again. The best thing now would be a good east wind that would blow the snow hard! Even if I had to sit in the igloo for 24 hours.

Do you know how I am passing the long evening? I have my [Immanuel] Kant with me and am studying him so that I shall not be too uneducated when I come home. Life here truly transforms people (but only temporarily; when I get to Kikkerton, I am quite sociable). When I think that this evening I, *your* Franz, was contemplating how good a pudding with plum sauce would taste, I almost have to blush. You have no concept of the effect of deprivation and hunger on a person. Perhaps Herr Kant is a good antidote!

And when I think, on the other hand, of how a year ago I was among Berlin society and was following all the fine rules of 'bon ton,' and tonight am sitting in a snow house with Wilhelm and an Eskimo, eating a piece of raw, frozen seal meat, which first has been cut into pieces with an axe, and in addition am drinking hot coffee almost greedily, one can scarcely conceive of greater contrasts. (...)

[Notebook]
Monday 17th [December]   Surveyed the coast northward in cold[,] clear weather. Ssigna went to the polynyas, but got nothing. Very tired in the evening.

18th [December, Tuesday]   Cold and windy. To the north the snow and the ice were such that it would cost futile effort to make any progress. I will wait at the Kikittens [islands in the north of the Sound] or go to Anarnitung. I took some bearings from the hill; in the meantime Ssigna tried to make a repair to his rifle and broke it completely.

[FB/MK]
(...) Yesterday morning [17 December] Wilhelm and I went up to American Harbour; much of the way we were travelling through soft snow and the shore ice which had largely broken up. Ssigna had gone south to look for seals in the polynyas but found few and got none. He saw a duck there, which had probably got lost. Today I really wanted to go back to the previous igloo to fetch some things, but turned back because with a temperature of −40° and a south wind I could easily have frozen my face and it was not an urgent matter. So I later went up the hill behind the igloo with Wilhelm and took some so-called sun altitudes (the sun was only 45° above the horizon) and bearings towards the south and towards Imigen. (...)

Now, if the sledge does not come tomorrow, we are obliged to turn back and to go to Kikkerton because we do not have enough fuel. (...)

[Notebook]
Wednesday, 19th [December]   Am still waiting for the sledge, which must almost be here. Wilhelm and I went northward again. Since the sledge is not here I am preparing everything for travelling to Anarnitun. Ssigna has fetched some things from the last igloo. Everything absolutely necessary will be packed in the bearskin which Ssigna's dogs will pull, and in this way I shall set off tomorrow morning.

[FB/MK]
(...) We are still sitting in our third igloo. This morning Ssigna went to the previous igloo at Ssednirun to fetch some tobacco, tea and *Carne pura*. He still has *one* shell for the Mauser and with it he will try to shoot a seal. Wilhelm and I went north to American Harbour. We finally got so far! At 7.30 a.m. at a temperature of −48° [the lowest Boas recorded this winter] we set off following the track of the sledge and came back at 2 p.m. Soon after us Ssigna appeared; he had not even been able to fire his 1 shell because there was too much fog rising from the polynyas in the intense cold. (...)

When I relate this adventure later, it will sound so bad and dangerous, and now we are laughing at our misadventure, and at our anticipation of the faces of the people at Anarnitung when suddenly three men on foot, with 2 dogs, arrive from Kikkerten; so what will Mr. Mutch say when his sledge arrives here and finds the birds flown! But tomorrow we must crawl into an Eskimo family's bed and finally get some dry things!

We have a substantial hike ahead of us, about 15 miles without a trail! (...)

[Notebook]
20th [December, Thursday]   Got up at 3 a.m. and by 5 we were ready to start. We set off with a temperature of −45° and clear weather, and reached Ssarbukduk. But here fog obscured any distant views so Ssigna could not find Anarnitun. The ice along our route is very rough and bad. The dogs finally refused to pull so we had to leave them and the bearskin behind. It was only after it got dark that we found the land, with some difficulty. Here we heard a sledge, but it only led us astray, taking us in the wrong direction. Finally we abandoned the search at around 1 a.m., ..

The First Time in an Inuit Camp: Anarnitung

[**21 December, Friday**]   .. only to begin again when the moon rose. I found a sledge track, certainly, but we followed it in the wrong direction, thus heading for Ssarbukduak [Sarbuxdjuax]. From here we finally reached Anarnitung at 6.30 after a hike of 26 hours. Wilhelm has slightly frozen two toes on the right foot and the big toe on the left foot seriously. I have slightly frozen my finger tips and my nostrils; Ssigna his cheeks and the tip of his nose. We went into Ocheitu's igloo and fell asleep immediately. Ocheitu [who in 1882–3 was employed by the German Polar Station as 'local labour'] went out to look for the bearskin and the dogs and at 11 came back with them and Kanaka. The latter had left Kikkerten the day before yesterday. He had reached Alikun the first day. On the 2nd he emptied the igloo and came as far as Itu's bearskin.

[FB/MK]
(...) He [Kanaka] had slept on the ice for two nights. He brought only one seal ..., dogsled, Shorty's boat! So I can certainly stay here longer. He has no dog food. This morning I have just eaten some cold seal. (...)

[Notebook]
4 p.m. 21st. Ocheitu feeds the dogs and promises to go to Kikkerton with

me. So tomorrow I want to go to Ssarbukduak and stay there for 1 or 2 days. In the afternoon Ocheitung showed me the sights of Anarnitung and took me to Mitirk on Idlungajung [Igdlungajung], a nearby island.

[FB/MK]
(...) In the afternoon I first went out with Ocheitu who showed me the igloos of Anarnitung as well as the boats, an old tupik in which a boy had died last fall, and the old house mounds, which all have names here. These are the first of their kind I have seen here. Afterwards we went to the nearby island of Idlungajung, where 5 other tupiks were standing, to visit Mitik, the oldest man in the Sound. I hoped to obtain some first-hand information from him about Foxe Channel [no Inuktitut name given], but got very little. Mitik had been here already this morning, and received a piece of tobacco from me, for which he was very grateful. When he was young the Inuit went from here in the spring, before the ice went out, to Netilling [Nettilling] and hauled their boats on sledges to Koukdjua [Koukdjuax]. From there the women went north across the lake, while the men descended the Koukdjua in their kayaks, then north up the sea coast for 2 sleeps, and from there hunted caribou.

He gave me a selection of names from that area, but is unable to draw, because he has very poor eyes. He does not look very strong, but he has grey hair and according to accounts he must be 80 years old [born around 1800!]. He knew Amarok and Ssigiriak and called the land to which they went Irgnirn [location not ascertained], which is part of Aguni [Aggo, North Baffin] and where many Eskimos live. Esk. drew the map he made. (...)

Now I am sitting here very comfortably on caribou skins on the sleeping platform in the igloo. Wilhelm is sleeping to my right; the woman of the house is sitting to my left, drying my things; in front of me Kanaka (who came from Kikkerton), Ssigna and my host Ocheitu are sitting on the floor, eating frozen seal meat, while I am thinking of you and your love. But now I too must have some raw, frozen seal meat for my supper, and then we will have tea and eat bread. It is the custom here that the guest, the 'Kodlunak' (white man) [I. *qallunaq* = white man ('big eyebrows')] provides the bread and tea, while the host provides seal meat and looks after all his things. (...)

[**22 December, Saturday**]   Ssarbukduak (Kingawa). As I had intended, this morning I came here with Ocheitu, Ssigna and Wilhelm. –44.5°. It was very cold with a very strong north wind, which made our faces freeze, one after the other. All of us are suffering from frostbite more or less. Here at Nudnirn (name of an island in Ssarbukduak) I found it impossible to walk against the wind and to observe *and* write, so I have to abandon my work. ἐκὼν ἀὲκ ντί νὲ δυμὼ [Greek = 'Even as I yield freely to thee, yet unwilling.' Homer, *Iliad*, 4:44 (Smith 1944: 44); see also 7 January and 25 June 1884. Boas used this quotation from the *Iliad* three times in exactly the same form during his stay with the Inuit when he felt he needed to adjust to certain conditions against his will. This well-known Homerian phrase was a standard part of the school curriculum that students had to learn by heart.]

Wilhelm, who has frozen both his big toes, insisted at Anarnitung that he would be able to travel; but here he is so ill that I can undertake nothing with him and sent him straight into the igloo which Ssigna and Ocheitu built. I went off alone, but had to turn back after about 1 hour, without having achieved anything. I cannot alternate between compass and pencil.

When I came back around 2 o'clock the igloo was finished, and we soon had lunch. Later a sledge came past with a young seal which he [Ocheitu] had taken. He came in and I gave him soup and bread. Wilhelm was lying in his sleeping bag. I hope he will be a bit better tomorrow. It was here that Ssigna first told me that Ocheitu had taken Mutch's sledge. I hope there will be somewhat less wind tomorrow so that I can at least do something. Tomorrow the sledge will bring our dry courletangs, since the sealskins are too cold for outside. Whether I will be staying here any longer will depend on the state of Wilhelm's health. This evening Ocheitu told me that he had been to the Koukdjua [Koukdjuax] along the north side of Nettilling. What a difference between today and the night before last. Now we are in a comfortable igloo; then outside, half freezing and half starving.

Do you know what we had for supper. Butter, which was so hard that we had to chop it with our strongest knife as if splitting wood, and a piece of sugar. Ocheitu who went out yesterday to fetch our bearskin tells me that we had initially been near Anarnitung, but then had wandered to and fro, and then had headed up towards Kingawa. The most vexing thing is that we once crossed the sledge route without noticing it. I would now prefer to go back to Kikkerton the day after tomorrow with Ocheitu and our sledge. If only Wilhelm will not get sick; the last few days have been really trying. (...)

23rd December [**Sunday**]   Anarnitung. Now I am again sitting in Ocheitu's igloo celebrating a great feast with him. Today Ocheitu caught two seals and now every man in camp receives a piece. Isn't it a fine custom among these 'savages' that they endure privations together, but all happily share in the eating and drinking communally when some game has been killed?

I often ask myself what advantages our 'good society' possesses over the 'savages' and the more I see of their customs, I find that we really have no grounds to look down on them contemptuously. Where among us is there such hospitality as here? Where are there people who carry out *any* task requested of them so willingly and without grumbling! We should not censure them for their conventions and superstitions, since we 'highly educated' people are relatively much worse.

The fear of the old traditions and the old conventions is truly deeply implanted in humankind, and just as it controls life here, it obstructs all progress with us. I believe that in every person and every people[,] renouncing tradition in order to follow the trail of the truth involves a very severe struggle. But what am I struggling for?

The Eskimos are now sitting alert, their mouths full, eating raw seal liver, and the blood stains on the other page will tell you how I was assisting them. I believe that if this trip has a significant impact on me as a thinking person, then it is the strengthening of my notion of the relativity of all *education* and the conviction of how the value of people lies in the guidance close to their heart [*Herzensbildung*], which I find, or miss here, just as at home, and that thus all service which a person can render to humanity must depend on the furthering of *truth*, which may be sweet or bitter for humanity. Yes, whoever furthers it, whoever widely pursues the search for truth, may say that he has not lived in vain!

But now back to the cold Eskimo country. Yesterday evening it gradually became quite comfortable in the igloo[,] and I hoped I would sleep well, but I couldn't get warm in my sleeping bag, which is not yet quite dry.

This morning I travelled with the sledge up to Kingawa, accompanied by Ocheitu and Ssigna; thus I got as far as I went in the fall with the boat [close to the German Polar Station, 7–9 September]. I had hoped to complete the map as far as Nudnirn, since yesterday I made such a thick grip for my pencil that I was able to hold it despite the cold. But unfortunately it broke off, and I was unable to get a point on it again and thus had to return to the igloo without having achieved anything. It was -45° again with a strong north wind. Along the way I met Nuvukdjua (Mitik's brother), who had brought Wilhelm's and my courletang. I travelled back the last part of the route with him. Ocheitu and Ssigna arrived soon after me; they had 2 seals, as did Nuvukdjua and we had lunch.

Unfortunately Wilhelm's left foot is still very badly frozen, so I probably cannot take him to Kikkerton. We stuck him in his sleeping bag, lashed it on Nuvukdjua's sledge, and travelled home together. Tomorrow morning I shall travel with Ocheitu directly to Kikkerton, while Ssigna and Kanaka will have to travel via Pamiujang and Ssednirun. I agreed with Ocheitu that I shall come back with him, live with him and will then be driven around the area by him; in return he will receive shells for his rifle, which he obtained from the German station. I hope, then, that from here I will be able to get the addition to Kingawa as well as the next two fiords. Wilhelm will have to stay here, since it is too cold to transport him to Kikkerton. Thus, I hope to spend Christmas Eve at Kikkerten and New Year here. Also today I could not protect my nose and face from frostbite, because the wind is lashing so viciously, but I find that the Eskimos are in no better situation. Now the Eskimos are sitting around me here, telling each other old stories. What a pity that I cannot understand any of it; when I come back I shall start collecting here too. (...)

[Notebook]
On the **24th** [**December, Monday**] on the way to Kikkerten. Kanaka and Ssigna are going via Pamiujang in order to fetch my things. Ocheitu, Nuvukdjua and I will go via Imigen [Imiling] direct to Kikkerten.

[FB/MK]
.. at 2 o'clock I wakened the Eskimos at Anarnitu. Ocheitung called his kuni and by around 3.30 the coffee was ready.

[Notebook]
Set off at 4 a.m. The route to Tichannirtu [Tikeraxdjung] is good and from there all the ice as far as Kikkerten is fine and smooth. In the meantime it is very foggy[,] and we had some trouble finding Kikkerten. In the evening magnificent northern lights over the islands, which then stood out very clearly. No Christmas tree. I arrived at 2 a.m.

[FB/MK; written on 26 December]
(...) Near the Seven Islands [the group that includes Pujetung] we landed in rough ice, but it did not extend very far. Presumably this is the limit of the pack ice, which Padloaping reported, and the pack ice has only just been driven south with the north wind, so smooth ice has formed on the

open water. Unfortunately it soon became foggy again, so we could not identify any land at all, and we could not find the tracks of Keiju, who had come from Anarnitung the day before, so had to search for a long time again. Around 12 midnight, however, we ran across the sledge route from Kikkerton, and then we proceeded across the rough ice. At 2.30 [a.m.] we reached the island safely. (...)

[Notebook]
[**25 December, Tuesday**]   [K'exerten] I saw Ocheitu to his mother's igloo [Macky's wife], took my bag on my back and went home. Naturally Mr. Mutch was wakened by the noise and immediately got up to cook something. I certainly could use something to eat; I had eaten nothing in 22 hours and had lived rough for 14 days. Hence cocoa and a caribou leg tasted superb. I went to bed around 4 and slept until 10.

I immediately set about unpacking; I took out our Christmas gifts from home and a little Christmas tree, assembled various good cans for lunch and invited Capt. Roach's cooper, Rasmussen, who was looking after the American station (he is a Dane). Thus, at 5 o'clock, by a Christmas tree with lights, we had a pleasant Christmas dinner; we spent the evening over punch and wine as if we were at home. Unfortunately Betty, Ssigna's wife, came into the house drunk, and greatly disturbed us. Around 10 Ssigna and Kanaka arrived with their sledge. They had spent the first night at Ssednirun and have come on here today.

On the second day of Christmas **26th Dec** [**Wednesday**] I took cases into the house and took out everything necessary for a stay at Anarnitung. On this occasion it turned out that the cases of bread contain only 123 lbs. instead of 144! I also gave Mutch back the bread that he gives Ssigna every Friday. By about 11 p.m. I had everything ready. I told Ocheitu and Nuvukd-jua to be ready at 4 a.m. then drank another bottle of wine with Mutch.

Second Trip to Anarnitung and K'ingua

On **Thursday** [**27 December**], however we were not ready to set off before 8 o'clock, since we had overslept. We easily found the route from Kikkerton and made rapid progress. Thus we were at Tichannirtu by about 8. Here Nuvukdjua lost the way and I preferred to stay overnight. Tyson and Johny Penny that same day had stopped here en route to Imigen and there were only 2 igloos left here. Last night 11 of us slept in one igloo, as tight-packed as herrings in a barrel. Here I heard that Tyson and [blank;

the person's name not inserted by Boas] will go to Padli next spring in order to see a ship if possible. They want to return here in winter.

This morning [**28 December, Friday**] we set off again and arrived here safely at Anarnitung around 3.30. Wilhelm's toe does not look as bad as I had feared. The nail and part of the ball have dropped off. Tomorrow morning I shall go north with Ocheitu and start surveying the coast. I have bought some old Eskimo articles.

Saturday 29th December   In the morning I travelled north with Ocheitu and another Eskimo, who always goes seal hunting at Ssarbukduak in the spring. At a small island I got off and hiked back to Anarnitung, while surveying the coast at the same time. I got back around 2.30, tired and hot despite the cold weather. All my things are being dried immediately, so tomorrow I will feel just as warm as today. Since I was very tired I slept a little[,] copied out my observations and had lunch. Ocheitu did not bring back a seal.

If it is clear enough I will take the latitude of Anarnitung tomorrow and take some photographs, and also survey the position of the kaumang [I. *qarmait* = houses made of stone, whalebone and sods] (old huts). If Ocheitu catches something I shall go up the fiord to Kingawa on Monday [31 December] and Tuesday, despite the fact that it is New Year's.

Sunday morning [**30 December**]   It is now just 7 o'clock, but just as dark as at midnight. The stars have deceived me so I shall write something in the evening instead of now. Tomorrow I shall go north with Ocheitu's sledge to survey Ssarbukduak. Nobody has caught anything today because the seals which the Eskimos shot were carried under the ice by the powerful current. Today the current was breaking ice up to 1 foot thick. In the evening Appak was here and told me some stories about the man in the moon [Boas 1888:598–9]. This morning I finished Audnerbing [Bon Accord Harbour]; my intention to take photos has been foiled by the dark weather.

[FB/MK]
(...) You must not think that a snow house like this is a cold dwelling. It is completely lined with skins; 2 large lamps burn inside, spreading light and warmth. We all sit on the large platform which is covered with caribou skins. But I think I still prefer a European home! Just 2 more days and we'll be in the year that will finally bring me back to you. Here the time is passing almost too quickly for the amount of work. If I calculate everything, I barely have enough time left to complete either the map or

the ethnographic work. But I am attaining my own goals quite well. I now have a very accurate knowledge of the migrations of the Eskimo and their routes, how they travel, coming and going, as well as their relations with neighbouring groups.

Yesterday evening I again had a long conversation with an old woman who has come here from far to the north and whose knowledge extends as far as North Greenland! Gradually I can make myself understood somewhat with the Eskimos. Their language is horribly difficult! (...)

Ocheitu has still not got a seal. Nobody got anything today, because the seal they did shoot was carried under the ice by the powerful current. It was breaking up thick ice this morning. In the evening Appak was here and told me some stories about the man in the moon etc. It is very difficult for me today to grasp the sense of the story. (...)

[Notebook]

31st December [**Monday**]   I am going to Kingawa with Ocheitu. While he was hunting seals at the Kangidliuta polynya, I went back along the west coast to Ssarbukduak. There I crossed the fiord and went back to Innukschuling [Inugsuling] via Nudnirn; about 1 mile beyond we caught up with the sledge and we got home around 4 o'clock tired and hungry. Here lunch was waiting for us. I gave Ocheitu a bottle of cognac while Wilhelm and I drank a bottle of Swedish punch and chatted until midnight. In keeping with old custom I greeted the New Year with three shots and woke up on 1st January to begin the new year with the old work.

In 1884 Boas kept the two diaries (D and D2) in parallel, along with the Notebook and the letter-journal (FB/MK); the text passages marked [D] and [D2] are derived from these diaries. Each entry in the diaries was prefixed by the date, without the year or the day of the week, and there was space for two days' entries per page. Boas kept the diaries generally as originals; until 2 February 1884, he transcribed all the entries from D and D2, with supplemental information, to the Notebook. By preference, the Notebook's text is reproduced here because of its greater completeness. In both diaries, Boas usually noted where he spent the night; here this is stated at the beginning of the day's entry from the Notebook if it is not indicated elsewhere. The date prefixed in the diaries is always presented in square brackets.

[Notebook]

[**1 January**] **Tuesday**   Kangirtuktuak [Kangertlukdjuax]. As it began to get light[,] Ocheitu and I headed up the fiord. [D: .. sledge team of 7 dogs.] I surveyed the south shore. In very clear, cold weather, by about 4 o'clock we had reached the end, where we built an igloo. Nearby were 2 very old graves. [D: Here there were some old Tudnirn graves. Very cold and windy today.] One can barely find a spot here where there are not traces of former residents, which the Eskimos generally ascribe to the Tudnik, a mythical people who are supposed to have once inhabited this land. The fiord is very narrow in places, whereas the head of it is again a wide basin, surrounded by vertically dropping cliffs; towering darkly out of the snow they produce a magnificent scene. The hills are not high; only near the head of the fiord do they rise to 100–125 m. A river, which flows from a large pond, debouches at the head of the fiord. Right now the river does not carry any water, whereas the deep ponds do not freeze to the bottom. In the evening I promised Ocheitu I would give him some more shells if he tells me old stories. Since then he has been uncommonly eager to tell stories. Last night our igloo, which had turned out to be very large, was extremely cold, so we could barely sleep. Ocheitu was uncommonly amused by the fact that in our first igloo at Ssednirun Wilhelm had frozen his nose in his sleeping bag.

[**2 January**] **Wednesday**   Anarnitung. On the morning of the 2nd we travelled along the east shore back to Ssarbukduak. [D: On the north side of the fiord to the summit of Ssarbukduak.] When we reached the usual route here, near Idnitelling [Ingnitelling], the dogs could barely be restrained any longer and raced at a furious gallop as far as Anarnitung. Along the way Ocheitu lost his whip. But I could stop the dogs only by letting myself be dragged along behind the sledge thus making it too heavy to pull. By 3 [D:2.30] we were already back at Anarnitung. I rested a little, then took some astronomical observations, although at −40° this involved some difficulties. The mercury had to be warmed first and my fingers froze regularly during the observations. Fortunately Wilhelm could at least note the time from inside the igloo.

[**3 January,**] **Thursday**   Anarnitung. [D: Rest day] On the morning of the 3rd I took another star altitude to check the time, then, in daylight, a bearing on Kikkertaktuak. I do not know how often I froze my fingers while doing this and taking 3 photos. In the afternoon I learned that Joe, my poor patient for long weeks[,] has finally died of his afflictions. Hannibal Jack, who brought the news, was here in the afternoon and brought me some bone articles. In the evening Ocheitu told me some 'unicartúa' [I. *unikkaatuaq* = stories], i.e. old legends about the origin of the narwhal etc. [FB/MK: .. of the white whale etc.] [Boas 1888:625–7].

Tomorrow I want to get on the way southward again to survey a large fiord which Ocheitu drew for me in the afternoon. I like to have the route that I intend to follow drawn for me ahead of time so that I am somewhat better oriented with regard to the country. From him fortunately I also learned how far Dr. Giese's surveys extended[,] so I do not need to do any unnecessary work [see BSH:DPK, station journal; survey trip to Issortuxdjuax, 18–28 May 1883].

[D]
Apart from this I wrote a little, worked up my observations and collected old stories.

[4 January] Friday Audnerbielling (Kagiluktung) [Audnerbiellung (Kaggilortung)]. In the morning set off for Kagilluktung. Overcast, fairly warm, but a strong north wind. We reached a little farther than halfway between Anarnitung and the fiord head. The fiord is so full of islands that I am unable to produce a map of it and have to satisfy myself with the mainland. Built an igloo on a headland towards Audnerbielling.

[Notebook]
On the 4th I travelled up Kaggiluktung with Ocheitu. But in the meantime it became windy and snowy, so I could do nothing and thus on the 5th I returned to Anarnitung.

[D]
[5 January] Saturday Anarnitung. In the morning it was blowing strongly; the top of the igloo is almost entirely melted. When it got light it was revealed that the snow is drifting so heavily that we can see nothing. So I opt for returning to Anarnitung rather than a [D2: .. useless] stay of indefinite length in the igloo. We arrived here at noon.

[Notebook]
An unpleasant surprise awaited us there. Ocheitu's wife, who had previously had throat pain, was seriously ill so I had no option but to head back with a sledge that was travelling straight to Kikkerton next day [6 January]; I could then bring Wilhelm back to the station during the warm weather (−17°) at the same time.

[D]
O.[cheitu's] kuni very sick. Since Padlukulu has not yet left for Kikker-

ton, tomorrow I will set off with him and Wilhelm. I can then at the same time get Wilhelm back to Kikkerton and can work there, whereas there is nothing to do here as long as the woman [D2: Ocheitu's] is sick. Packed in the evening.

[6 January] Sunday   Imigen. Set of at 8 a.m. with Padlukulu from Anarnitung. It is overcast and foggy, but warm, with a slight southerly wind; hence a very fair day [D2: .. a good day for Wilhelm's feet]. Until we reached the old route to the South[,] the dogs were pulling heavily through the snow; the trail is also totally snowed in. By about 4 we were at Imigen, to where all the families from Tichannirtu have now moved. The route up there is very bad. I went into Tyson's igloo; he wants to come to Kikkerton tomorrow too. He had had to turn back the day before yesterday owing to bad weather. [D2: .. owing to the Kignait gale].

[Notebook]
Thus on the 6th, Sunday, we reached Imigen, a camp between Anarnitung and Kikkerten, where we stayed in Tyson's igloo; then on the afternoon of the 7th back to Kikkerten.

[D]
[7 January] Monday   Kikkerton. At 12 midnight Tyson gets up to leave. But I played tough and slept till 2. But the people made such a racket [D2: .. such a hellish racket] that I got up in desperation and at 3.30 set off against my will.

[D2]
ἐκὼν ἀὲκ ντί νὲ δυμῶ [Greek = 'Even as I yield freely to thee, yet unwilling.' Homer, *Iliad*, 4:44 (Smith 1944: 44); see also 22 December 1883 and 25 June 1884.]

Naturally we lost the route in the dark and reached Kikkerton at 4.30 p.m. after large detours. 4 sledges: Tyson, Nuvukdjua, Johnny Penny and ours. Tyson did not find his [seal]skins, which he [had lost] the day before yesterday owing to the Kignait gale, when he was unable to reach Kikkerton. Nuvukdjua brought his with him. Hungry and ate heartily. In the evening also drank some wine. Tired, in bed by 9.

[Notebook]
I was very happy to have Wilhelm back home again, although I myself had lost much time. We had agreed that Ocheitu was to fetch me again when

his wife was better. But the first thing was that I fell ill at Kikkerten, presumably because I could no longer stand the good life. But by Friday [11 January] I was in good health again and then began working up my observations – something that was very necessary. I am still not finished with this task, but it is somewhat clearer.

The entries in the Notebook and in the letter-journal to Marie stop here, beginning again on January 18. From January 7, Weike stayed at the whaling station, doing daily chores around the house until April 11, when Boas again took him on a sledge trip up Kingnait Fiord. During these three months Boas was alone with the Inuit, driving with dog teams from camp to camp in the Sound.

K'exerten

[D]

[**8 January**] **Tuesday**   Fairly exhausted. I have been putting my things in order; they all have to be improved and I have been lazy. The hut in which our supplies are stored has been completely filled with snow during a storm and it took a long time to clean it out again. Finally I was able to get inside and can now get stuff out. We are terribly stressed again. I think the period of rest here will do me a lot of good.

[**9 January**] **Wednesday**   Sick for the first time in the entire period! In the morning I fainted and all day I have been in no condition to do anything. Better in the evening. In the meantime, in my conversations with Tyson I have not achieved much.

[**10 January**] **Thursday**   Writing and working all day. Finished off the map etc.

[**11 January**] **Friday**   The same very bad weather. One of the children is again very ill with an inflammation of the throat. I am working up the stories I have collected and have got to No. 33 successfully [ball game by Mikidju and Aranin in Rink 1885, FB/Henrik Rink, 28 April 1885, Minden/Copenhagen; Boas 1888:609–41]. Tomorrow I will record the Ssaumia [Saumia] men, which I was unable to get today because they were 'ankuting.' Read Marie's letters, what a delight after such a long time!

There are no entries in the Diary between 12 January and 6 February 1884.

[D2]

[12 January] Saturday   I am now getting up so early that we have coffee around 8; Mutch does not seem very pleased at this. However, I have a lot of work to do and do not want to sleep away the whole day. A large slipper has been made for W.[ilhelm's] foot so that he can walk better! Today I was packing away things that have been lying around. In the evening the cooper was here. Went to bed at 11.

[13 January] Sunday   Got up late this morning. Wilhelm has a lot of pain in his feet, which I am now burning with jade stone. Otherwise did nothing, as usual on Sunday. Another child died.

[14 January] Monday   Mutch is making a coffin for the child; I am unpacking supplies and in the evening invited Shellback to my room to tell me about Ssaumia. I am now taking a sight on Jupiter or Mars every evening in order to check the time of my chronometers.

[15 January] Tuesday   Shellback and Tam [Tom] are travelling back to Ssaumia. My thermometers [at the station] were unfortunately smashed during the last Kignait storm [4 and 5 January], when I was at Kaggiluk-tung.

[16 January] Wednesday   Mutch set off to test his dogs, and is again preparing for a major trip. I was working in the house. Killak is sketching Padli for me.

[WW]
(...) Today we again got up to a temperature of −38° with a fairly steady west wind. J.M. [James Mutch] set out to test how his dogs ran in harness. He is equipped just as an Eskimo is when going on a long trip, with rifle, lance [harpoon] and a large knife on his sledge. On our winter trips we were running around without any means of protection. In the evening it was −41°. (...)

[D2]
[17 January] Thursday   I took a set of observations from the lookout. Mutch leaves for Tinninikdjua [Tininixdjuax] tomorrow. I asked him to take me with him so that I can complete my arrangements with Piera. In the evening another sledge arrived from Anarnitung to report that Ocheitu's wife is now very sick. At the same time they told us that Teson

[Tyson] had said that he did not want me in his tupik and that many Eskimos were blaming me for the sicknesses; hence J.M. has opted to stay here.

[18 January] **Friday**   Since Nuvukdjua is starting back very early and I am not yet ready, I cannot travel with him. However[,] Mutch will lend me his dogs tomorrow so that I can get to Tinninikdjua. Thus I had everything made ready and hired Ssigna for the trip.

[19 January] **Saturday**   Unfortunately I overslept and did not wake until 7 o'clock. So I have opted not to set off, but am going to Manitung in order to finish off the rest of the Kikketens [the islands in the K'exerten archipelago]. I finished this faster than I expected and was back by 2 o'clock.

[20 January] **Sunday**   Slept till 9.30, and then had coffee late. Did nothing all day except laze about and do some writing. Tomorrow, we will at last be on our way!

[Notebook; summary of events between 17 and 21 January]
On 18th January I wanted to travel with Jimmy Mutch to Tinirnikdjua, where I have things to do in connection with the trip to Kennedy Lake. On Thursday [17 January] somebody came from Anarnitung with the news that Ocheitu's wife was sicker, rather than better. At the same time he reported that many Eskimos are attributing the blame for the many cases of sickness to me. Some are said to have stated that they do not want to see me in their igloos.

[FB/MK]
(...) If I were superstitious, I might really believe that my presence has brought the Eskimos bad luck! In short, some are said to have stated they did not want to see me in their igloos and Mutch does not do anything. (...)

[Notebook]
Probably because of this the latter has become alarmed and so today, the 21st [January] Monday, I set off alone [without Mutch]. I have been welcomed here at Nichemiarbing [Nexemiarbing] (an island near Tinninikdjua) just as amicably as ever, and feel really at home here at Piera's [FB/MK: .. at Tinninikdjua].

Third Trip to Anarnitung and K'ingua

[D2]

[**21 January**] **Monday**   Kikkerten – Nichemiarbing. I set off early, at 6
a.m. with Mutch's dogs and Ssigna for Nichemiarbing. Wilhelm must still
stay at home, since his foot is still not better. The right one is sound again,
but there is still a substantial hole in the left one.

[Notebook]
It is really good that this has not happened to me; what would I have done
if I had lost all this valuable time.

[D2]
Ssigna and I arrived here in good weather in the evening at 4 o'clock.
About two hours from here we met the natives who were hunting seals
here. They showed us the route through the rough ice and we made fast
progress towards our desired goal.

[FB/MK; written on 22 January]
(...) You can't imagine how one watches out for the ice foot to appear on
the horizon, the best sign that one is close to land, and how gladly one
welcomes the comfortable igloo! One simply cannot express how comfortable and fine it seems as one crawls into this dirty, confined space, at
the appearance of which I turned away full of horror the first time! To my
great distress I heard here that Piera, for whose sake I am here, is at Naujateling, but is expected back this evening. In fact he arrived around 10. I
will have to postpone my consultation until tomorrow. I had already
decided to push on again tomorrow when we heard a sledge arriving,
bringing Piera. It was too late to discuss anything with him so I postponed
it until this morning [22 January]. However I bought various things from
Netteling. (...)

[Notebook]
[**22 January**] **Tuesday**   Nichemiarbing. This morning I have made my
arrangements with Piera. He will accompany me to Netilling next month
with 9 dogs. I now have to see if I can get another 15 dogs, and then
everything will be in order. I hope to set off around the 3rd February. I
now want to head for Anarnitung tomorrow, where I hope to obtain dogs,
do some more work there, then return here to buy seals. Then I have to
go to Imigen to see about dogs and seals and back to Kikkerten to pre-

pare for my trip. How far I progress with all this depends entirely on the weather and the seals.

[D2]
Kikker is going back with Mutch's dogs. I have assembled only 13.

[FB/MK]
(...) Well, Marie, I've finally got so far that I am about to complete what I came here for. I know now that it is only a very small part of what I originally intended but I have to be resigned to this. I have carried out my own plans well and can be satisfied with the results; also the cartographic work offers enough that is new. When I look at the sum total I am quite pleased with the results of the trip and at least I have the realization that I have done what I could. Just one more month and half my time is past, and it is the longer half; from now until I return there is not a moment of inactivity: in February a trip to the northwest; in March and April to the southwest. In May I leave the Sound and go north. Now, for some time, I have my own dog team which I have assembled here; I will go with it to Anarnitung tomorrow morning. (...)

Now I still have a few star altitudes to take, and to interview a woman, and then I am finished here and can get on my way! But let me quickly send you one more heartfelt greeting. Things are really totally upside-down here, compared to what we expected; when I am at Kikkerton I am in such great demand that I can't get on with anything; when I am travelling I have enough time in the igloo to tackle something. And then I shall use this time to chat with my beloved. (...)

Will fortune favour me, so that very soon I may anticipate the fulfilment of our most longed-for wishes? It is *not* my wish to attain a German professorship, because I know that I am not dependent on my science and the teaching profession, to which I have little inclination. I would much rather live in America so that I can also work for the ideas in which I believe. But how? That I don't know. Well I can do nothing about it now and must wait patiently to see how things turn out when I come back. And what I want, what I will live and die for, is equal rights for all, equal opportunities to [work] and strive for poor and rich! Don't you think that when one has done even a little towards this, this is more than the whole of science together? And that will certainly never be granted me in Germany. (...)

But too often the rude reality, the shouting of the Eskimos, the howling of the dogs, the crying of the children, even just the cramped igloo wakens me from the dream [about Marie]! I often find myself wondering, when I am with this company in the evening, in what company you find yourself? (...)

[D2]

[**23 January**] **Wednesday** Imigen. Naturally after the argument with Tyson I refused to back down, but let him know I am komachiadlu [I. *komakiádlu* = disgruntled; angry (FB)] and want to have nothing to do with him ever again.

[Notebook]
However, this morning I set off with 13 dogs. But they are all such pitiful animals that they scarcely make any progress.

[D2]
The dogs are pulling so miserably through the soft snow that we did not arrive here until nightfall.

[Notebook]
Thus I have stopped here at Imigen, because I have to come here again. I also want to order some seals here and see whether I can get any better dogs. The men are not yet back from seal hunting. I wonder what impression the message made here, which I sent to Tyson, the Eskimo who did not want to have me in his igloo. In summer he will be travelling the same route as myself [via Kingnait to Padli] and I had the messenger tell him that he would never get anything from me until he had first invited me to come into his house.

[FB/MK]
(...) .. never receive anything from me, even if I saw him starving before my eyes, unless he first came to me to ask me to come into his igloo.

[Notebook]
I hope none of my dogs runs away tonight. To my great regret I heard here that Ocheitu's wife has died. Padlukulu and Hannibal Jack brought this news. Throat ailments wreak terrible havoc here. A few days ago at Kikkerton a child [boy] died, whose mother died here in the fall. The day before he died a message was sent to the station with the request that a coffin should be made for him, since he wanted to lie beside his mother and asked for some tobacco which he wanted to take to his mother.

[FB/MK]
(...) I shall probably come up [to Anarnitung] tomorrow, but I still don't know where I shall stay. I just want to provide Ocheitu with provisions, because he may not go out for 3 days now [because of his wife's death]. I hoped I might now persuade Ocheitu to help me get to Netilling. (...)

Isn't that really touching? I have noticed quite often here how calmly the Eskimos look death in the face, although they are unbelievably afraid of the dead and even death, as long as they are healthy, and I have also seen such protestations of inner love between parents and children. I shall never forget coming into a small snow house in which a mother was sitting with her sick child which barely gave any sign of life, but still was voicing the most tender endearments to her child! And I'll always remember how Joe, who also is dead now, told me that thinking of his son, who had died the previous spring, made him so miserable.

These are 'savages' whose lives are supposed to be worth nothing compared with a civilized European. I do not believe that we, if living under the same conditions, would be so willing to work or be so cheerful and happy! I have to say that as regards character[,] I am totally contented with the Eskimos. (...)

I have obtained a couple of really good observations here and again know that I have to shift one point in the Sound. Ssigna has just come back to tell me that another Eskimo from Anarnitung is here and will be going back tomorrow, so we will certainly get there safely. (...)

[D2]
[24 January] Thursday   Anarnitung. With my poor dogs we travelled for 12 hours towards Anarnitung, arriving only after it got totally dark. Unfortunately it has become foggy again so I have been unable to survey the coast. The passage between Anarnitung and Idlungajung is now so filled with grounded ice that we could not get through. We hunted for Anarnitung for 45 minutes in the fog, when it lay only about 30 paces from us.

[D2]
[25 January] Friday   Anarnitung. None of my celebrated observations, since it is very windy and cold.

[Notebook]
It took us 12 hours to reach Anarnitung on the 24th. [FB/MK: .. travelled from Imigen to here (a distance of 24 miles maximum).] Today the dogs had to be fed and had to rest after their 2 days of work. Tomorrow morn-

ing [26 January] I want to set off for 2 days and to connect here with American Hrb. with new surveys. During the day and now it is clear, but it is very cold and windy.

Yesterday Nuvukdjua also travelled to Anarnitung, but somewhat later than us. At first we could not find the route into the island and had to climb over the grounded ice. I spent the night in Charlie's (Kakotscha) igloo. Charlie (Ocheitu's father-in-law), his son and Ocheitu were still in mourning in Ocheitu's igloo. I immediately sent word to ask what they needed and took them bread and coffee. [D2: .., since they had had nothing to eat for 2 days.] Due to this circumstance my supply of bread has become very meagre.

This morning O.[cheitu] has built a new igloo [D2: .. and I shall probably move in with him], while the old one has fallen prey to the dogs. He almost seems his usual self, though he is terribly sad at the death of his wife. He volunteered to go up Kagilluktung with me [D2: .., there I want first to go north with Ssigna in order to connect Kingawa with Ussuadlu] [Ussualung].

Today I have been examining my things which are still here, and yesterday I took a few observations. Today's, however, did not turn out particularly well, since the wind was disturbing me too much. Finally I have found a second person who at least knows the names from here to Iglulik. He is Mitirn [Mitik], the oldest man in the country, who knows it from travelling with Ssigjiviak.

[FB/MK]
(...) Mitik, whose knowledge derives from a woman who travelled there long, long ago. Gradually I have interviewed everyone, so I am now better informed about everything, like the older people, since I am also familiar with the map of the country. (...)

My census of the Sound is now making rapid progress; as far as I know I still need to check 2 camps, Nuvujadlu [Nuvujalung] and Naujateling, then I am finished [cf. Boas 1885:70, 1888:426].

[Notebook]
[26 January] Saturday   Anarnitu. At 6.30 on 26th January I went with Ssigna [D2: .. up to Ssarbukduak, to the entrance to Kingawa] in order to travel south along the east shore [D2: .. for 2 days]. Once we had got over the rough ice, the sun showed itself but so weakly and low that it was almost impossible to make progress and after we had pushed south about 4 miles [D2: .. in 3 hours] I had to turn back [FB/MK: .. with a sore heart],

because in fact it was not worth the trouble to continue labouring in this manner. The weather was quite thick and I could not take any bearings. Perhaps a better opportunity will offer itself later. Thus I came back to Anarnitung around 5 o'clock. [FB/MK: In the meantime Ocheitu had built himself a new igloo and ..] I now walked over to Ocheitu's.

[**27 January**] **Sunday**   Anarnitung. On the 27th the dogs were fed; in the meantime I went south with Ujo to survey some islands. But we had scarcely left when it got so thick that I had to turn back near Anarnituk-djuak [FB/MK: Look Out Isl.] [Anarnituxdjuak]. I had sketched in only three islands.

[FB/MK]
I inquired of the various men whether they would lend me dogs to go to Netilling.

[Notebook]
I have obtained about 5 dogs for Netilling and still need 10 more.

[**28 January**] **Monday**   Anarnitung. On the 28th I stayed at Anarnitung because of the bad weather. I asked Mitik and his wife for some things and obtained some information.

[FB/MK]
(...) Old Ssigjiviak has indeed been to Iglulik and even told me about the country beyond it. (...)

[D2]
The bad weather always thwarts my plans.

[Notebook]
[**29 January**] **Tuesday**   Ikeressakdjuak [Ikerassaxdjuax]. On the 29th, with Ocheitu and Ssigna I travelled with 2 sledges up Kaggiluktung, in order to return to Kikkerten from there. [D2: But we are barely back at Audnerbielling [Audnerbing] again.] We had barely got as far as I had been the previous time, when thick fog obscured any distant objects and it began snowing heavily. [D2: Since I do not want to sacrifice long days here, but want to get to Nettiling, I turned back, to go back to Kikker-ton.] Thus I again had to turn back with nothing achieved. I headed south with Ocheitu but was unable to reach Imigen. So we spent the

night on the ice near Ikerassatang. Built a small windbreak from snow blocks. Made coffee and despite a temperature of –20° in the evening and –34° in the morning, we slept superbly.

[**30 January**] **Wednesday**   Kikkerten. Set off at 6.30 a.m. One of the dogs in my team is sick; I had to lash it to the sledge and left it at Imigen. There we met Hannibal Jack, who was in the process of moving to Nichemiarbing. We followed Tyson's track, since he had gone to Kikkerten with Ikera; got on the trail at dusk and by 7 were safely at Kikkerten. I arrived quite unexpectedly, since Tyson had just reported that I was at Anarnitung. Capt. Roach has been here for about a week; he came up with the cooper in the evening and stayed till around 10. I did not get to bed until 12 although I was very tired.

[**31 January**] **Thursday**   [K'exerten] Kikkerten. Yesterday, the 31st, the first task was to fetch something to eat [D2: .. from the store house]; I spent the rest of the day calculating, transcribing etc and preparing things for Ssigna, who is to go back to Nichemiarbing tomorrow to bring on the dogs and to see if they have caught any seals for me. The presence of Capt. Roach does not leave me much chance of getting on with my work because he is up here a lot.

[**1 February**] **Friday**   Kikkerten. On 1st Febr. Ssigna left for Nichemiarbing. I gave him abundant supplies for 3 days.

[D2]
Capt. Roach is up here a lot throughout the day. Another of the dogs that I got from Nichemiarbing is sick and dying.

[**2 February**] **Saturday**   Kikkerten. I am afraid that I am having great difficulty in getting the {dogs} seals together. I now have enough dogs at a pinch. Moreover a large number of dogs is being kept at Tinninikdjua.

[Notebook]
Early on the 2nd C. Roach left for Naujateling [D2: Umenektuak] [Umanaxtuax] after he had asked me once again to visit him there. In the evening three sledges arrived from Nichemiarbing; Ssigna arrived with one sledge from Kikkertuktuak. Nobody had taken a single seal for me, and moreover the seal hunt this last while has been very poor, so they have probably been saving them. Thus it will probably still take a long time ..

[FB/MK]

.. before I have enough seals, and this raises the question of whether I wouldn't be better to go to Padli with Bob and Shangin, who want to go there in order to buy dogs for me. In the evening Shangin came up and ended a story he had begun to tell me. I sent for Bob, to ask him whether he wants to go tomorrow; when he didn't come I went to his tupik. He had been at Nuktukarlin's and had called Shangin. Since they had been told this evening that a boy who had had diphtheria was dead, they have to stay here for another 2 nights and would like to go on Tuesday [5 February]; so I have plenty of time to see what is to be done. (...)

The text transcribed to the Notebook breaks off abruptly here in mid-sentence on 2 February; the following pages, with the exception of the last four, which contain a list of fifty-seven Inuit place names (beginning with letter A) are blank. Boas continued the original and transcribed entries in his letters to Marie (FB/MK) and in the two diaries.

First Attempt at Crossing the Kingnait-Padli Pass

[D2]

[**3 February**] **Sunday**   Kikkertaktuak. Since I am having difficulties with dogs, it is probably better to travel to Padli with Bob and Shanguja [Shangin], who are leaving for there tomorrow to buy dogs; the trip should last 5 nights. I spoke to Bob about it; he told me they could not leave tomorrow, because a boy was dying of diphtheria. But he was still alive on Sunday morning, so they wanted to leave quickly before he died. I therefore packed my things at breakneck speed and we set off at noon [without Wilhelm Weike, who recorded that the boy died after they left].

But we made slow progress. We had to spend the night at Kikkertukdjuak, where I had slept in the fall. Travelling with the first sledge are Padlualu and wife [FB/MK: .. named Marie] and child [FB/MK: .. Nilli, in the mother's hood] [apparently, Boas gave the Inuk woman the name Marie]; with the second sledge Bob, Shanguja and I; and with the third Mitu. Since we are travelling so slowly, Mitu is to turn back.

[FB/MK]

(...) Here Mitu and Padlualu built an igloo on land, we built ours on the ice. Mitu wants to go back tomorrow. (...) Bob would like to as well, but I want to go on. (...)

[D2]

[4 February] Monday   Akkinikjua [Axtinixdjuax]. Despite all my efforts, we did not get away before 11 o'clock. The ice here is full of little stones and we made very slow progress. When darkness fell we were below the first bend in Kignait. The weather is very bad; the Eskimos have no more dog food; Bob does not want to go any farther and I cannot foresee how we can keep going. So tomorrow Bob and I shall turn back because as things are the bread bag cannot last as far as Padli. In the evening we found barely enough snow for an igloo.

[FB/MK]

(...) The ice here in Kignait is completely free of snow; there is scarcely a trace of it on the land. Thus our progress is greatly hampered and by evening we found ourselves barely 4–6 miles above Torgnait [Tornait] at the bend in the fiord. (...)

We searched for snow here, but hardly found enough because what little there is is blown too hard, so one cannot penetrate it with a saw. Finally around 3.30 the igloo was finished and we spent a cold night here. Since the prospect of travelling to Padli is so poor, I prefer to turn back and, if Ocheitu is at Kikkerton, to head out again. I shall then easily catch up on these remains. So I again have to turn back here at Akdinikdjua! [as Boas did on 23 September 1883] On the other hand it would take me 14 days to travel to a camp in Padli. (...)

[D2]

[5 February] Tuesday   Kikkerten. Since Sh.[angin] and Padlualu wanted to carry on, I commissioned them to [FB/MK: .., let the Padli Inuit, especially Kenningna and Shangin [Padli-Shangin] know that I want to buy 18 dogs at the time of the hunt for young seals, which somebody might bring here. Sh. said that if I go to Padli, he wanted to go with me in order to travel with me up to Tudnunirn [Tunirn].

[FB/MK]

(...) It would not be unpleasant to have him as a companion. Thus Bob and I set off around 11 o'clock, especially since Shangin and Padlualu wanted to hunt seals. (...)

In Kignait it was blowing full-force down the fiord and thus, although I had only 6 dogs, we made rapid progress; but then a stiff east wind with heavy snow drifting began blowing. At 8 we reached Kikkerton safely. Unfortunately Ocheitu is no longer here, so I shall have to stay here still. (...)

[D2]

Favoured by the wind we arrived back at Kikkerton late in the evening. Mutch had lent me a dog, but it had escaped on the first evening.

[6 February] **Wednesday**   [K'exerten] Gale and blizzard all day long; I am glad to be back again.

[FB/MK]

(...) After the storm had persisted all night, it is now beginning to improve. I have given my things to Betty, to put them in order somewhat, especially my comings and caribou stockings. In the evening the cooper came over and we played cards. In the morning I want to go and look for seals. I hope that Ocheitu will soon come to Kikkerton to take things to Nichemiarbing, since thereby we will have a better chance of getting seals. Jimmy Mutch wants to give me an entire walrus. (...)

[D]

[7 February] **Thursday**   In the evening some sledges arrived from Tinninikdjua; Kikker was among them. The weather is now abominable. A gale out of the east with snow and bitterly cold. I wish Ocheitu were here so that I could get on with things.

[8 February,] **Friday**   Ocheitu has finally come. The wind is southerly and with it 2 sledges came from Idjikuakdjin [Itixdjuangin], and finally, in the evening, Ocheitu. He had been at Imigen the previous night and arrived here today. Apart from him, Appak also arrived; he had not been in Kikkerten for years. Keitju and Kakotscha's son, who wants to marry Jenimi's daughter and will now be living here at Kikkerten in Jenimi's igloo.

[9 February] **Saturday**   Wilhelm surprised me this morning with the news that Ocheitu already wants to leave, since the weather has become fine. I therefore passed the message to him as quickly as possible that he should stay here and all the others should stay with him. I want to send him down to Salmon Fiord for Mutch, because Mutch would like to get some meat here and spoke about this recently. He will then give me two bags [of walrus meat]. [D2: .., if Ocheitu can bring them. He should then set off tomorrow.] At noon I asked Mutch about it, but all of a sudden he does not want to send his dogs off for this purpose. He wants Ocheitu to fetch some [meat] and send it himself next week. Since Ocheitu does not know where the meat is located, Kikker wants to go to show him the spot.

[**10 February**] **Sunday**   Although yesterday O.[cheitu] insisted that he had enough dogs, this morning he was short of 4, because Charlie's son did not want to lend him his. I therefore went to Pakkak and obtained the missing number from him. Finally they [D2: .. Kikker and Ocheitu] set off after sunrise. At noon a sledge arrived from Nuvujen; with it came Kakotscha's (Mutch's) daughter Annalukulu [FB/MK: .. Naniculu], who had been visiting there for a few weeks. Ocheitu and Kikker came back around 9 o'clock. They could dig out only 1 bag because the remainder was too firmly frozen. Mutch is now thinking of sending a few men who will keep working until the meat has been chopped out. The dogs are very wretched so I shall stay here now.

[**11 February**] **Monday**   I bought a seal from Mitir, and this morning Ocheitu gave it to them [the dogs].

[D2]
Ocheitu fed the dogs in the morning. Tomorrow I want to go to Anarnitung to supply all the men there with powder and lead so that they may finally get some seals at the polynyas.

[D]
At Anarnitung all the men, to whom I will give powder and lead, are to go to the polynya to hunt seals. Wilhelm and Jenimi were pouring bullets on Saturday [9 February]. Once my preparations were finished, I wrote and calculated a little, just as on any day in Kikkerten.

Fourth Trip to Anarnitung and K'ingua

[**12 February**] **Tuesday**   Imigen. I woke Wilhelm at 5, called for Ocheitu and Ssigna and was able to set off at 6.30.

There are no entries in the Diary between 13 February and 10 March 1884.

[D2]
A very cold north wind (face mask). Set off at 6.30 and arrived here at Ikera's fairly quickly.

[**13 February**] **Wednesday**   Anarnitung. It was getting dark before we reached A[narnitung]. I am also starting to drive [the dogs] a little, but am not managing it properly. The whip is quite long and my voice is not accustomed to the shouting and cursing. It is again so thick that we can see nothing.

[FB/MK]
(...) Ocheitu now has a new igloo on the north side of the island, one that is very fine and comfortable. A few days ago he told me that they once had pitched tupiks near the grounded ice on Tiratirak [Teratirax] (Middlis), and that when the ice broke away, it had buried everything; one man had escaped to the island's hill, naked. On Pojontai (Seven Isl.) [Pujetung] some tupiks had once stood on the summit of the hill when the driving ice surged over the island and carried away tupiks and people. The pack must often possess terrifying force. Ocheitu also told me he had once seen floes 20′ [6 m] thick above high water mark on Warham's Island. (...)

[D2]
[**14 February**] **Thursday**   Headed for Ssarbukduak to hunt seals. The ice was breaking up violently under the influence of the strong current; very cold and windy. Today took a total of 1 seal. There are not many in the water today.

[FB/MK]
(...) Today I went hunting for the first time, although not with brilliant success since the only [seal] I shot was carried under the ice by the current. I sat there just like the Eskimos at the water's edge behind my ice floe and waited patiently for a head to appear. You can't imagine what an impression it makes, to sit so near the water at this cold time of year, and to hear the roaring and rushing again. (...)

I will try my luck again tomorrow to see whether I can get a seal; there are certainly not many in Ssarbukduak. (...)

[D2]
[**15 February**] **Friday**   Anarnitung. Calm and warm, so it is better at the polynya. The only seal I shot [FB/MK: .. tore loose from my harpoon and ..] went under [the ice] with the strong current. Ocheitu took 2, which I claimed firmly for myself. I hope I can still get the 7 seals I need and then I will quickly set off for Nettiling.

[FB/MK]

(...) I went out today exactly like an Eskimo with my harpoon and all the accessories and sat by the water just as patiently as they. Today it was cloudy, with no wind at all; and the water made a totally different impression. It now flows peacefully and quietly; one can hardly believe that these quiet waters could smash the ice with such force. I felt it only when I could hardly hold onto my seal pup. Since it was warmer today one could see farther, almost to Kingawa across the water. (...)

In the evening Mitik was here and told me eternally long stories, which corrected Mikidgu in reference to Ssikonilan [Sikosuilax?, NW Baffin] and the surrounding area. As far as I know this is the only point about which my assembled information is still inadequate.

This morning my young friend Tokaving brought me a seal slaughtered by bloodletting, since he wanted some tobacco, which I gave him. Akunitok, whose wife died very recently, had a sealskin and the intestines on his sledge this morning. On inquiring I learned that it is the custom that in such a situation the man keeps only the meat of the first seal he kills; the skin, blubber and intestines are thrown into the water.

As you see, my Marie, I am now truly just like an Eskimo; I live like them, hunt with them, and count myself among the men of Anarnitung. Moreover I scarcely eat any European foodstuffs any longer but am living entirely on seal meat and coffee. But I have high hopes that in this way I will at last manage to accumulate my required number of seals so that I can soon set off for Netilling. Although I am heartily bored with seal hunting, I have no option, because it is the only possibility of obtaining the necessary number. I hope to still be able to get away this month. Perhaps I will obtain some more dogs from Padli before then, then I would be really happy! – to be finally free of this dog nonsense. (...)

[D2]

[16 February] Saturday Anarnitung. Since yesterday evening it as begun to blow strongly from the NW[,] in the meantime the sledge dogs went to Ssarbukduak. Since owing to a misunderstanding, the sledge with which I had meant to go left without me, I remained at home.

[FB/MK]

(...) In fact I have lost nothing, because the Eskimos brought nothing back with them and I certainly would have caught nothing. They said 'Ssarbukduak komakiádlu udlumi,' i.e. Ssarbukduak [the current] is very angry today, and I imagine that the wind which became even stronger during the day would have inconvenienced the hunters quite badly. I hope that it is calmer tomorrow. Aniksirn, Ocheitu's cousin, also made a wise choice and stayed at home to build an igloo.

Thus today I have simply listened to stories and collected words. My glossary is now expanding rapidly. But it was certainly about time that I began it. I wish I could draw well, in order to give you a picture of an igloo such as this. You can see the exterior from a photograph, but not the interior [Boas 1888:541–3]. Think of a round room 12' in diameter. Conically arched and entirely lined at the top with sealskins. (...)

The background is formed by a snow platform about 3' high, which occupies half the space. On it lie smoothly spread caribou skins and in the background there is a large heap of all kinds of items, skins, clothes etc. and all these beloved Innuit! The front part of the space is filled with 2 snow blocks of the same height, one right and one left, and with two lamps. The lamps stand on the snow blocks and above them hang the kettles; above them are the essential drying frames, wooden frames with a mesh of string, which are filled with drying clothes, day and night. To right and left of the entrance, in front of the two lamps, lie on the one side the supply of seal meat, and on the other the offal, and it really requires some practice to get accustomed to this sight.

In the remaining space, which ... is about 6' long and 4' wide[,] stands a large block of snow[,] with which the door is closed at night[,] and usually 2 or 3 dogs[,] but I myself have seen 6 or 7 of them. After some practice we can just about get through the door without resorting to using a bitch to distract the rest. Beyond it there are another 1 or 2 small igloos, which serve to keep the cold out and at the same time to store provisions.

Now you should just see the long-haired, dirty fellows sitting there! They sit there, their arms folded across their bellies, usually with their heads held a bit to one side, and they chatter, laugh and sing unrestrainedly! From time to time one of them grabs a knife and cuts himself off a good chunk of seal meat which he consumes and, if it is frozen, it is chopped up and eaten by everyone – not excluding myself – with greatest relish. Remarkably, when eating and talking, they almost always look at the wall and seldom at each other.

There is an old man called Mitik (eider duck) [I. *mitiq*] here, who provides me with particular pleasure. As soon as he sees me coming from a distance[,] he shouts 'Arko *you* tidli!' [How are you?], and begins telling me all kinds of stories in his finest pidgin of English and Eskimo, because English words hardly occur.

So this is my daily life here; can you believe that I really long for a sensible conversation and for a person who can really understand me! Unfortunately this time I have no book with me to read so can't do anything in that direction. I have already read the advertisements and everything else on a page from a Cologne newspaper. (...)

[D2]

[17 February] Sunday   Anarnitung. Yesterday's bad weather is followed by worse today. A NW gale, so that one can see only 10 paces. I sat all day with the Eskimos in the igloo.

[FB/MK]

(...) And do you think that I can write in these circumstances? When I try to start, I deliberately throw the book into a corner; everything just looks too disagreeable to me. Whatever I might start goes awry, and it doesn't take much for me to feel really depressed. (...)

[D2]

[18 February] Monday   Anarnitung. Although it is still blowing strongly we are going out to the polynyas. The Eskimos simply have to, because they are half starved.

[FB/MK]

(...) You should see the voracity with which they usually consume the hard, dry ship's biscuits that I give them. (...)

[D2]

I am feeding Ocheitu's family and 2 sick children, but I can't supply bread to the 43 residents of the camp [14 men, 13 women, 8 boys and 8 girls; Boas 1888:426]. Since it is nigpei [I. *nigiiq* = east wind] there is still much young ice; it was not until 1 o'clock that it was completely broken up. The time for hunting at the polynyas has passed ineffectually. In total 3 seals were taken at the {Nudnirn} Putukin polynya.

[FB/MK]

(...) O.[cheitu] has now taken another wife, but she is not yet living in his igloo. (...) Some Eskimos, who were at another polynya, brought home 3 small seals. (...)

[D2]

[19 February] Tuesday   Nichemiarbing. A detestable day: a blizzard out of the north so that one can see nothing; below Imigen it is slightly better. We arrived here before sunset. Here there is another unpleasant surprise. The illness affecting the children is raging terribly here and Piera, my main support, now has only 7 dogs! What is to happen? He does not want to travel with me to Lake Kennedy.

[FB/MK]
(...) Yesterday evening I successfully assembled a dog team and this morning at 9 o'clock we set off. I will suffer seriously from the sicknesses that are prevailing here, since I know that many Eskimos only reluctantly have any dealings with me, though they dare not express it to my face. Now none of them wanted to lend me any dogs, but when I asked for them, they did not dare refuse.

[**20 February**] **Wednesday**   Kikkerten. Ocheitu is going back to Anarnitung and I to Kikkerten with Hannibal Jack. We travelled fast and safely. At first there was a cold north wind, but then a calm; finally we were in the realm of the south wind, which we had seen blowing on the mainland for so long. Last night it blew ferociously! In the evening Mutch's sledge came back from Salmon Fiord after me; they were supposed to be fetching walrus meat from there.

[FB/MK]
(...) Now it is comfortably possible to make all our trips by daylight, no matter what stops one makes. (...)

[D2]
[**21 February**] **Thursday**   [K'exerten] A severe southerly gale, which swung round to a north wind at noon. Hannibal Jack cannot get back owing to the bad weather. Valuable stories about the turgnak [I. *tuurngaq* = protective spirit; Boas 1888:634–8].

[FB/MK]
(...) In the evening Kikkertaktuak was here and told me a story which I wrote down as quickly as possible; I also heard another from Kakotscha; also I learned something more about the turgnang, the Eskimos' spirits. (...)

[D2]
[**22 February**] **Friday**   Hannibal Jack has gone back. I gave him seal and

walrus meat for the doubtful trip to Nettiling. Tomorrow Mutch himself will be travelling to Salmon Fiord for meat, and I with him.

[FB/MK]
(...) Wilhelm's foot is now almost better again; only at the tip, where the wound has extended to the bone, is it still refusing to close. (...)

[D2]
[23 February] **Saturday**   At 7 a.m. the weather looked so bad that I opted to stay at home, since I can do nothing outside. When Mutch set off there was a southerly gale with snow. At 5.30 he came back without even having reached Salmon Fiord. I had a good meal prepared for him. [FB/MK: In the evening he talked so much that I got nothing done.] The cooper did not come up, probably because of the bad weather.

[24 February] **Sunday**   Mutch had occasion to send a sledge to Warham Island and has promised to let me go with it; I look forward to getting to know the coast to the south in this fashion.

[FB/MK]
(...) Today at noon it was calm, but now there is a north wind; the thermometer is reading −17° (Celsius). I have now compiled everything that I have worked up cartographically thus far and have just finished this evening. (...)

I hope the *Red Lion* from St. John's will be the first [ship] I catch sight of. In all my diaries I have heavily underlined the 1st of November, since by that date I want to be home with you. (...)

[D2]
[25 February] **Monday**   I brought bread inside and repaid J.M. [James Mutch]. I have packed for the trip to W.[arham] I.[sland] tomorrow.

Trip to Milixdjuax

[26 February] **Tuesday**   Middlikdjua. Woke Wilhelm and Jenimi at 4 a.m. and by 6 were ready to depart.

[FB/MK
(...) Day was already dawning when we left the harbour and headed rap-

idly south. We reached the land near Kedliridjen [K'adliridjen] and then travelled south along the coast. Soon, around Rocky Fiord [Kangertluk-djuax] I entered an unfamiliar area and it was a real joy for me to see and observe something new for a change.

I was able to determine the entrance to Rocky Fiord clearly; thereafter there were icebergs along the coast near Ilichisimarbing [Iliximisarbing], Shake Head Pt., or Shomeo Pt. Allegedly a boat full of Eskimos was killed by falling rocks there long, long ago, and every Eskimo who travels past has the obligation to shake his head and say 'Brr!'; my good Jenissy certainly did so. He showed me on the steep, high cliff the spot from which the rocks broke loose and at the foot one could still see the rock masses piled high. By about 7 we had passed Ilichisimarbing and then a magnificent fiord opened out.

I thought I had already seen the most beautiful landscapes in the fiord but I had never imagined such magnificent cliffs extending for miles, or such massive towers. Unfortunately everything was too confused here and I was able to plot little of it on my map. By 3 o'clock we had passed the fiord, had left the coast and were heading across to Warham's Island [Milixdjuax]. Whereas it had been fine weather all day, here it began to blow strongly and continued to do so all night; but this was only a local wind that is said to prevail here frequently. (...)

[D2]
I was able to survey the entire coastline of W.[arham's] Island in superb weather. Jenissi built an igloo here, while I climbed the hill to get my bearings in terms of the ice situation. It lay off Nuvukdjua [Nuvukdjuax; Ragged Point, also Queen's Cape] across to Kachodlui [K'axodluin] about 7 miles from Warham Island. Bears, whose fresh tracks could still be seen, had eaten 2 large and 1 small barrels of blubber. Here at Middlikdjua there was an abominably cold wind.

[**27 February**] **Wednesday**   [K'exerten] Kikkerton. Travelled back home in fine weather. The dogs ran well and fast[,] and thus we arrived at 5 p.m., having set out at 8. In the evening Wilhelm [Scherden], Capt. Roach's second mate, had arrived, bringing the sad news that on his return trip to Naujateling the Capt. had frozen both feet. He will probably lose both big toes. He slept out on the ice overnight and got frozen as a result.

[**28 February**] **Thursday**   Kikkerton. Have worked up my observations from the trip. In the morning I visited Wilhelm [Scherden] at the American station. In the afternoon everything was made ready for the trip to Naujateling; Mutch's dogs are heading there now and I along with them.

Second Trip to Naujateling

[**29 February**] **Friday** Umenaktuak [Umanaxtuax] (*Lizzie Simmonds*). Kanaka and I travelled across in superb travelling weather. It was very clearly and magnificently summerlike. Near some icebergs that were stranded in the middle of the Sound off Idjuchuaktun [Idjorituaxtuin], I lost a box in the rough ice and had to spend an hour travelling back for it. We arrived at 9 p.m. and were welcomed in very friendly fashion.

[FB/MK]
(...) Now I am ready to depart again; the sledge stands harnessed in front of the door. I am just waiting till the Eskimos have drunk their coffee and then we are off to Naujateling. Yesterday morning, after I had completed my observations I went to the American station to visit Wilhelm [Scherden], the mate. It feels quite wonderful to be able to speak German to some person other than my Wilhelm [Weike] once again! Then in the afternoon I got everything ready and this morning I woke at 4.30. Now it is 6 and high time to get on our way. So goodbye for now. I shall write to you again from Naujateling, or rather Blacklead.

In the evening. Blacklead on board *Lizzie P. Simmonds*. Today the weather was ideal for travelling. The sun was shining so warmly and there was not the slightest wind. At the same time it was so clear that we could make out the land with its valleys and mountains very clearly. At noon we travelled through some rough ice near a stranded iceberg, and on this occasion I lost a box and had to spend an hour going back for it. (...)

[D2]
[**1 March**] **Saturday** Umenaktuak. Today I must give the dogs a rest, and because yesterday evening it was too late to arrange anything, I shall remain here on the ship today. During the day I asked Peter, my last hope, about Hudson Bay [no Inuktitut name given], but could get nothing out of him either. The right Peter died 2 years ago! Capt. Roach's feet are indeed very badly frozen [FB/MK: .., so that I am afraid the poor man will spend the entire summer sitting as a result]. In the evening I took a latitude and hope to get a bearing tomorrow. Foggy all day; in the evening it cleared up.

[FB/MK]
(...) At 8.30 the second mate, Bill [Wilhelm Scherden] arrived from Kikkerton. He had met Tyson in the rough ice near Kikkerten. Tyson is in the process of travelling to Padli. (...)

[D2]
[2 March] Sunday   Umenaktuak. Naper, one of C. Roach's Eskimos, hitched up the team early and around 10 we got under way. I surveyed the coast from Kikkertelling [K'exertelung] and Naujateling Harb. Unfortunately it was not possible to see across the Sound and so I did not get any bearings.

[FB/MK]
(...) It is difficult always to converse in English when both mates [Fred Grobschmidt and Wilhelm Scherden] prefer to speak German, but for Capt. Roach's sake I make an effort to speak only English. (...)

[D2]
[3 March] Monday   Umenaktuak. Tomorrow Kanaka will be starting back via Nuvujen, for the sake of the planks for which he came; he is to pick up skins at Nuvujen. Fred [first mate] is going with me to Kachodlui [K'axodluin]. A superb, clear day.

[FB/MK]
(...) The sun is so warm that I had the greatest desire to lie down and have a little nap on the top of the island we had climbed (−15°F. [−26°C]). From the summit we obtained a good insight into ice conditions. (...)

[D2]
The ice has essentially broken up, and now extends from 8 miles below Kachodlui to Nuvukdjua, forming a bay whose end lies between Kautak and Ilichisimarbing. By 7 o'clock we had returned, after having got a look into the interior of Kachodlui Bay.

[4 March] Tuesday   Umenaktuak. We gave the dogs a rest. Bill[,] Fred and I went [FB/MK: .. to the camp and climbed] to the top of the island[,] from where I took a bearing on Middlikdjua. Unfortunately Kikkertukdjuak was enveloped in fog. I had to show the mate [Fred] how to take observations with the sextant.

[FB/MK]
A mate who can't take observations and a captain who cannot read or
write represent a fine phenomenon!

[D2]
[5 March] Wednesday   Nuvujen. Fred [Grobschmidt] and I started back
[FB/MK: .. at 7.30]. Although he had promised that we would travel along
the island, he is now going past Margarethen Isl. [Margaret Island;
Umanaxdjung]. We were at Nuvujen by 2 p.m. Fairly windy and cold.

[FB/MK]
(...) There we entered Keppignang's igloo, where Mutch's daughter
Annalukulu (correct name unknown) was also visiting. I read a little in
books I had swapped with Bill [Wilhelm Scherden], and slept excellently.
(...)

[D2]
[6 March] Thursday   Kikkerten. Set off at 8.30. Near Nuvujen there was
some drifting snow, but farther out there was little wind, whereas towards
Kikkerten it was thick. But we found Kikkerten easily, since the tracks led
directly to it. We arrived around 3. Jimmy Mutch was at Salmon Fiord
[FB/MK: .., to fetch walrus meat] and returned around 6 o'clock. At the
moment there are two men here from Ssaumia; perhaps I'll go there with
them to buy dogs [FB/MK: .., if I do not have the opportunity to go to
Padli]. It appears that I might be able to acquire 5.

[7 March] Friday   [K'exerten] Kikkerton. Have been finishing off the
map. In the evening Anarsin, the second of the men from Ssaumia, came
back from Tinninikdjua. Unfortunately he had also sold a dog there, as
well as 2 to Jimmy Mutch previously. In the evening I called Bob over to
ask him whether he wants to go to Padli with me, but he now has no
desire for further travelling. Hence, if the sledge does not come from
Padli, I will have to go to Ssaumia.

[FB/MK]
(...) Today Mutch has once again gone down to Salmon Fiord to fetch a
fully loaded sledge. I asked Muckelmann [Mummoachia; apparently
descriptive name given by Boas; G. *Muckelmann* = somebody who mum-
bles] and the Ssaumia Eskimos about dogs and it appears that I could
probably get 8. (...)

Now I have not managed to do any writing for days, my Marie. I could not seclude myself on board the ship and chat with you. I am back at Kikkerton and this afternoon do not wish to be disturbed from the unpleasantnesses and worries that overwhelm me day and night, in order to fly to you. It is easy to say that one should always hold one's head high, but actually even my retreat to Padli has been severely jeopardized by this unfortunate dog disease! (...)

The illness has been prevalent here for about a month with outstanding virulence, and Piera, with whom I wanted to travel west, has lost 7 of his 10 dogs, so I have abandoned all hope. At Blacklead, the sum total of surviving dogs is 15 among 10 men; in another camp, the largest [Anarnitung], it is scarcely possible to assemble a single dog team; in short there can be absolutely no thought of my getting away from here without assistance from Padli. And just think how terrible it would be to have to sit idly here all summer, with the prospect of not being able to get away in the fall. (...)

Yet often I can scarcely add a word to you to my dry daily reports. Often I might be able to but, when I hear the conversations between Jimmy Mutch and his Eskimo wife [no name given], this vapid, often trivial chat, the pencil drops from my hand; how can I transpose your pure image to these surroundings. It often appears to me superimposed on everything that I am seeing and hearing around me. And yet Mutch is a relatively good man, to whom I must do justice in that during a sojourn of 17 years [since 1866-7] with very few interruptions, he has learned much in this country and is an open, honourable character, who moreover does not attempt to conceal his weaknesses.

But the people on board the American ship! [*Lizzie P. Simmons*]. I turn away with disgust from this bunch of blokes and am heartily glad that I am not condemned to spend the entire winter with them. Only the second mate [Wilhelm Scherden], a German American, is a truly good, acceptable fellow; I feel sorry for him that he has to live and work for years in such company. I like him best of all the people I know here in the Sound. I am ashamed to acknowledge the first mate [Fred Grobschmidt] as a countryman.

I realize it increasingly from day to day. I am not born for loneliness. I need people too much, or those of them who really have a claim to the name. (...)

[D2]

[8 **March**] **Saturday**   Kikkerton. Foul weather. In the afternoon tidying up the provisions room. The sledges [from Padli] have not come and thus I will get prepared for Ssaumia in any case.

[FB/MK
(...) Mutch is prepared to lend me one of his own dogs when I go over to Padli and try my luck there. If only I can acquire a good team!

[D2]
[9 March] **Sunday**   Kikkerton. Everything has been made ready for the trip. The sledges from Padli seem not to be coming. We want to set off tomorrow if the weather permits.

[**10 March**] **Monday**   Kikkerton. A southerly gale so we have not set off.

[WW]
The Dr. bought the first dogs, two from Arne, but he had no more to spare. Major sledge repairs.

From 11 to 20 March, Boas again wrote original entries in the Diary, which he transcribed, with additions, to Diary 2.

[D]
[**11 March**] **Tuesday**   In the morning it was snowing, so we have not left yet. Later it turned fine and thus I have unfortunately lost a good day.

Trip Southeastward to Saumia

[**12 March**] **Wednesday**   [D2: Below Rocky Fiord.] Kikkerton iceberg behind Akku [Akugdliruk]. Since the sledge is very heavily laden, we are making only slow progress despite our 16 dogs and have not even reached Ilichisimarbing. The two Eskimos [Muckelmann and Shellback] quickly built a snow house [D2: .. near an iceberg] and we slept quite well [D2: .. superbly]. Travelling is now very pleasant in the strong [D2: .. fine] warm sunshine.

[**13 March**] **Thursday**   [D2: Itidlirn to Ugjuktung.] We set off around 8 o'clock, travelled up Kouakdjua [Kouaxdjuax] and began climbing overland. The route here is very bad and rocky. We often had to lay a bearskin under the sledge to avoid smashing it. But as soon as we got out of the valley of the narrow stream, it got better. We camped near the top of the pass.

[BN; here, from 13 to 15 March, Boas made notes that are almost illegible.]
Itidlirn 13th March 1884. At Ugjuktung and Kouakdjuak. Woke around 7 a.m.; by 9 everything ready. Today we made rapid progress since the snow and ice were better. Went ... up Koukdjuak with its massive rock cliffs and in the evening reached Itidlirn. Here we went ... through the middle of a deep, wide valley with enormous notches carved in it, and stopped up at the top. Fed the dogs. Built an igloo. Fine, fresh caribou tracks .. [Text breaks off here.]

[D]
[**14 March**] **Friday**   Itidlirn, Ugjuktung. Today we covered only a short distance because the dogs were tired and are to sleep at Ugjuktung. The view from the top of the pass is magnificent. At Ugjuktung we found a tupik still in usable condition and slept warmly and well in it. [D2: It was even thawing inside!] I left a seal here. Yesterday the dogs were freezing.

[BN]
Friday 14th. In the morning the sun woke us from our slumbers; we got up, readied the sledge and caught the dogs. One of Jimmy Mutch's pack ran off and came back only as the sledge was leaving. I welcomed him back with a sound thrashing. We headed uphill with good going, and reaching the top we could see beyond into the spectacular Ugjuktun Fiord. In the foreground lay Kikkertaugak [K'exertaujang], and to the right Innukschunne [Ijiksune]. Now we headed downhill like the wind and soon we were back on ice again.

   We crossed the fiord [to the] narrow point, first to Tessiujang then to Ugjuktun and reached the old camp. One tupik stood there undamaged and we made it our quarters. How wonderfully warm it felt then; how comfortably we were able to stretch our limbs! An old boat still lay here and a lot of provisions; some equipment was piled on top of the boat. Among other things even a walrus skull. An attempt at climbing Kikkertaugak was unsuccessful because the snow was too smooth and I did not have [ice] chisels with me.

15th [**March, Saturday**]   We and the dogs are now rested and we can now continue. I hope we reach the land today! [End of the original entries in the Black Notebook.]

[D]

Ugjuktung, Ssersokdjuak [D2: Tessijua{raluk}lukdjua] [Tessialukdjuax]. Initially we made rapid progress. As we headed up inland the going was good and thus despite many steep climbs we progressed rapidly. After we had crossed a large lake [D2: Tessialukdjuak][,] we made a halt on a small one in which there was open water. An old igloo located there was in such bad shape that we could not stay there. The dogs were fed in the evening as well.

[16 March] Sunday   Ssersokdjuak. Kairoliktung [K'airoliktung]. (In the evening). We set off around 9 a.m. The going was very bad so we made only slow progress. Ultimately the Eskimos [D2: natives] lost their way completely but luckily we at last reached the river, which was still flowing. Then finally we came to a large pond at the end of Kairoliktung. We made a halt there, near the water, at 6.30. 65°34′ N lat.

The First 'White' among the Inuit of Ukiadliving

[17 March] Monday   Okiadliving [Ukiadliving] 65°39′. In the morning we carried all our things down to the ice with [D2: .. great] effort, but then we progressed rapidly. Near Kikkertalukdjuak [K'ekertalukdjuax] we encountered Muckelmann's father [D2: and Angutikatan] and now we are making great speed [D2: .. and now we are heading home as fast as possible]. Later we met another Eskimo and by 3.45 we were at Okiadliving [D2: Okkiadliving].

I was welcomed with a great deal of shouting, singing and dancing as the first white man to come here. The women shouted and danced outside till I was deafened. I was quartered in the kagmang in which Muckelmann and his father [D2: Angutikatan] lived, as well as Shellback. I obtained 2 dogs from Muckelmann and 1 from Shellback. The dogs were fed.

[18 March] Tuesday   [D2: Okkiadliving.] Today the Eskimos are going out hunting. I remained here to give the dogs a rest. I went up the hill with Muckelmann and at noon I got a good latitude. When the Eskimos came back in the evening (Angutikan had shot a bear) I began bargaining for dogs. Although I cannot pay generously, everyone is glad to sell to me [D2: .., everyone is keen to sell]. I obtained 2 from Angutikan[,] 2 from Mummiachia[,] 1 from Shellback, 1 from Mummiachia's father, 1 from Tom and 1 from N.[iguaitung]. Tomorrow I want to travel along the coast to the NE, because I want to get over to Aniralung [Angijaralung].

[D2; names of Inuit men living at Ukiadliving]
Angutikan: Atichelling, Okkaliriak.
Mummiachia: Ututitung, Piulak. [Muckelmann]
Father: Kirmidliak.
Shellback: Nirdnirng.
Tom Tom: Tachtocholang.
Pudlaujang: Pikkuiling. [Sugarloaf or Sugarloafy]
and Aranin [Anarsin]:   Niguaitung, Tacholik.

[D]
Tomorrow I want to travel northeast a little because I have no idea where I am on the map.

[**19 March**] **Wednesday**   In the morning I travelled north with Sugarloafy (Pudlaujang) to try the dogs and to survey something of the coast. Anarsin is travelling the same way to hunt bears. P.[udlaujang] has volunteered to go with me to Kikkerton, at which I am very glad. I now have 10 dogs of my own and 6 in Kikkerton [D2: .. from J. Mutch and Shanguja]. Altogether a good team.

Unfortunately the ice as far as Udlimaulitelling was so bad that I was unable to get a [D2: the last] bearing which I [D2: .. very much] wanted. I cannot find where I am on the map. At noon a very strong W wind blew up and by evening had reached gale force.

[D2]
Probably my farthest point was Cape Mickingham [Cape Mickleham; K'exertuxdjuax].

[FB/MK; written in Nichemiarbing on the way to Nettiling Lake on 29 March]
(...) I would have liked very much to travel an hour farther since I would then have been sure where I was on my map. But unfortunately the bad ice that filled Djákiak [Sakiak] Fiord prohibited any further advance. I

had hoped to perhaps encounter a bear along the way, but I had no such luck. We saw only fresh tracks. On the return trip a very strong northwest wind began to blow, making travelling anything but pleasant. I was back by about 6 p.m. The hunters had arrived back before me and a noon meal of bear meat and the warm kagmang soon restored our degree of comfort. In the evening a little girl told me a large number of stories for which I paid her with beads. (...)

I have not previously written to you from so far from home as I am today. I am here in Okiadliving on the shores of Davis Strait, having come here to buy dogs. It was a tough journey, sleeping in cold igloos, but finally I got here. You cannot imagine the shouts and amazement with which I was greeted here, since I am the first European who has visited this corner. Fortunately my business has succeeded better than I had expected. I now possess 10 dogs, and thus the basis for leaving Cumberland Sound. I hope to be able to acquire a couple more so that I have a good team.

20th [March, Thursday]   Yesterday morning I went out to get to know the coast a little to the north, and at the same time to try out the dogs, with a view to possibly giving back or exchanging some. At noon the weather became quite foul with drifting snow and a cold north wind. I had really expected to find this side of Davis Strait plotted fairly accurately on the map.

But from the map I cannot find out where I am at all. I really believe, Marie, that I have never experienced a spring that made such an impression of spring on me as this one. Everything is still so wintry, but I am very indifferent to the effects of cold. You should just see how magnificently warmly the sun now shines on everything, and how good it is to *feel* its warm rays again for the first time! (...)

In the optimal situation it will be only another 4 months until I hear from you again, because by then the Dundee ships will have reached this coast and you surely will have sent *your letters* with them. When I return to Kikkerton the first thing I will look at will be your picture. Just another month and I will begin my travels. I shall then travel up Kignait Fiord, so I will be in Padli in early May, then I shall hang your picture up in my igloo wherever I stay anywhere for any length of time. It will be a tough task to haul all my things overland to Padli! (...)

[D]
[D2: Okkiadliving.] This morning we first caught the dogs, then fed them; this took until 11 o'clock. The Eskimos went seal hunting. Tomor-

row I want to go over to Kikkerton with Pulaujang's and Angutikatang's sledges. I hope to get there in 4 days. I should very much like to see Uibarun (C. Mercy) but this is impossible, since the time is too short. I saw the promised land from here yesterday. [D2: Yesterday I saw the Promised Land!] [which Boas had seen the first time from the *Germania* on 16 July 1883]

Boas made no entries in the Diary between Friday, 21 March, and Monday, 5 May 1884, but in the same diary (from Wednesday, 28 March, until Thursday, 5 April), there are notes from 1883 related to his attendance at the Third German Geographers' Congress in Frankfurt and his visit to Marie in Stuttgart (see above).

Return Trip to K'exerten

[D2]
[21 March] Friday   Tessialukdjua. I set off in the morning at the same time as the hunters. Another sledge, driven by Tom Tom took advantage of the opportunity to travel with me to Ugjuktung to fetch tupik poles. Since the route I had used in coming here was so bad, I am returning via Poalakdjua [Poalukdjuax].

[FB/MK]
(...) .., where a man from Capt. Roach's ship, who died of scurvy 2 years ago [1882], lies buried; by this route I reached Ujaradjiraichjung [Ujaradjiraaitung] Fiord. (...)

[D2]
The route via [Poalukdjuax] took only about 1 hour but it was very difficult. By 12 we were at the head of the fiord[,] then we headed inland up the channel of a mountain stream which, however, was very evenly filled with snow. When we finally reached the old valley, we had avoided the greater part of the bad trail. We reached the old igloo as it was getting dark. The pond was so swollen that it was almost lapping at the door.

[FB/MK]
(...) I took another astronomical observation and by about 12 we were ready to go to sleep. (...)

[D2]

[22 March] Saturday Ugjuktung. Today we travelled very comfortably, heading downhill and arrived here fairly early and slept in the well-maintained tupik. In the evening we fed both my team and Tom Tom's.

[FB/MK; written on 29 March]
On the 22nd we travelled across the large lake, Sessialukdjuax [Tessialukdjuax], crossed the pass then down to the Sound. In the evening we got back to Ugjuktung, where we slept in the well-maintained tupik.

[D2]

[23 March] Sunday Near Ilichizzimarbing. We parted early. [FB/MK: Tom Tom went back to Ssaumia, Pudl[auj]ang and I went north.] A miserable north wind was blowing straight into our faces and enveloped everything in thick clouds of snow. Up in Kouakdjuak we found the warm remains of a seal partly eaten by a bear.

[FB/MK]
(...) But there was no sign of the bear and I had no inclination to look for him, since I wanted to get to Kikkerton as quickly as possible. (...)

[D2]
We made only slow progress against the strong wind. Behind Naujakdjuak [Naujaxdjuax] we had some shelter, but then near Ilichizimarbing the wind swept down from the mountain in terrifying gusts, throwing one of the sledges onto the dogs and capsizing it. We were unable to reach the old igloo [12–13 March] beyond Shake Head and at Nechzekdjuak [Nersexdjuax; not included in the list of place names or marked on the map; Boas 1885:90ff., plate 1] we dug ourselves into a deep snowbank, although the old igloo was barely half an hour away.

[24 March] Monday Kikkerton. The force of the storm had slackened, but it was still blowing in strong gusts from Warham's Island to Uichizimarbiung [Unasiarbing]. It quickly cleared up to the north. We soon saw Middliakdjuin and Kikkerton and at sunset reached the house safely.

The Padli Esk. [FB/MK: .. Innuit] have been here and, unfortunately, have left again [on 23 March]. Mutch has bought 5 dogs from them for me, so I now have 15 in total.

[WW; written on 22 March]
[James Mutch bought three dogs from Kenningna and two from Shanguja for Boas. According to Weike, who observed the deal, they received in exchange the following items.]

Coninak [Kenningna]: 2 cans of powder, 1 package of matches, 2 cans of syrup, 1 can of coffee, 10 lbs bread, 2 knives, 2 handkerchiefs, 8 lbs lead, 1 piece of soap, 60 plugs tobacco.

Schangu [Shanguja]: 4½ lbs lead, 200 ship's biscuits, 40 plugs tobacco.

[D2]
Fred [mate of the *Lizzie P. Simmons*] is here and wants to leave again tomorrow morning. Iwi, an Esk. from Padli[,] has come here with him, but is now at Naujateling. I let it be known via him that I want to set off on 25th April and will need 2 sledges [from Roach] to help me.

[25 March] Tuesday   [K'exerten] Kikkerton. I am staying at home to feed myself up a bit. Last year [1883] 6 ships were seen at Padli. 2 Americans! Hurray!

[FB/MK; written on 29 March]
I stayed at home on the 25th. Now I felt it necessary again to *feed myself up* a bit, since the long trip had run me down quite badly. On the 25th Mutch told me that 5 or 6 ships had been at Padli and you can imagine with what feelings I heard that there were even 2 American ships! I felt as if all the blood was running to my heart when I could again hope of coming to see you! Oh Marie, how happy I'll be if my good luck leads me to an American ship! However it will be going to St. John's in Newfoundland, rather than to New London [Connecticut], but that doesn't worry me. St. John's is not the end of the world, like this country, and a few days will take me to you from there. In all my diaries and ephemerides I have underlined November 12 [1884] as the day on which I hope to be in New York or Minden. Another 6 months in this country. (...)

[D2]
[26 March Wednesday]   Kikkerton. Mutch wants to go to Warham's Island[,] but since the weather is not good enough, after long reflection he went to the Pangnirtu polynyas. I still have work and drafting to do.

[27 March] Thursday   Kikkerton. Today W.[ilhelm] and I began packing the things for the homeward trip, as well as getting the sledge ready for the morning. Heavy drifting snow.

[FB/MK; written on 29 March]
(...) I have underlined this date in red in the calendar as being the day on which I began preparing for heading home. In the evening I was really tired and went to bed early.

Trip to the Northwest to Nettilling Lake

[D2]
[**28 March**] **Friday**   Nichemiarbing. Ssigna and I travelled to Nichemiarbing in superb weather [FB/MK: .., from where I wanted to survey the fiord]. At the spot where the tracks diverged westward earlier, we were met by Jimmy Mutch, who had spent the night at Ocheitu's site on the Ikirn [I. *ikiq* – small narrows; probably at Ikerassaxdjuax]. When we arrived in the evening[,] the weather did not look exactly brilliant.

[FB/MK]
[**29 March**] **Saturday**   Nichemiarbing. Last night a vicious blizzard arose. In the afternoon a south wind with snow which unfortunately made the going very poor. I spent the entire day in Piera's {tupik} igloo.

[FB/MK]
(...) Today, dear Marie, I caught up on a whole series of days in my letters to you. When I am travelling and living in a little igloo, it is usually so late, almost midnight, before I get to bed, that I am quite happy if I have even written my entries in my diary. I am now on a trip to Lake Kennedy and after the very first day have been halted here by a south wind and heavy drifting snow. (...)

[D2]
[**30 March**] **Sunday**   Kassijidjin [K'assigidjen]. Although it was still snowing in the morning I set off with Ssigna to travel to Netilling. Piarang was setting off at the same time with a wretched team, so I lent him 2 dogs in order to make better progress. Because of the snow the going has become very bad. It cleared up a little. Passing Tudnun [Tunukutang] we bypassed Ssarbakdualuk [Sarbuxdjulung], then crossed the fiord [Nettil-

ling]. Through Kassijidjen we avoided Ssarbukduak [Sarbuxdjuax]. We bypassed the beautiful Ssarbukdjukulu [Sarbaxdjukulu] easily on the good fast ice. There was very deep snow in Kassijidjen, and we built an igloo on the isthmus.

[**31 March**] **Monday**   Kangia{nga} [Kangia]. In the morning we travelled on against a strong north wind. At the little polynyas at Kognung [K'ognung; the narrows of the lower river] P.[iarang] tried to kill a seal, but got nothing. At the upper Kognung S.[signa] told me the story of the 2 bears that have been turned into stone here. In the evening we reached Kangia and were able to spend the night in an old igloo. I will leave all the things here and tomorrow want to hurry up to the lake.

[**1 April**] **Tuesday**   Netilling (Issoa) [Isoa]. Since the dogs were constantly scenting caribou, we made very rapid progress uphill. At Amitok [Amitox] Ssigna shot a caribou. At Armaktong [Angmartung] there are open rapids with a lot of water. We were easily able to cross the small isthmuses. The lake is about 50′ feet above sea level. In the evening we stopped at some fairly old igloos, put one of them into habitable condition and slept in it. P[ia]rang killed another 2 caribou.

[FB/MK]
(...) Without my having in any way intended it today is also the day on which I was to reach the long-wished-for Lake Kennedy. [Marie and Boas had met in Stuttgart on 1 April 1883 as marked in the Diary.] And the day again appears to be turning out fine. Yes, even here amidst the snow and ice it is spring. The sun is shining so warmly and I can feel the spring in my heart. (...)

Today I am writing to you from the uppermost end of the long fiord that forms the route into the interior, and today I should see the lake. I am really looking forward to it. (...)

[D2]
[**2 April**] **Wednesday**   Nettiling. Kangia{nga}. Since there have been reports of other rock types here, I pushed on for another 2 hours to Iglun [Igdlun], but found only granite. It is not possible to survey this country right now, because one cannot distinguish water and land. Unfortunately, due to lack of food [for the dogs] and blubber for the lamp, I had to turn back again, and reached Kangia in the evening.

[FB/MK]

(...) So finally! Here, almost at my goal, I have to turn back already, just where I had intended actually to begin. (...)

This morning we travelled up to Kangia via a chain of lakes that are separated by narrow strips of land. These water basins are surrounded just by low granite hills with steep cliffs. Before we set off every little scrap of walrus hide, in the shape of thongs on the sledge, was set aside, because the Esk. may not take any such items into caribou country. Soon we saw tracks of a large number; the dogs scented them and set off after them over hill and dale. I stayed up with the dogs and Ssigna killed a large caribou for me. After it had been cut up, we continued and spotted a herd of 7, which Piera and I fired at in vain. We were unable to get close enough to it. There are also several more tracks here. (...)

First we saw a herd of 7, then another of 6 and finally another 3. The second herd came so close that I hoped to get within range, but the dogs broke away with the sledge, and the caribou fled. Fortunately Ssigna managed to grab the sledge, but was unable to stop it. The lead dog broke away, but fortunately came back after 15 minutes. In the evening when Ssigna was trying to chop up the seal meat for the dogs, the axe handle broke, so I was unable to feed them until this morning (the 3rd.) (...)

(D2)

[3 April] Thursday {Kangianga} Kognung. We did not get away until 1 o'clock because the dogs had to be fed in the morning. It was dull, snowy weather and bad going. Since Piara's and my sledge is now very heavy, we made only slow progress. In the evening, when we were at the Kognung polynya, we saw 4 seals, all of which we shot. The dogs immediately ate 2 of them. We built an igloo and slept well.

[4 April] Friday Ssarbakdualuk. Unfortunately it snowed all last night, and also through the day today. As a result we can scarcely make any headway. Especially in Kassigidjen the snow now lies about 3' deep. Although I was walking ahead the dogs could scarcely move the sledge at all. Built an igloo near Ssarbakdualuk.

[5 April] Saturday Ssarbakdualuk. I want to stay here today to shoot seals while Piarang goes home [to Nexemiarbing]. We got only 1 seal[,] which the dogs ate immediately. Today is a very fine day. Tomorrow I want to go south along the coast to Nuvujen. In the evening there is unfortunately thick fog.

[FB/MK]

(...) You ought to see me sitting here right now. Dirty (since I left Kikkerton no water has touched my face or hands, and in any case fuel is too valuable) and burned black by the sun, so that I can scarcely recognize myself. Here I am sitting in an igloo. It is so warm that the air hole in the roof has melted out till it is quite large and through it I can see the beautiful blue sky. (...)

[D2]

[6 April] **Sunday**   Nichemiarbing. Since there was still thick fog in the morning and no prospect of improvement, we headed for Nichemiarbing. Around noon it cleared up and I am very upset that we did not go south. Spent the night at Piarang's.

[FB/MK]

(...) Yesterday evening we experienced thick fog so that we could not even see the land 200 paces away. Since it was still foggy today, I opted to go back via Tudnukutan [Tunukutang]. It was heavy work to haul the sledge across country and through deep snow. (...)

[D2]

[7 April] **Monday**   [K'exerten] Kikkerton. We set off around 7 a.m. and made only slow headway. To top it all, we landed twice more in polynyas, which develop as a result of the tides. If one tries to cross them, the sledge sinks in deeply and can be pulled out only with great difficulty. We did not reach Kikkerton until 11 o'clock; I woke Wilhelm and had him prepare me a meal [FB/MK: .., since I was very hungry].

[8 April] **Tuesday**   Kikkerton. From all the reports I have gathered about the land I have to cross on the way to Padli, the section to Kignait is very bad. Since we can anticipate that what little snow there is will have gone completely by the end of this month, and since Mutch is willing to lend me dogs and a sledge, I shall take everything up and over the rocks in one haul. I think I shall finish packing tomorrow and the day after.

[FB/MK]

(...) Thus, today I was still working out my observations, and had Wilhelm start packing. Mutch is modifying a large sledge for me so I hope to be able to set off on Friday [11 April]. (...)

[D2]
[9 April] Wednesday   Kikkerton. Packing all day.

[ww]
(...) Today we were again packing the boxes that are to go to Padli, while three men were working on the sledge to complete it. J.M. [James Mutch] wanted to lend the Dr. his dogs so that the Dr. can travel with two sledges. We worked today as never before. It was 7 o'clock when J.M. said that the sledge would not be ready. It was reasonably fine weather; I had already got my sleeping bag and everything practically ready. (...)

[D2]
[10 April] Thursday   Kikkerton. Also took the boxes down to the ice in the evening so that there will be no delay in the morning. I offered to trade the small boat [*Marie*] for one of Mutch's sledges, to which he agreed. He is modifying an old one for me to the point that it is quite new.

Second Attempt at Crossing the Kingnait-Padli Pass

[11 April] Friday   Below Niutang. I woke Wilhelm at 5 a.m., called Pudlaujang and Ssigna and was ready to start by 7 a.m. Yesterday evening I asked Fred [Roach's mate], who is here to cook blubber, whether he wanted me to take some letters with me [FB/MK: ..., whether he or somebody on the ship [*Lizzie P. Simmons*] wanted to send any news to Europe,] and asked him whether he wanted rum and alcohol from me. I also asked him for two iron stakes for the sledge on land. Despite the heavy loads we made fairly rapid progress and camped for the night below the second bend in Kignait [FB/MK: .., where we built an igloo]. Unfortunately one of the [whalebone] runners of my sledge was smashed on the rough ice.

This was Weike's first sledge trip since his confinement to the whaling station at the beginning of January. The day before, 10 April, he had loaded the sledges on the ice and gone for a short distance with Inuit, returning the same day. From his entry it is clear that there are discrepancies between his and Boas's recordings of who did what!

[ww]
At 5 o'clock in the morning 27 degrees when I had the fire blazing. Went

out and woke the Eskimos who would come along. At 7.30 a.m. the sledges left Kikkerton [the station] for the ice to be loaded; we had in all 33 dogs and five men for two sledges. On the way one of Herr Dr.'s dogs fell ill; it did not take long and he was better; still we did not let him pull. It was beautiful weather and we got farther fairly rapidly. We stopped and ate some bread and bacon. And then we drove farther into the Kineit [Kingnait]. I was glad when it was 5 p.m. that I could take off my snow goggles; on the land there were a good many black spots, so they were not necessary any more. At 6 we stopped to build an igloo; it was already quarter past midnight when we ate our supper.

[D2]

[12 April] Saturday   Kitingujang. In the morning it was blowing down the fiord a little, but as we travelled farther we ran into a fine example of a Kignait gale. At the head of the fiord the ice is very bad, full of rocks and earth, then elsewhere so smooth that the dogs were unable to make headway into the storm. Fortunately there was at least no drifting snow here, since there was no snow. In the evening we got through the pressure ice safely with all our things and I travelled about another mile up the river with some boxes.

[FB/MK]

(...) Since there was still good snow here I had Ssigna and Kikkertaktuak build an igloo, while Pudlaujang and I went back to fetch the rest of the things. We could not haul everything in one load. (...)

[D2]

As he was fetching it in the evening Wilhelm ripped the bread bag and everything was scattered along the trail. We will have to go to retrieve the bread tomorrow morning.

[13 April] Sunday (Easter)   Kitingujang. A terrible storm, against which it is impossible to travel. So we simply fed the dogs, brought all the boxes up the mile [from the shore] and collected the bread.

[FB/MK]

(...) Steep cliffs but – ugh! I had no luck [Boas sketched them in his diary]; my hands were cold, the snow was drifting[,] the wind was howling, the dogs were raising a terrible uproar. As you can see from the sketch Ssigna was tenderizing blubber and all I want to do is crawl through the black hole of the igloo, where it is better than out there. Then, inside I can chat with you, *uman*! [I. *uumma* = heart; for Boas meaning figuratively 'my heart, my love'] (...)

[D2]
[14 April] Monday   Kitingujang. The gale is still blowing but it is somewhat milder than yesterday. We hauled our things farther and with the help of the bearskin we got across the bad spots on the trail safely, though they were rather rocky. Up on top we twice had to unload and carry everything across; this was a tough job. Ssigna insists that we have passed all the bad spots, so the country is not as bad as all reports have indicated.

[FB/MK]
(...) This morning I sent Kikkertaktuak back to Kikkerton. (...) (The trail crosses a small river and 2 ponds.) Tomorrow I want to return to Kikkerton. (...)

[D2]
[15 April] Tuesday   Kachzak [K'arsax]. Favoured by the wind we made fairly rapid progress. After a few hours we met Robby, who had left Kikkerton with Iwi a week before. I had thought he would have been in Padli long since. Soon we also came upon Iwi's igloo. I went up and gave him some tobacco, coffee and bread. He wants to stay here today because the travelling is too bad. Behind Neivan [Naivaun] the wind left us. I did not want to stop at Iwi's old igloo above Kachzak, but continued on, so as to be close to Kikkerton tomorrow. Slept on the ice.

[16 April] Wednesday   [K'exerten] Kikkerton. Ssigna went around Kikkertaktuak to hunt young seals. We continued on and reached Kikkerton around noon. One of Mutch's dogs came from Kignait crazy [FB/MK: .. and died]; I just hope mine are spared!

[17 April] Thursday   Kikkerton. Poured bullets and prepared other items for the journey home.

Trip to the West Coast of Tinixdjuarbing: Tarrionitung

[18 April] Friday   Imigen. Probably my last trip in the Gulf. Off Haystack

[Umanax] a wide crack had formed and we crossed it only with great difficulty. [Boas was accompanied by Ssigna; Weike stayed at the station.]

[FB/MK]
(...) I want to survey the large Kaggiluktung Fiord and the south shore of the nameless water body as far as Nichemiarbing. If time and weather permit I should also like to go to Naujateling, but I am afraid that this will be impossible because, come what may, I want to set off on about 1 May. (...)

[D2]
[**19 April**] **Saturday**   Tulannirtu [Tarrionitung]. In the morning we headed north inside Imigen, although the weather was thick and it was snowing. The snow was about 2' deep and the going very bad. Thus we were happy to reach Tulannirtu around 4. Built an igloo and unharnessed the dogs. I hope it will soon clear up. In this weather my plans for Kaggiluktung will probably not materialize. We continued heading south, but since the weather was quite thick and Ssigna could not find the polynya, we had to turn back.

[**20 April**] **Sunday**   Tulannirtu. I hope to reach at least Anarnitung today [FB/MK: .., to fetch my dogs,] but even in this I was disappointed. The farther north we went the worse the snow became. I soon had to unload everything from the sledge in order to make any progress at all. The new polynya at Ikeressakdjuak deceived us. The ice was so bad that we could not get to the edge of the water. In the evening it again began to blow strongly out of the south and to snow.

[**21 April**] **Monday**   Imigen. The storm continued, but around 7 o'clock the wind dropped; however it had not improved the snow because even more had fallen. With the heavy going it took us 4 hours to reach Imigen (normally 1.5 hours). We had scarcely arrived here when the blizzard began again. We fed the dogs.

[**22 April**] **Tuesday**   Imigen. A heavy fall of snow and again another terrible blizzard, though one hopes it will ultimately improve the going. Sat in Ikera's igloo all day and in the afternoon fed the dogs in John Penny's [Ussukang's] old igloo.

[FB/MK]
(...) The time is now flying by too fast, and because of many misadven-

tures, lack of dogs and bad weather[,] I have not finished my work here, but at least I am conscious that I have done what I could. In the last 2 months I have slept in a bed for only about 7 nights; and otherwise I have never undressed! (...)

Not much longer! It would be terrible if I had to stay here for another year, abundantly supplied with provisions, certainly, but without any possibility of travelling, because my trade goods would be exhausted. No, I cannot think about it; it is too improbable. Why should there not be ship over there this year, when normally 7–8 ships come every year. But only 1 American ship. I hope that they all come together and I can get aboard it. (...)

Now we cannot sit on the sledge as we did earlier but have to walk the whole time, because the snow is too deep; as a result I am more tired in the evening than I was earlier. Even then, I have scarcely been driving the dogs at all [done mainly by Ssigna], a task that is now unbelievably strenuous! (...)

[D2]
[23 April] Wednesday   [K'exerten] Kikkerton. The snow is really hard and we drove to Kikkerton in clear weather. Ssigna had become snow-blind so I had to drive. The old crack [at Umanax on 18 April] had closed. We reached the station fairly early.

[24 April] Thursday   Kikkerton. The dogs ate and rested. Tomorrow Wilhelm is to go with Ssigna to Nuvujen [FB/MK: .. and Nichemiarbing] to buy young sealskins that I need. I will go myself only if the weather is very good [FB/MK: .., although I cannot tell you how fed up I am of travelling here.]. It is snowing almost constantly. Packed.

[25 April] Friday   Kikkerton. A raging storm out of Kignait. My big chest is packed ready. I wonder whether the weather will be better after this storm.

In Diary 2 there are no entries between Saturday, 26 April, and Monday, 5 May, inclusive.

[WW]
Today [probably 26 April] the Dr. travelled to Tinitschua [Tinixdjuax] for dog food and skins. The weather was not exceptional, though it did clear up a little; immediately afterwards snow began falling again and the wind

swung from one side to the other. Today I finished packing the large chest and nailed up other boxes so as to be able to put them out of the way; I have also packed the photographic things; in the evening I visited the cooper [Rasmussen].

The Last Trip on the Ice of Tinixdjuarbing: Nuvujen

[FB/MK]

26th [April, Sunday]   Nuvujen. Now I have made a trip on my own. I wanted to at least not have to reproach myself later that I had not done everything I could to complete the map of the Sound. But I can say that I have not approached any trip more reluctantly than this one. The continual bad weather of the past month and the slow going across the ice have often driven me to desperation. Even today was a foul day. We had barely left Kikkerton when it became so thick that we could hardly see the dogs ahead of the sledge. The trail across the Sound was no longer visible so we had to steer by compass. But Ssigna told me that a crack ran right across to Nuvujen; we went to look for it and lost our way; as a result we reached the other side about 4 nautical miles too far south. Around 6 it cleared up; we could see Nuvujen and could steer straight for it. (...)

27th [April, Sunday]   This morning I heard the pleasant news that Hannibal Jack [Innuakjung] who wants to go with me to Padli and whom I now want to pick up has departed from Nichemiarbing with all the other Eskimos. Nobody knows where to. So we quickly had to set off in search of them. First of all this morning I bought 2 young seals and 2 adult seals. Since it was extremely thick weather, this trip too has been fruitless. I was able to fix only one reef about 8 miles from Nuvujen. Here, unfortunately, the snow was very soft and because of our heavy loads it was impossible to make any progress. Around 7 o'clock we reached a large iceberg near Nichemiarbing where we expected to find the igloos; but in this we were disappointed so we had to camp on the ice since the driving had been too tough to expect Ssigna to build an igloo as well. Hence we had to content ourselves with a small piece of dry bread; I had forgotten to take bacon with me.

28th [April, Monday].   Today there was thick fog again. We travelled around searching all day, but did not find an igloo. Off Nichemiarbing almost all the ice had disappeared so it is no wonder that they [Inuit] have left the island. There was a large number of seals lying on the ice, but we didn't have a rifle to shoot them with. This evening we built an igloo in order to at least be able to cook something; since yesterday we have eaten only some bread and unfortunately we oversalted our soup so much that it was inedible even for my hungry stomach.

[WW]
(...) This morning I went out early, since they had begun making preparations at J.M.'s [James Mutch's] for going to Warham's Island; they were making the boat ready; he had 13 Eskimos at work. In the afternoon I was still down at the harbour and finished it. In the evening [29 April] the Dr. also arrived; another three sledges were made ready, which were to come down here [onto the ice].

[FB/MK]
29th [April, Tuesday]   Today I headed back without having found Hannibal Jack, but there is nothing I can do about it. Of course all the fog has disappeared now and we will at least find Kikkerton. (...)

[WW]
(...) This morning three sledges travelled to Warham's Island[,] the others [Inuit] were here working again. We have packed; in the afternoon it began snowing again; after work the men went outside to play ball. At 8 in the evening it was only –11°; a trifle at the end of April.

K'exerten: Preparations for the Trip to Davis Strait

[WW]
30 April [Wednesday]   It was not very clear today; the Dr. sent two Eskimos with one sledge and dog food to Kineit [Kingnait]. In the morning I finished packing the large chest; afterwards I had to clean the steel tape. The Dr. took photos today. Towards evening I soldered up the large chest.

[FB/parents; this letter, a summary of Boas's winter activities (and also his inner feelings), reached his parents in Minden, courtesy of James Mutch, via Dundee, in November 1884.]
Kikkerton, 30th April 1884. Dear parents! The time has now come that I am leaving Kikkerton in order to head homeward. You can't imagine how

my heart is beating when I think that in a few months I shall hear from you again, that in barely six months I shall be back, whether I land in St. John's or Dundee. A long, work-filled winter lies behind me since I dispatched my last letter to you [on 3 October 1883].

Happy days, when I could see that my work was making good progress; anxious times when I could see no prospect of doing anything or of finding my way to Davis Strait, from where I am to return home because probably no ship will come here. Yes, it is a long, long separation but it has not lessened my love for you. I feel more warmly than ever the love which you, dear parents and sisters[,] cherish for me when I still hope I shall find the only American ship that visits Davis Strait so that I can hasten aboard it to my Marie, and then return to you. You know how much I love her and how I long to see her for the *first* time since she became my Marie.

I hope that kind fate, which has protected me this winter through all the perils and adventures, has also watched over all those whom I love, and that I will be able to greet you happily and without any painful feelings. Yes, dear loved ones, I shall be coming back just like the old Franz. All disappointments, all the serious worries of this, the most anxious year of my life, have not bowed my courage, or dampened my cheerfulness. I can see a beautiful life lying ahead of me, full of tasks that are worthy of applying all my strength to. I can see myself striving steadfastly, with Marie at my side, towards my goal, which I have identified, and finding satisfaction in working towards it, whether I am successful or not.

Yes, whoever freely wants to ride out the trivia of life and who wants to see that happiness will be found by working and striving, independently of those trivia, should go out into solitude and work under conditions that we at home would think intolerable and will see how even these miserable people [the Inuit] can live happily and cheerfully here! None of the hopes with which I came here have been fulfilled, for fate has not favoured me much.

I arrived just when many dogs had died from an illness that has flared up now here now there, for a long time; these dogs represent the only mode of travel. But it was precisely during this past winter that it raged especially virulently, so that at the time when I was able to start on my major trip, absolutely no dogs were to be had, and I could not stir from the spot; I even had doubts that I would be able to reach Davis Strait. Then a sledge arrived here from the northern part of Davis Strait and I went back with it on an arduous trip to buy dogs [in Saumia]. I came back with 10, and these I soon augmented to a full team by a further 5. Thus I was at least able to reach the long-wished-for lake (Lake Kennedy).

During the past month I was unable to do anything more although I was constantly travelling, since the snow was too deep and the weather was constantly bad. Thus my work was confined to surveying the eastern shore of Cumberland Sound, part of Davis Strait [along the coast of Saumia] and the fiord [Nettilling] leading to Lake Kennedy, as well as a small part of that lake. On the trip on which I am now embarking I shall probably survey another long stretch of the Davis Strait coast. My work on the Eskimos has given me more satisfaction than my trips. I have a fine collection of their traditions and songs and precise information on their migrations.

Now I am heading east. My boxes and maps have already gone and in 5 days I shall follow. I hope to reach the most northerly camp in 8–10 days; by then I shall have overcome all serious difficulties. I shall probably occupy a station at about 69° N. latitude [at K'ivitung], then I shall go north from there to encounter the ships as early as possible. I am longing so much for news! I shall leave this letter here to let you know that if I miss the ships, which is very probable, and a ship should call here, that I am well and happy. The same applies to Wilhelm. On our very first trip in December he froze his big toes and has had to sit in the house all winter, while I have been constantly on the move.

Spring is arriving here too. The sun is starting to melt the snow on the land, so in about 2 weeks there will probably be nothing but water. The temperature in the shade is now about −10 to 12° Réaumur [−12.5 to −15°C], yet we feel very warm and at times the heat of the sun is unbearable. The very cold winter has altered our level of sensitivity. The lowest temperature was −40° Réaumur [−48°C], but I easily tolerated it.

I hope that this letter will land in your hands long after I am safely back. May it reach us all, in the joyous, happy awareness that we are united in civilized countries. I have sampled enough solitude that I now long for people, real people! What shall I tell you now to describe my life at this spot for you; it has no sense, yet one thought surfaces above all others: never was my love and friendship for you all greater than now, and the time when I will see you all again appears to me as a golden, rosy future. Right now my thoughts barely extend beyond the present moment!

To the best of my abilities I have held at bay all thought of what possibly may have been happening at home, and have retained images of all my beloved, just as I left them[,] and I hope that you also have always been following me valiantly! And if ill luck should dictate that this letter should reach home this year while I have to remain sitting here, do not despair. I am supplied with sufficient provisions for a further year and just as I have remained healthy thus far, I will survive the second year hale and hearty too and certainly will not let my courage sink in despondence. But this situation is so improbable that the possibility can scarcely be contemplated.

Let us look confidently to the future; the will to pursue what I have undertaken to a successful conclusion will also make it a reality.

Till we meet again, happy and safe! – as always, with love and friendship, your son and brother, Franz.

Boas made no entry in any of his journals from 1 to 4 May.

[ww]
1 May [Thursday]   May has begun very fine; it was fairly good weather, and even warm. In the morning J.M.'s [James Mutch's] sledges came back. We have been continually packing things in order to get our boxes ready. In the evening the cooper was here and we had a little farewell celebration.

2 May [Friday]   The weather was very fine again today. The natives had to make ready the things for dressing skins today. In the evening the boats were loaded on sledges. Captain Rosch [Roach] also came.

3 May [Saturday] Ascension Day   [*sic.* It fell on 22 May in 1884.] It was very fine weather today; very warm. We are making quite good progress in getting our things organized; there is only one chest left to pack. In the afternoon I was cleaning. Towards evening the sledge came back from Kinneit [Kingnait]; the dogs looked so miserable; they had not had enough food. It was 10 o'clock before we came into the house and by then the curs were fed.

4 May [Sunday]   This morning at 5 Captain Rosch came to say goodbye, since he wanted to go back to Neuantilik [Naujatelling]; we had a Kignait wind although it was not very strong. Around noon we had a south wind with heavy snow which lasted all afternoon. The water was running off the house, it was so warm.

5 May [Monday]   Today there was still a lot to do to get our things together, since we wanted to set off on the 6th, weather permitting. Herr Dr. had invited the cooper for the evening. All day long the natives came running with all sorts of things to sell to the Dr. Towards evening we took the chests over to the storehouse.

[FB/MK]

(...) Now many days have passed without my writing anything. On the 30th [April] I had recovered somewhat from the rough living on this the most miserable of all trips and now all the remaining work of packing will quickly be completed.

On 1st May I sent my dogs with 7 seals up to the head of Kingnait so that I would have a food cache there. It was not until four days later that the two Eskimos who hauled them came back; in the process they had let the poor dogs starve so miserably that I now have to stay here for another 2 days. (...)

Overland to Davis Strait: From Kingnait to Padli, May 1884

From 6 May until 5 June, Boas continued the Diary in the original. There is a transcription for this period in Diary 2; the place names that he recorded only there are included here in brackets following the date.

[D2]

[6 May] Tuesday   [Kachzak] Set off from Kikkerton with 2 sledges, J.M. [James Mutch] and the cooper escorted me out onto the ice. Then we set off with Appak in the lead. The thick fog cleared just at the moment we set off, but soon enveloped everything again. We tried hunting seals but got nothing. In the evening we halted off Kachzak and erected a tupik on the ice.

[WW]

This morning we got up around 4.30. The natives were wakened then. J.M. and his men went down to the water today with the boats to go whaling. It was around 9 o'clock when we left the station. J.M. and the cooper escorted us as far as the harbour; we had flags flying from our sledge; the snow was soft so that we made only slow progress. We were travelling with two sledges; one was driven by little Appak; Singna's Batti [Betty, Ssigna's wife][,] the other by the Dr. and me; this was the entire party [plus Ssigna]. We had 25 dogs in total.

It cleared around noon and then it became so hot that we took off our kolitans [fur coats] and sat on the sledge just in our shirts. At the southern tip of the large island [K'exertukdjuax] I had to hunt for kumans [I. *kumak* = louse] in the Dr.'s shirt for the first time. There were quite a number of seals on the ice, but the dogs raised such a racket that we were unable to get close to them. In Selungenut [near K'arsax?] we made a halt at the same iceberg where we slept on the previous occasion [15 April]; it was the first time since last fall that we used our tupik, because one could no longer build an igloo.

[D]

[**7 May**] **Wednesday**   [Kachzak] While Appak and Ssigna hunted seals, I made various observations. Today is a superb day. Warm sunshine and innumerable seals on the ice. But they are so wary that we got only an old seal, which Ssigna killed just as we came back to Kignait. Appak and Wilhelm at the same time brought some boxes ahead.

[**8 May**] **Thursday**   [Niutang] Set off between 6 and 7 a.m. and travelled slowly on while hunting. It was again very fine and clear. I obtained good observations. By the evening we were at Niutang, where the old settlement and the kaggi [I. *qagi* = singing house] are located, which I could now take a look at. They are built of round boulders, not of flat stones like the other kagmangs [D2: *kaggis*].

[FB/MK]

(...)I really must take care now not to lose any days when we are outside every day and there is no fixed schedule. Indeed this is the only way of keeping my journal with the utmost regularity. So far we have had the most magnificent weather; the sky is blue, the sun is shining warmly and one can hear the water roaring down from every rock face; even the snow on the ice is beginning to melt from the sun or at least is becoming soft.

I drove the team all day without wearing my sealskin jacket. Simply a woollen shirt sufficed to keep me completely warm. We made only slow progress because I wanted to hunt seals at the same time; but two very young seals were all that we managed to pick up. The seals lying on the ice always take alarm, so that they always dived when a hunter approached. We got up this morning between 4 and 5 and by 6.15 had finished loading the sledges. We now glimpsed Kikkerton from a great distance for the last time, and the bulky island of Kikkertuktjuak for the last time, which I have also sketched for you, and now we are near the head of Kignait.

Here there is a deep valley, in which there was a large settlement earlier; one can still see the remains of the huts in which, according to tradition, long ago Tudniks and Eskimos lived together until the former were driven out. Many other traditions and myths are linked to this spot, concerning the singing house in which the old Eskimos celebrated festivals and the quarrel with the Eskimos of the west shore of the Sound and battles between themselves. Opposite it lies a rock named Kaminguang [Kamingujang]; i.e. something resembling a boot. This is a vein of light-coloured granite in the steep cliff of the northeast shore of Kignait; at its foot there is a talus cone that is pierced through a side crack into the other trough. (...)

I have [just] been interrupted because supper is ready, a young seal which Appak shot today and which tasted excellent. (...)

[D2]
[9 May] Friday   [Above Kitingujang] Today we were travelling uphill inland; I left Appak behind hunting, but he got nothing, whereas Ssigna shot a small seal. When we reached the fast ice, it was almost high tide so the trail was deeply flooded. However I soon found an alternate route. Here we met Tyson with his wife and son. He still has some things at Tessikdjua [Tessixdjuak], which he now plans to fetch and he described the going as much worse than in winter.

[FB/MK]
(...) They helped us up the steep spots and I gave them supper as a reward. (...)

[D]
[10 May] Saturday   [At the same place] [Kitingujang]. Except for the seals yesterday everything was at the site where the chests that had arrived earlier were standing. This morning Appak and I brought chests across the first bad stretch [on the steel sledge] while Ssigna and Wilhelm held onto [D2: .. and fed] my dogs then followed with the remainder [seals]. Once they were past the first bad stretch, Appak and I again hauled the things onward. In the evening we slept, very tired, at the same site.

[FB/MK]
(...) Last night we had snow and now it is blowing violently out of Kignait, but despite this the snow is melting very quickly; where there was good going this morning, there is now nothing but water. (...)

[D]
[11 May] Sunday   [Torngnatelling (Tornatelling)]. After we had taken the tupiks down, we began bringing the large sledge up over the rocks. It was heavy work, and it was not until towards evening that we got every-

thing across. Then we loaded the small sledge with everything required for the night and reached the spot to which Appak and I had hauled the chests yesterday, around 9 p.m. Supper at 11 o'clock. I had to leave some boxes here and thus began unpacking bread and repacking other things.

[**12 May**] **Monday** [Torngnatelling] Today we simply hauled the remainder of the boxes here. As we began to push on, Ssigna and Appak took a wrong route which led through a narrow valley over massive boulders, and they got no farther today. I was still packing and they called for me to come and search for the route with them. From the summit of a hill that lies in the middle of the valley, I found the old tracks, which led along over the east slope of the hill.

[**13 May**] **Tuesday**   [Near Kikkertelling (K'exertelling)] Yesterday it was too late to go any farther; so we fed the dogs and this morning we set off early. We made barely 2 miles of progress all day along this steep, narrow route, but now we have reached a fairly large pond, so hope that tomorrow we can make progress across it. We were travelling from 8 a.m. to 2.30 a.m.

[ww]
This morning we began to haul the stuff over the mountains. Hr. Dr. had packed things in such a way that a large part of our stuff could stay behind because we did not know if we could transport it. This was strenuous work and we could hardly notice that we got ahead. For each time we had the stuff on the sledges, we had to carry it three times as far. Except for a few boxes we got the stuff to Kikerteluk [K'exertelling], where we stopped and prepared supper. When I called for supper, the Dr. asked me what time it was; it was quarter past one a.m. Since there is no night any more, one does not know what the time is; and we move constantly, again two boxes had to be prepared to stay behind.

[D]
[**14 May**] **Wednesday**   [Tessikdjua] At 8 a.m. we began bringing up the sledges. Then we repacked them once again and left two boxes behind. Thus I now have only the *absolute* essentials with me. The three strips of land that we crossed today made for easy travelling; however at the first Kitinguasirn [Kitingujausirn], a narrow canyon, the route was so narrow that we had to unload the entire sledge to get across the rocks. [D2: But this took us barely an hour.] Afterwards we kept searching for another

hour. At 7 o'clock I spotted Tessikdjua, and we travelled halfway across it.

Boas recovered the contents of the two boxes (which also included items owned by the German Polar Commission) through the help of James Mutch, who retrieved them and brought them to Peterhead, Scotland, in November 1885. From there they were forwarded to the Deutsche Seewarte *in Hamburg, Germany.*

[**15 May**] **Thursday**   [Tessikdjua – Ssinimiutang (Simiutang)] Last night we slept safely on Tessikdjua. From there we made rapid progress because the going was very good. Towards evening Appak saw 2 caribou. We all went hunting, but were unable to get close to them because they ran off. Appak went after them on his own and killed one. As we continued with the sledge, we met a herd of 8, with the dogs again racing like mad after them; they had probably run back most of the way after the animals like this. Since it was so late, I stopped for the night.

[**16 May**] **Friday**   [Below Ssinimiutang] Broke camp around 10 a.m. For a short stretch the route lay along the riverbed and was very rocky; later there was only thin ice on top of the water, through which the sledges frequently broke, so that for half the day we were standing in water pushing the sledges. In the evening my dogs again scented caribou. We drove the sledge straight into the rocks and Ssigna and I went hunting. We soon saw 5 caribou, of which we killed 3. I killed my first animal. Thank God, I now have enough dog food. Appak went hunting alone and shot one caribou; a second wounded animal escaped.

[**17 May**] **Saturday**   [Same location (Simiutang)] Rested and washed. It is windy and sunny, so it is possible to at least dry some things. I was involved with this until the afternoon then I read and wrote a little. Ssigna and Appak were out hunting [D2: .., but killed nothing]. We are now only a few miles from salt water and the going is fairly good. I hope to reach the settlement [Oxilejung] in a few days. 66°47′N. lat.

[FB/MK]
(...) Thank God that these days are behind us. We are now quite close to Davis Strait, and I have brought with me what I absolutely essentially need. But what days those were, Marie! From morning till late in the evening we had to sweat and toil to make any progress at all. Even on the second day I realized that it was impossible to continue travelling with all

my boxes and therefore packed up what I *had* to have, but even this I had
to cull once again because the going was too bad. Now I am obliged to
head north as fast as I can in order to make contact with the ships as soon
as possible.

You can't imagine how relieved I feel to be here now. I have now overcome the worst and in 8–10 weeks I shall hear from you again. Can you
imagine how happy I feel to be able to count just weeks? I hope that in
this short time I shall still achieve a lot.

I am quite satisfied when I cover a daily average of 12 miles (nautical
miles); at this rate I shall comfortably reach my goal. Occasionally I am
now very impatient to hear from the ship, but this is not often! This long
trip has taught me patience. (...)

[D]

[**18 May**] **Sunday**   [Ochilejung (Oxilejung)] Set off around 9 a.m. At
Kangianga, which we reached at 11.30[,] we met Iwi, who was in the process of coming with his sledge and his son to help me. Now he turned
round and we reached the camp at 5 in the afternoon. 6 men had arrived
there with 3 sledges; they were all in the act of heading inland to help me.
We pitched the tupik and made it very comfortable.

Along the East Coast of Baffin Island: Survey Trips on the Sea Ice, May–July 1884

From Padli to Padloping

[D]

[**19 May**] **Monday** [Ochilejung] Since Piukkia [woman], whom Appak wanted to see[,] is in Kivitung [K'ivitung], the latter and Ssigna want to start back from here. I sent Wilhelm and 2 Eskimos [Appak and Ssigna] inland with one sledge to fetch a few more things [from Tessixdjuak]. In the meantime I want to push on and take a look at some of the land to the south. I hope that they will reach the area to which I will be travelling tomorrow by Sunday [May 25]. Among others the Kikkerton Inuk Shanguja [who accompanied Boas north] is also here. Thus, in contrast to my expectations I obtained *abundant* provisions here.

[**20 May**] **Tuesday** Ochilejung. Padlobing [Padloping]. [D2: Padloping]. Wilhelm and the rest of the group went for the things while Iwi and I, each with a sledge, travelled to Shanguja's place. The farther we went the worse the snow became. Finally I could no longer move with my heavily laden sledge[,] but just as I unloaded [D2: 2 boxes] Shanguja (Padli) [D2: .. who was going seal hunting] arrived and took part of my things [D2: .. my boxes] from me, and thus I reached his place with everything fairly quickly.

[WW]

(...) Today we split into two parties. The Dr. headed on with two sledges while I headed back with 1 sledge to Kineit [Kingnait] to fetch things. Singnar [Ssigna] and Apak [Appak] also travelled back with me to Kineit while two sledges from the island [Oxilejung] were going to hunt caribou. It was very hot today. As we travelled farther from the head of the salt water, we encountered a strong wind; right at the head everything was covered with water and the snow had all melted so that we had great difficulty in making any progress. I went to the site where we had last slept [Simiutang]; in the meantime the natives had cut up Appak's caribou and had harnessed all the dogs to Singnar's sledge.

When I saw that they did not want to take their sledges, I told them I wanted to go back. Then the dogs were harnessed in anticipation and our things were brought back again; once we had loaded everything we headed back. The two sledges that were hunting caribou also headed back with us. Towards evening it began freezing again and the snow hardened. It was 10.45 p.m. when I reached the camp [Oxilejung] from which I had started; I wanted to travel through the night, to join the Dr. next morning, but the natives refused because they had not slept the night before since they had been hunting; I pitched my tubik [= tent] and brewed coffee; it was after midnight by the time it was ready.

[D]

[**21 May**] **Wednesday**   [Padloping] Fed the dogs in the morning. Kunnorsirn [woman], who is living here now, washed my pants and repaired Wilhelm's stockings. In the afternoon I was sleeping outside, because I wanted to leave in the evening when Iwi [D2: .. Shanguja's mother] woke me with the news that 2 sledges were coming. It was Wilhelm and the Eskimos, who had been unable to get to Kignait because there was too much water [D2: .. in the river] there. Appak had even caught a salmon already. Since it began snowing and storming in the evening, we are staying here.

[WW]

(...) At a little after 4 o'clock I got up again and got ready to push on, but I could not drag the natives out; I had already drunk some coffee but they still didn't want to come out; they got up at 7 and took the tubik and everything with them. They had arrived there only shortly before we reached the island; they lived at the camp [Padloping] where the Dr. is now. The natives said it was so close, but we drove hard all morning but it was still after 3 in the afternoon before we reached the camp. Fortunately the Dr. had not left for Ekzeter [Exeter Bay/K'armaxdjuin][,] which is located on Döver Island [Durban Island/Aggidjen] at 67°3'.

[D]

[**22 May**] **Thursday**   [Padloping] In the morning there was still a gale blowing; but it soon calmed down and I went with my sledge to Kangi-chukluak [D2: Kangirtsukdjuak (Kangertlukdjuax)]. But I did not get very far since I sank belly-deep in the snow and was very happy to finally crawl out of the hole again.

[**23 May**] **Friday**   [Padloping] Snow-blind so I am staying at home and can do nothing. Somewhat better in the evening. Severe blizzard in the evening.

[ww]
First I wanted to drive today, but I did not like the weather. The Dr. was snow-blind today; my eyes were also sore, that's why I did not want to go out. I went with Shanguja to feed the dogs and afterwards I stayed at home. The natives collected berries the whole day, so we ate them constantly. Towards evening it began to snow. (...)

[D]
[**24 May**] **Saturday**   [Padloping.] Since my eyes are slightly better[,] I again started out for Durban Harbour [Exaloaping] and surveyed part of the coast there. 2 dogs ran away, but turned up again during my absence. In the evening I arranged with Shanguja that he would go with me to the next camp. It is still abominably cold, unfriendly weather [D2: .. and abominable mauja [I. *maujaq* = soft snow].

[**25 May**] **Sunday**   [Padloping] Since it is very foggy and since my eyes are still very painful, I am not travelling. I have spent the day mainly writing and doing other small tasks. We have been making new lids [D2: .. with screws] for the boxes because they had split badly due to the nails.

[FB/MK]
(...) The Eskimos here tell me that the *Wolve* [*Wolf*] is the only American ship that comes here, but is always the first; how delighted I shall be when I see her funnel smoking! (...)

It is now already full spring or even summer with you. Here too we can again hear the clear calls of the gulls; on the land the snow is melting and even on the ice it is starting to settle; this is good since here one sinks hip-deep in the soft snow. But the sledge still glides across the top, because it is the surface that is melting. I hope to be at the next camp [K'exertak-djuin] in 3 or 4 days; I shall probably stay there a week, then continue on north. The next place thereafter is the harbour [K'ivitung] at which the ships call. (...)

[ww]
First I had to fix the boxes. Since we have to open them every day, their lids had got totally out of shape. When I was finished I had a thorough scrubbing and a haircut. After supper I went hunting, when I returned I had to cook again. We waited for the natives returning from their hunt because we wanted to feed the dogs. It was already 22.30 when I left by sledge, one of the natives came along, we returned by 2 a.m.

[D2]
[**26 May**] **Monday** [Padloping] Very bad weather; lazing around at home. Snow and a strong north wind; a very distinct water sky. We cannot light a fire.

[**27 May**] **Tuesday** [Padloping] Weather approximately the same, and thus *still* not travelling. But it is clearer today, with no snow. If only it would finally get better! But the wind is no longer packing the snow firmly, since it has already melted too much on the surface. But I shall not travel until the weather is better.

Between 28 May and 5 June, Boas recorded in the Diary the entries from 1883 and 1884 together under the same date (see May and June 1883). In Diary 2 there are no entries for 1883; from 27 May 1884 onward, it contains original entries written in pencil.

[**28 May**] **Wednesday** [Padloping] Atrocious weather! So we are not travelling. Shanguja's two-week-old child died suddenly last night. In the afternoon I sketched and wrote. This is the anniversary of our engagement; drank a bottle of punch.

[D2]
Drank a bottle of punch to celebrate the day.

[ww]
(...) Each time I went for an outing, the dogs came along. Once Pilulak came running with my big knife [in his mouth]. When I got him, I gave him a thrashing and then let him go. In the evening, we had a holiday with a bottle of punch.

See Boas's entry in the Diary for 28 May 1883, when he received the letter from Marie Krackowizer in Minden in which she accepted his proposal of marriage. To commemorate the day, he wrote her a letter in which he reflected on the past year.

[FB/MK]
(...) Occasionally I look back over what I have achieved in order to contemplate it through the eyes of my expert colleagues, and without boasting I find that it is a respectable achievement, which deserves to be recognized. I have told you often enough what I think of it myself, i.e. that above all I respect the reputation of an explorer of strange parts of the world very little; one is nothing more than a drudge! But where there is a field that is worthy of a man's work, I know how to help myself whenever I am successfully or unsuccessfully striving to attain my ideals. (...)

My work is now just child's play compared to the winter; as soon as the warm sun eventually reappears it will become as warm as if we were at home. Now I still have to survey 3 fiords before I travel to the harbour [K'ivitung] at which the ships call.

Northward: From Padloping to Tunirn

[D]
[**29 May**] **Thursday** [Padloping] Very fine weather so we set off in the morning: Shanguja, Sirinirn and ourselves. In addition Akotu and Bob came with us to hunt. We passed high, steep Kachodlui [Kaxodluin] and crossed the fiord [no place-name given] which still displayed rough ice and deep snow, to the site where Tyson's igloo [D2: tupik] had stood earlier. It was not an interesting route, but at least I now know where I can find myself on the map. (After sun rose above the fog [D2: .. written at 1] [a.m.]).

[**30 May**] **Friday** [Kikkertakdjuin (K'exertakdjuin)] Set off around 11 a.m. Near Kikkertakdjuin we met Tauto, who [D2: .. now] is travelling to Padli. When we were about 2 hours from Kikkertakdjuin, it became impenetrably thick, so we could see nothing. I was afraid that Sirinirn, who had gone for a seal[,] had lost his way, but he turned up around 9.30. We had arrived at 9 [D2: ..8.30]. Today 2 men arrived here (Kikkertakdjuin) from Kivitung. We pitched a tupik and slept very well [D2: .. excellently].

[**31 May**] **Saturday** [Kikkertakdjuin] In the morning Sirinirn and Shanguja started back. While they were still here, another sledge arrived from Kivitung. The latter told us that the people at {Kivitung} Cape Kater [Kouktelling] had half-starved over the winter, because the ice had not formed until very late. They had killed [D2: .. slaughtered] their dogs and eaten the frozen meat. Now there are only 6 dogs left there. In the evening Robby also arrived from Kivitung. Nachojassi and Tyson are here now. It snowed in the afternoon.

In the evening Tyson and I fed the dogs. It was clear and fine again later. Unfortunately I was still unable to determine any latitude. Spent the day drafting my map [D2: .. and writing and] working up data just like yesterday and the day before.

[**1 June**] **Sunday. Whit** [Kekertakdjuin (K'exertakdjuin)] Harnessed the dogs in the morning and went for a little drive; what was to have been a short trip became a fairly protracted journey [D2: .. since I got into deep snow and thus made only slow progress], so I did not get home until 9 o'clock. Surveyed Kokiirbing [K'orxirbing] and another island, as well as Angiuk. [Weike stayed behind in the camp because he was snow-blind.]

[**2 June**] **Monday** [Kekertakdjuin] Snow-blind, so stayed at home. In the evening I climbed to the top of the island to take a look around.

[**3 June**] **Tuesday** Pushed on in the morning. Overcast sky and cold, hence good going; I must be about 40 miles from Kikkertalukdjuak [K'exertalukdjuax]. In the meantime Pegbing [one of the dogs] began to have pups; there were 9 of them by Wednesday morning, 4 of which were dead. A snowstorm in the afternoon.

[**4 June**] **Wednesday** Stayed home; have lent Tyson my rifle to hunt seals; there have been very few seals here in the past few days. At noon the natives went hunting since it was fine; I stayed to write and draft. My eyes are badly affected. In the evening Shanguja arrived, but he wants to push on tomorrow to Kikkertukdjuak [K'exertuxdjuax]. Tyson got 4 seals.

[**5 June**] **Thursday** [Kikkertukdjuak] In the morning Shanguja set off, while I first fed the dogs. Tyson [Nappikang], Salmon, Wilhelm and I then set off with 2 sledges and arrived here after 3 hours. A very beautiful campsite.

[D2]

.. (very pleasant after that vile Kikkertakdjuin.) In the evening I shot a tern. Ssangdloping who has also arrived here also brought in 2 ptarmigan. Snow and a strong south wind. If the weather is tolerable we want to go to Maktartudjennak [Maktartudjennax] tomorrow.

The entries for 1884 end here in the Diary. From 6 to 20 June, entries in the Diary also appear for 1883; see the text for 1883. The journal for 1884 is continued in Diary 2.

[FB/MK]

(...) Dear Marie, please don't be angry with me for writing for you so irregularly. I really cannot help it since I am almost constantly snow-blind and dead tired from travelling. I always drive my dogs myself now and when I have been travelling for 10 hours in soft, deep snow, I am more than happy when I have put my notes in order and can go to sleep. I am now only 2 or 3 days' travel from the harbour at which the ships call. (...)

Today I travelled here in very bad weather and am afraid of being held up here for longer than I would like, since it is now blowing violently out of the south. From here I want to travel with Wilhelm for 3 days to survey an area of land, then proceed quickly to Kivitung and from there to Cape Kater [Kouktelling] and back. It is really distressing that my great travel plans have been reduced to such a modest scale and yet I *must* be satisfied. (...)

6th [June, Friday]   Morning. I want to set off from here at noon today; I have only one more latitude to take here. I think I can have everything finished in 3 days and then I'll go to Kivitung, where all my things are. My chests and boxes have become significantly fewer in number since I packed things better and used up all the voluminous provisions and barter goods. But this is not a matter of great concern to me, since I can be at my goal in 2 days' travel.

I cannot now believe that it could happen that I could stay here, because all the Eskimos agree that the ships are coming. They are now all beginning to move to Kivitung to rendezvous with them there. I have promised 1 lb. of tobacco to the person who first brings me news that there is a ship there after I have travelled by sledge to the floe edge! (...)

[D2]

Kikkertukdjuak – Kokiirbing. Around 2 p.m. we set off in very fine

weather. At 4 o'clock we got into very deep snow and it was 9 before we
reached a headland [no place name given] where the route for Maktartudjennak goes off. Since it was snowing too heavily and we were tired, we
pitched the tent on the sledge and slept excellently. I really wanted to
travel at night when it froze again, but it did not freeze and it snowed
until 5 o'clock and so we ..

[7 June] Saturday   Kikkerton [K'exerten]. .. set off only at 7 o'clock and
travelled to a nearby island [K'exerten] where we stopped to cook. From
the descriptions, there ought to be a small camp here, so we travelled
around the island until we finally found it around 11 o'clock. We cooked
here and I said that I wanted 2 seals in the evening; I bought a piece of
caribou meat from Kenningnu and travelled up Maktartudjennak, and
returned from there around 11 p.m. A strong wind up above. When I
came back[,] the seals were already cut up and the dogs fed and we
crawled into our sleeping bags at 1 o'clock.

[8 June] Sunday   Kikkerton. Vile weather. Despite this around 10
o'clock set off for Pangnirtu [Pangnirtung, the counterpart to the one on
the west coast]. Near Aupallukissa [Augpalukissax] it cleared up somewhat and we travelled about a further 10 miles into Pagnirtu, but then a
superb east wind and heavy snow arose so that we could do nothing but
turn back and travel home, where we arrived at 7 o'clock. Behind Aupal-
lukicha [Augpalukissax] we tried firing repeatedly at a gull colony, but
got nothing since they were much too high. On the way back we met
Johnny Rae at the entrance to Pagnirtu and we travelled back together. In
the evening we had caribou.

[9 June] Monday   Kikkertukdjuak. We got under way at noon, after we
had fed the dogs. We travelled with great peace of mind since we were in
no hurry. Beyond Kokiirbing we travelled in Kenningnu's tracks, because
there was better snow there. Near Kokiirbing Johnny Rae's son overtook
us; he was going to K. [Kikkerton, the whaling station] to pick up his pay.
    Near Ijekdjua [Ijexdjuax] we met Nachojaschi and Mirka, who had
been hunting seals and had fed their dogs. There is now a large camp
here. Shanguja [from Kikkerton], Shanguja [from Padli], Nachojaschi,
Ikerajang, Iwi, Tyson, his son-in-law, Tessivang, and Mirka. The tupik was
intact (I had bolted it). In the evening I quickly worked out my observation and slept like a log. Iwi brought me a whaling lance, and Shanguja
and Iwi's son a ptarmigan.

[10 June] **Tuesday**   Kikkertukdjuak. Today is a rest day. Lazed about, wrote and calculated. A glorious day; I obtained a latitude of 67°29′. I now have 6 ptarmigan and a caribou leg.

[11 June] **Wednesday**   Kikkertukdjuak. Got up at 5.30 a.m. and travelled to the outer side of Kikkertukdjuak [Cape Broughton]. Took the latitude and azimuth from the eastern tip of Kachodlui. Yesterday I surveyed as far as ... W.[ilhelm] did some washing yesterday, and I have just put on a clean shirt! In the evening I again climbed to the top of the hill with Wilhelm, and obtained a fine overview over the region. Saw 5 caribou on the flat summit.

[FB/MK]

(...) It is really terrible how little chance I get to write to you now, but with the eternal travelling[,] by evening I am usually so exhausted that I am quite happy if I can get my notes in order. In this connection I have to be very careful with my eyes, because otherwise I inevitably become snow-blind.

Yesterday was foul weather; a strong gale and snow out of the north; I had to sit in the tupik all day. I probably could have written there if I had not been too cold. We are unable to cook in bad weather so it was extremely unpleasant.

By contrast today was a glorious day! The wind dropped around midnight and by 12.30 the sun was shining so strongly and it was so warm that we got up. Wilhelm made coffee for the entire family. Shanguja, my inseparable companion, and I harnessed the dogs and were able to set off by 3. Then I surveyed a fiord, which I could not have visited during the day because the snow is too soft then, whereas at night the surface crust is frozen. By 12 I was back here and was able to quickly determine the latitude of this spot.

You simply cannot imagine how pleasant it is to be aware that I am at the harbour where the ships call annually. Now it will probably be not more than 7 weeks before we see the ships. Hurrah! I have to travel only a few miles more from here to reach the actual harbour. The snow there is still too deep to pitch the tupik, so we have camped here on an island Tudnirn [Tunirn], about 6 or 7 miles from Kivitung. (...)

But I can still keep working actively! I want to complete [the survey] of the coast as far as Cape Kater. Even though my original plans have been distressingly foiled, at least I have travelled and mapped a substantial stretch of country here. If I had travelled as I had originally intended, I would have been able to make only cursory outlines of the country. The stretch to Cape Kater will fill my time completely! (...)

Yesterday Wilhelm and I were picturing how it will be when we arrive; we have no clothes, because they are on top in Kignait [in the boxes left behind]; for better or for worse we will have to go ashore in Eskimo clothing. How warm will the welcome be? (...)

I have just been interrupted because the sledges have come back from hunting. I quickly bought 2 seals and fed them to my dogs, which have received nothing for 2 days. Now meat is abundantly available again, whereas yesterday there was absolutely none available and the Eskimos were very hungry. My pups are now giving me a lot of fun; they can see now and are crawling around very amusingly. Perhaps I will bring one home with me.

[D2]
[12 June] Thursday   Set off with Shangin [Shanguja] in the morning. Got safely past the spot where the polynya is located and around 5 o'clock had reached the new camp [no place name given] where we also pitched our tupik and cooked a meal. Tomorrow we plan to push on to Kivitung. The going was fairly good. Unfortunately there are no seals at all.

[13 June] Friday   Tudnirn. Set off shortly after Shanguja. [WW: .. This morning 7 sledges left the camp to drive north.] It is very fine weather again. On the open side of Kikkertukdjuak initially; a large iceberg has stranded here and has formed a massive crack. Here we eventually overtook Shanguja. We arrived here in Tudnirn at about 5. The site on which the settlement is located is covered with deep snow, so we have just arrived there after ... hours, but it is very wet here. Tyson came with us and went to the tupiks in which the two Shanguja's [from K'exerten and Padli] and I are living here. In the evening Jack and Shorty arrived; I got another seal from them so was able to feed my dogs well.

Establishing the Base Camp at K'ivitung

[14 June] Saturday   Tudnirn. A delightful blizzard introduced an abominable day. At noon an *avagnanirn* [I. *avagna'nirn* = wind along the land, north wind] began with gale force and now it is still the same. Hence I crawled into my sleeping bag with my cold feet and have been writing a little. Today Shanguja was visiting me a lot and vice versa.

[**15 June**] **Sunday** Detestable weather. Wilhelm in his sleeping bag all day, and I almost as much. *Avagnaniradlo akssadlo! Mana miktiliviangtu. Erk!* [I. = It is blowing strongly out of the north! Now ... Ah!]

[FB/MK]
(...) We are now at last at the destination of our journey, the harbour at which the ships are always in the habit of calling. I cannot conceive that it is at all possible that we will remain here; the Eskimos, in all their activities, are focusing on the arrival of the ships. They are packing seal blubber in barrels and are collecting skins for trading with the whalers. Everything is focused on the arrival of the ships; surely they won't leave us in the lurch this year? The day after tomorrow I am planning to set off once again on a fairly long trip; I have only 2 more fiords to survey [based on the British Admiralty charts] and then my travelling will be done. (...)

[D2]
[**16 June**] **Monday** Tudnirn 67°53′. Around midnight the weather improved. At 7 the sun appeared, but then the wind died. Thus we got up at 12.30. I harnessed the dogs and travelled to Maujaorsirn [Maujatuusirn] and Mauj[atung]. Quite good going. Last night Shanguja went to Kivitung, where there is a good camping site; we now want to move there. When he came back he slept; I got back at 12 and got another latitude. I hope I will get the longitude tomorrow morning. I slept a little in the afternoon, fed the dogs, worked and wrote.

[**17 June**] **Tuesday** Tudnirn. Set off again at 10 a.m. [without Weike]. Shanguja is moving to Kivitung and also took my boxes [WW; .. two seals] with him. I shall follow tomorrow, but today want to survey a further stretch of the coast here. I travelled until 4 p.m. Heavy going in Kaijongnamg [K'ajongnang], so did not get far. The campsite is now very wet and unpleasant so I was quite glad to get away. Shanguja will come back tomorrow morning to fetch me. Iwi sold me another seal. In the evening Wilhelm went up the hill [on Tunirn] again.

[**18 June**] **Wednesday** Kivitung. Shanguja arrived at 7.30 a.m. Then we packed up and set off. After travelling for 90 minutes we arrived here in Kivitung, or rather Pamiujang, opposite Kivitung. A very fine tupik site. We pitched the tupik very well, since it will be standing beside an old one and a new one. In the afternoon the curs got 2 seals. I had received a seal on the morning of the 17th.

[**19 June**] **Thursday**   Kivitung. Tomorrow I want to go out to the point, but first I had occasion to become violently angry at the dogs which first of all ran away, then wouldn't move or stop when I wanted. Finally I got away around noon, but could see little. Just as I came back, Ikeraping and Tyson passed through. In the evening Tessigang arrived. From their description Niachonanjang [Niaxongnang] is now Cape Raper. Now, finally I shall really find out 'which is which' [written in English in the original].

From K'ivitung to Siorartijung

[**20 June**] **Friday**   Atteraélling [Attereelling]. Today we are leaving the harbour just as we did a year ago! [Putting to sea from Hamburg on 20 June 1883]. But this time only to go north for a few weeks. The tupik was packed full and bolted, then Shanguja and I set off [with Weike]. We progressed only slowly across the isthmus; below the mauja [I. = snow] was not so bad. We arrived here at 5; it then became very foggy; in the interim it had cleared up after a snowy night. Akshudlo, Ikeraping and Tyson are here. Old Piukkia [Ikeraping's mother] is almost dead.

[ww]
.. When we reached the ice again, we moved faster driving along the trail leading to Ikeraping's tupik on an island [Attereelling]. We stopped; he had driven here yesterday so that his mother, Piukkia, could die here without being devoured by dogs immediately. In the afternoon we saw the first flower. We had plenty of caribou meat.

[D2]
The first flowers! Fed the dogs. In the evening Ikeraping and Shanguja were in my tupik. The small tupik with poles and spars for a door works very well. I now have no idea where I am on the map. In the morning Shanguja showed us a letter from the *Thetis* [a Scottish whaling ship which was at this coast in 1882 out of Dundee], in which it said that she would come to K. [K'ivitung] next year [1883] to fetch barrels [of blubber] so that no other ship gets them.

[**21 June**] **Saturday**   Nedluchseak [Nedluxseax]. Set off around 11 o'clock. Prior to that received some more caribou legs. I climbed the hill to orient myself. A very fine day. We travelled through between Atterrael-

ling and Alikdjua [Alixdjuax], but could scarcely see Alikdjua and Manitung from here. Maujadlu! [I. *maujaaluk* = deep, soft snow]. In the
evening shot another rabbit. A great deal of water here. I do not know
whether we will reach Nudlung tomorrow. Today we saw the island of
Ssettiksun [Satigusn], off Nudlung, from which Kikkertukdjuak ought to
be visible, distorted by refraction. I have no idea where I am on the British [Admiralty] chart.

[**22 June**] **Sunday** Tupirbikdjuareitung [Tupirbikdjariaitung]. After I
had taken a latitude sight, I set off at 12.30. Sh [K'exerten Shanguja] has
gone ahead with his 3 wives to hunt seals, while Padli Sh [Shanguja] set
off with us. In the morning I obtained more bearings from the hill, but
there was nothing but boulders up there, very difficult to climb. Today we
made quite rapid progress and at 9 arrived here, where there was a fine
tupik standing. Shot another young seal and 1 *nauja*. In the evening I had
a horrible toothache, so could not even finish my map. The numerous
islands are making my task very difficult.

[FB/MK]
(...) There is still deep snow lying all around, and it is still freezing at
night, but they [the first flowers] and the rushing of water are true har-
bingers of spring. In the past few days we have made only slow progress,
since the snow is *very* bad. At every step one sinks hip-deep and the dogs
cannot pull; as a result driving a sledge is a terrible job, and often I almost
lose my voice.

The country here is hellishly full of islands and is giving me fearful
trouble; and then I don't know at all where I am, whether south of Home
Bay or in Home Bay [no Inuktitut name given], since there is absolutely
no connection with the map! Well, tomorrow or the day after will probably show us where we are! But now I must hurry and take a latitude; otherwise it will be too late. I have been waiting here just to get this very
latitude.

[D2]
[**23 June**] **Monday** Tupirbikdjuareitung. 68°19'5". Do not start out due
to bad weather, fog and snow. At noon Shanguja went off hunting caribou. My teeth are now slightly better, whereas last night I barely slept a
wink. Worked at the map. Shanguja came back at night with a caribou. In
the afternoon it cleared up. I went up the hill and took bearings on the
various islands and points.

[FB/MK]

(...) Now I know where I am on the map. Quite close to the Sound at the entrance to Home Bay. From here I can reach the next settlement in one day and from there Cape Kater probably in one day. But I hope to be there in 4 days from now. Then I want to come back along the coast, which will take me at least 8 days, and rendezvous with Shanguja again here, i.e. at Nudlung. I can probably be back in Kivitung on about 8 July. [As it happened, he did not get there until 19 July.]

Unless there is unusually little pack ice outside and a high swell rolling in, the ice will probably break up with the spring tide on 22 July or 6 August; then I may hope to see a ship soon thereafter. Already all the ice outside is seamed with wide cracks which we usually can barely cross with the sledge, so I presume that the outer ice will soon break up.

I will be really glad when my travelling ends in a month, since I have no desire to be constantly hanging on a sledge! Oh! how happy I shall be when I can once again sit in my quiet study and work! Here one gets deprived and becomes totally demoralized! (...)

[D2]

[24 June] Tuesday   Nudlung. In the morning the fog was still thick, so we did not start out. At noon the sun broke through; but still it remained fogged in. But I was able to get a latitude. Around 5 p.m. it suddenly cleared up. I immediately harnessed the team, but it immediately became thick fog again. Shortly before Nudlung it was snowing heavily and only now, at 12 midnight[,] has it cleared up again. I hope that we will soon enjoy fine weather. On the way, in addition, I obtained the necessary directions for my itinerary.

[25 June] Wednesday   Nudlung. C.[ape] Hooper. Foul weather again! Fog[,] strong wind. Cold, clouds. Shanguja got 2 caribou and the other [Shanguja] 2 seals and 1 ptarmigan. Lazed about. In the evening we sang and played checkers. ἐκὼν ἀὲκ ντί νὲ δνμῶ [Greek = 'Even as I yield freely to thee, yet unwilling.' Homer, *Iliad*, 4:44 (Smith 1944: 44); see also 22 December 1883 and 7 January 1884].

[26 June] Thursday   Filthy weather! Avagnanirn [north wind]. Wrote something for the [*Berliner*] *Tageblatt*. Scarcely left the tupik all day. Fed the dogs in the evening. I hope to be able to get away in the morning, since the wind has died this evening.

[ww]

(...) .. Schangu [Shanguja] came back with 2 caribou. We have idled away the day. (...)

[D2]

[**27 June**] **Friday**   Idjutung [Idjortung]. Last night it snowed heavily, but towards morning it cleared up and it has become a very fine day. We crossed half of Home Bay and stopped in the evening on a small island [Idjortung]. Quite close to this lay an ice ridge about 15′ wide, which we were able to cross only with great difficulty. Many birds in the pressure ice. In the evening I went up the hill for a bit to get an overview of the region. Then I worked up the map[;] this took a long time because of the many small islands. But the British map is totally useless! We are now quite close to Arbaktung [Arbaxtung] (perhaps Cape Bisson) [place name uncertain], where more Eskimos are still living. We have to cross the land [isthmus] there.

[**28 June**] **Saturday**   Near Iwissak [Ivissax], a small, red island. In the morning it looked quite good, but it clouded over during the day. Since the dogs had to be fed, Shanguja went seal hunting and killed one. In the meantime it had become very thick, so we could barely see 30 paces. The water is lying up to 2′ deep on the ice here, with a thin ice crust on top. Today it was not melting, so the going is very bad.

Suddenly it cleared up, to the extent that we could see Arbudjuktung [Arbaxtung], but then we reached the Kingilung [K'ingniellung] crack, which fortunately led us there. Wind; quite thick. But there we spotted a small island, which we take to be Itidjilung [Itidliellung]. But as emerged later, it is another island [Audnirn] near Iwissak[,] which we fortunately reached despite the fog. This morning the sledge fell into a lead. A thick blizzard as we arrived.

[**29 June**] **Sunday**   Kouktelling. Last night it cleared up and this morning it was very fine weather. Thus I first took bearings on the summit of the island for the latitude so that I could correct the position of some doubtful [islands] and improve my bearings of yesterday. From up there I could also pick the best route to the mainland, but even this route lay through a lot of water.

Near Niachongnan [Niaxongnan] there was another lead 20′ wide, full of ducks. W.[ilhelm] and I got 3. We then headed along the land. In the evening there was a miserable, rough southeast wind; around 9 we reached the isthmus that we have to cross here. Since the going is very bad on the ice now I will gladly give up on this region and camp here; I want to carry on only to fetch my guide.

[FB/MK]
Cape Bisson? (...) Fortunately, however, I have at least obtained quite good compass observations; this ... region is causing me enormous headaches. (...)

[D2]
[**30 June**] **Monday** Kouktelling. When we woke this morning it was snowing and avagnirn. So we had to stay in our sleeping bags. During the day it was blowing terrifyingly. Shanguja's dogs ate part of their traces, but not yet mine. Wilhelm was able to cook in the morning, but not thereafter, due to drifting snow and wind.

[WW]
Herr Dr. woke us at 6:30, when I looked out of the tubik, it was foggy and snowing. The Dr. then said [using the formal address as he always did with Weike]: you can sleep as long as you want. I went back to sleep till 10:30, then I got up to make coffee. At noon the sun appeared enough for the Dr. to get a latitude. Then a strong wind arose and it started snowing. In the afternoon I tried to get the fire going again, but the wind was too strong and I did not succeed. I twice got a fire going with gunpowder, but before I could get it to catch, it was blown out again. Now we had to open one of our cans of meat and dig into the bread bag, which has already shrunk seriously. Campsite at 69°12′ (...)

[FB/MK]
Tuesday, 1st July At the same place [Kouktelling]. When I woke yesterday the weather had changed abominably; it was quite thick fog, snowing and blowing with all its might. During the day the storm intensified, so we were left with no option but to remain in the tupik and in our sleeping bags and live on dry bread again. I hoped for a change from hour to hour, but there was no let-up until this morning at 10 when the sun finally shone through. Now it has become almost totally clear, though the wind is still blowing quite strongly. In the meantime Wilhelm has managed to get a cooking pot going, so we probably may get something cooked to eat again. Also, earlier, I was able to get a latitude for this location, and to my

great delight I discovered that despite the fact that I have had no astronomical observations for a north-south distance of 53 miles, my dead reckoning is correct to within 0.4 miles. We are at 69°12′ N lat. and with luck will finally reach Niachonaujang [Niaxonaujang] and the Eskimo camp [Siorartijung].

My supplies are starting to run very low, because originally I had calculated on a trip of only 14 days, and now it has stretched to almost 4 weeks. But there are enough seals and I hope also to get some salmon in Niochonaujang. My dogs are in the worst shape; the poor animals have not eaten for 2 days and now unfortunately we are seeing no seals at all. I plan to cross the little isthmus here this evening[,] and if the weather finally improves[,] we will probably reach the long-awaited camp tomorrow evening. It is truly terrible how much bad weather we have experienced here; constant wind and fog, only half a day at most of really good weather! I wish I could be back in Kivitung very soon, since I am now *thoroughly* sick of travelling; if at least it was resulting in something decent, but the constant fog prevents all work. (...)

[D2]
Kouktelling. Exactly the same. When it cleared up a little and the wind relented at noon, we set off; but immediately the foul weather broke with renewed strength. When we had driven for about 2 hours, my sledge landed in a pond[,] which was covered with snow. Then I lost Shanguja's tracks so I erected the tupik on my sledge, since there was nothing else I could do.

[2 July] **Wednesday** Kouktelling. Clear in the morning. Hence we set off; immediately the fog and storm began again. Sh. lost his way completely. It was so thick that we could not see for 50 paces. Stopped again after about 3 hours. Now, in the evening, the wind has dropped, but the snow is still drifting and there is totally thick fog. Our rations: 12 oz. of meat and half a biscuit. If it is still the same tomorrow morning I will have to shoot Neinessuak [dog] in order to feed it to the other dogs.

[WW]
(...) .., then Schangu lost his way[,] so we were on a mystery trip until we had overtaken him; then we stopped and pitched the tubik on the sledge and made ourselves at home. The Dr. wanted to shoot a dog and feed the rest with it, but Schangu suggested that it would be better for the sledge; so his life was spared until tomorrow, if it had not got any better.

The Dr. went off to get a drink of water; in the meantime Schangu told me that he was hungry and wanted to take some of the meat that he was to take for the natives. When the Dr. came back, we told him this; the Dr. was happy with this and so that's what happened. Schangu removed the cross-pieces from his sledge; they were used as firewood and we made soup. (...)

[D2]

[**3 July**] [**Thursday**]   Ssiroartüjung [Siorartijung]. Last night the wind dropped, but in the morning the weather was still quite thick. Around 8 it seemed to me to be clearing, so I had Wilhelm brew coffee so as to be ready to set off. It really improved, but as we were starting off, it became just as thick as ever. I had Sh.[,] who does not know where he is, head north-northeastward[,] and we soon began to travel downhill. Eventually our route dropped very steeply to the water, where the sledges were almost smashed.

As soon as we were at sea level it became quite clear and warm. *Utos* [I. *uuttuq* = seal on the ice] were very numerous, but Shanguja got only the fourth one. One, at which he had fired and wounded, surfaced again at its hole, but I was too late with the harpoon. I had us drive to the first small island; soon we spotted people's tracks and found 1 tupik, Utoaluk. [WW: .. The camp consisted of one man and one woman.] I bought another seal and was able to feed both lads [Weike and Shanguja]. Kunu and all the other men are far up [north], hunting caribou, behind Nia-chonaujan [Niaxonaujang; probably Cape Hewell; uncertain information]. Neinessuak [dog] has escaped with its life again! Foul toothache; face swollen.

The Inuit Settlement of Siorartijung: The Most Northerly Point

[FB/MK]
Friday, 4th July   Ssiroartüjung. 69°32′ N. lat. (...) I have now reached the most northerly point of my journey and am heading back. (...)

But we had a couple of difficult days on the way here. My dogs had last eaten on the 29th and then there was bad weather for 4 days. Shanguja, my Eskimo[,] lost his way in fog and storm on the isthmus, so it took us 3 days to cover a distance of 7 miles. We finally reached the ice again yesterday afternoon. We spent the entire afternoon hunting and fortunately procured a seal.

You can imagine that the poor dogs were almost starved, nor were we in the best of shape. We were unable to cook for lack of blubber and thus our daily ration was half a ship's biscuit and 12 oz. of beef. Around 7 we suddenly saw footprints on the ice, and quite unexpectedly found a tupik here on an island. Here we were informed that the entire settlement of Niachonaujang had moved. Naturally, I am not now going farther north, but [will attempt] to head back.

The weather is so fickle here that I shall be content if I can complete [my survey of] Home Bay. Tomorrow both Eskimos [Shanguja and Utoaluk] are to hunt seals while I shall look around the surrounding area a little. Then, the day after tomorrow I want to head back and, I hope, will be in Nudlung by the 10th, perhaps even on the 9th. Here I have had to endure yet another great pleasure, namely unbearable toothache, and today a badly swollen face, but it is already getting better.

Just think, this man [Utoaluk] whom I met here, probably the last strange Eskimo I will encounter, finally gave me the information about the longed-for north. He comes from Igluling and has quite often travelled down the entire coast of Foxe Channel as far as Netilling. So I was right the first time, back home, when I wanted to sail from Dundee and then travel from north to south! Well, now it doesn't matter and I will be glad when I am home again. (...)

[D2]
Last night the left half of my face swelled severely, so that this morning my eye was almost closed, but the pain is abating. In the morning I was writing in my sleeping bag, and then the swelling in my face began to go down. Otuadlu [Utoaluk] comes from Igluling and tells me that the Igluling residents commonly visit the coast as far as Piling, and often go even as far as Koukdjua [Koukdjuax]; he himself has seen Netilling in this manner! You could have knocked me down with a feather! I can't go outside, as I had intended, because of my swollen face. In the morning U.[toaluk] and S.[shanguja] want to go hunting so that we can take some seals with us.

[5 July] Saturday Ssiroartüjung. Since I was better, in the morning I went over to Aulitiving [Aulittiving] with the sledge to fetch firewood and do some surveying. There was an old sledge runner and ship's planking lying there. At the northern tip of Aulitiving I was unable to go any farther because of a wide lead. Utuadlu and Shanguja got 4 seals. U.[Utoaluk's] wife has been to Tudjan. I am now unsure whether it is Cornwallis or North Devon, but I think it is the latter. U. knows Netshillik [I. *natsilik* = those, who have seals], i.e. those known as the Sininirmiut [I. *siqnirmiut* = people of the sun]. They have not visited Akkudling [Akudlirn], because it has very manilary [I. *manilara'dlu* = very rough (FB)] ice inshore.

[WW]
(...) After 13 hours' sleep I crawled out of my sleeping bag at 8 a.m. The natives went hunting; the Dr.'s cheek was a bit thinner. The Dr. left to get wood and he brought some back soon; he had four thick planks on the sledge. At noon, being bored, I made cocoa. When the two Eskimos returned, they had four seals; two were immediately prepared and fed to the dogs and the meat for us. We now eat meat with the coffee every morning since our bread is gone. (...)

Southward: Excruciating Sledging on Late-Summer Ice

[D2]
[6 July] Sunday   Woke at 5.30, but it was not until 9.30 that we were ready to set off; thereafter a great deal of carrying things to the land etc. I gave U. a letter for the ships [FB/MK: .., in which I stated that I was at Kivitung and was waiting for them]. At first the dogs did not want to run, but then we made quite rapid progress and by 9 o'clock had reached the entrance to Home Bay, where we stopped because of fog before rounding the point.

The fog is quite intolerable[,] it hinders me in every aspect. If only I could reach Home Bay. Around noon it suddenly cleared again. Afterwards, for safety's sake I took a bearing on Pilektuak [Pilektuax; Hang Cliff (FB)]. S. saw 7 caribou; and along the way went off hunting to the west. The caribou fled[,] but S. brought back 2 ducks. Kouktelling.

[FB/MK]
(...) So I quickly pitched my tupik and am now sitting in my sleeping bag with at least my legs warm. Despite the sun (which we *never* see, however) it is perceptibly cold at night and by 7 or 8 it has already begun to freeze. (...)

And now it is 11; supper is now ready and I am terribly hungry; I have eaten nothing since 7 this morning and I had only 2 small seal ribs then! (...)

[D2]

[**7 July**] **Monday** Niachongnausirn [Niaxongnausirn]. Since S. was still trying to shoot some seals in the morning[,] it was around 11 before we set off. Near Kouktelling, where a large river is debouching now, the ice is very bad; we shot a few ducks. It was the same at Niachongnang, and here, too, finally. There are now innumerable eider ducks here, but we did not get any. Since there is again a lot of water on the ice and it all starts freezing at 7, we stayed here, rather than trying to cross to Abüdjelling [Avaudjelling]. Got to bed around 1 a.m. half snow-blind.

[**8 July**] **Tuesday** Small island [Kiporkain] north of Idjuktung [Idjortung]. We were travelling all day along leads that run from island to island. Near Abüdjelling the lead from Niachongnausirn disappeared, so we had to travel through water, which made for slow progress. I shot another duck. Unfortunately, because of the water I *cannot* get into the inner parts of Home Bay, and I get a glimpse of it only from time to time because of the high fog and *rain*, our first rain. Off Agirobing [Agdliroling] we soon reached the small islands. Sh. found a tern's egg.

[**9 July**] **Wednesday** Ssaviksunitung [Saviksonitung]. Ipsimissus [Boas turned 26 years old]. To celebrate my birthday we brewed {coffee} the last chocolate, and had bread and canned meat. As a result the dogs were also half-sick next morning. I am almost totally snow-blind. We were able to travel along leads to the small islands this side of Idjuktung, but when we got into the rough ice we again had to go through the middle of the water, which is still very deep here and forms a tide that rises very quickly. Off Idjuktung S. shot a walrus that was sleeping by the lead, but we were unable to recover it since the lead was too wide and we could not get across it anywhere. It is raining again. [WW: .. In the evening we had six ducks in the soup.]

[**10 July**] **Thursday** Nudlung. It rained all night. In the morning we had to cross a stream of water to reach the large Ssaviksunitung, but we made faster and better progress than I could have hoped. We reached land near C. Hooper [part of Nudlung]. Here the water was streaming off the ice into the fast ice in great rivers. Once again the sun is trying to shine on Home Bay, but I am not turning back to that abominable [country], where I have had nothing but vexation. S. really wanted to leave some meat here, but we have found nothing. We have almost nothing for a decent soup. [WW: .. For supper I made a strong pea soup with meat from caribou that were shot here] [by Shanguja on 26 June].

[**11 July**] **Friday**   Upper end of Nudlung Fiord. I woke around 6, since we probably have a long drive ahead. At first the going was good; but once we got farther into the fiord, everything was under water. We left our wood on a small island [no place name] then Sh. guided us to the wrong side of the fiord, which is indented by many bays. Thus I twice had to wade through water. It was about 4′ deep. The dogs and sledges were swimming! Finally, around 9, we spotted the tupik here at the head of the fiord, but there was nobody in it; presumably they are at the salmon pond. In the evening Sh. went out again and presumably has gone there now to fetch the others. Mika [K'exerten Shanguja] is here too, as I can tell from his dogs. Everything is horribly wet; so we will probably have to stay here.

[FB/MK]
(...) Our days of starvation are over I hope, since we suppose that Shanguja is abundantly supplied with caribou meat and salmon. Unfortunately I was able to survey Home Bay only very cursorily, because the ice was covered with water up to 2 feet deep, so we could make no progress with the sledge. Now I anticipate another 6 days of travelling, then it is finished.

You cannot imagine how happy I shall be when I no longer have to sit on the sledge and am free of that torture at least. Then I can pack my map away in a trunk and begin some ethnographic work, which is less strenuous, until a ship arrives. (...)

[D2]
[**12 July**] **Saturday**   Shanguja came back last night. I shouted to him when I heard him singing in the other tupik this morning and he came over with 2 salmon. He had met Mika and one of the wives of [K'exerten] Shanguja at the salmon pool while Sh. himself was hunting caribou. But he plans to come back today. And indeed in the evening the whole group came down with a lot of meat and many salmon. Now, happily, our days of starvation are over.

[FB/sister Toni; on the occasion of the birthday of his sister and mother]
Nudlung, 12th July 1884. Dear sister and friend. This is probably the only time during the long, long period of my journey that I shall write to you personally, but do not think because of this that my thoughts have not

often been with you and have not often been in an intimate conversation with you. But the tasks and troubles of daily life barely give me a chance to make my essential daily notes, and when I have worked up my observations in the evening, I am glad to be able to go to sleep. In addition I am constantly tormented by snow-blindness, which prohibits any major strain on the eyes. When I tell you how I have been living this summer you will understand, I think, why my reports have thus been confined to the most essential. But today a lucky fate has granted me not only to be able to think of you right on your birthday, but to be able to send you my best wishes in writing.

Yesterday we landed in so much water with our sledge that I have to dry all my things[,] and in addition the Eskimo with whom I want to travel back to the harbour at Kivitung is still away hunting caribou. You can't imagine how happy I am that my travels are approaching an end, since with the eternal bad weather, water up to 4' deep on the ice, and the monotonous, exhausting sledging, I am really thoroughly sick of it. But our thoughts are no longer here; they are with the ship that we can now expect soon. I have selected three weeks from tomorrow [3 August] as the earliest date; I can scarcely believe that I shall then hear from you all again! But I can see that I am not writing what I want. This is the daily litany that occurs often *ad nauseam* in my letters to you all. (...)

You once feared that when I came back I would again be as reserved as I once was; that my protracted solitary life would have made me taciturn, but don't believe it. Send a person into the wilderness such as I have been living in (for Wilhelm is scarcely company) and he will experience the need to communicate, the need to see people around him with whom he can *live*, and *how* I long for my work. You have no idea; and how I long (I'm almost ashamed to admit it) for vegetables and potatoes. The life we are living now (for a week we have had no bread) has a totally {unnerving} demoralizing effect on a person. I often catch myself noting that we are talking about good things such as savoy, peas, cabbage, fruit, things that ought to leave one quite indifferent! But when you live for 2 months on seal and caribou and very little bread[,] then you know what sort of effect it can have. We are already revelling in the thought that we'll get some rice from the ship!

I stopped [writing] at noon today, because there were all sorts of small jobs to be done. Will we really see a ship in three weeks? I can scarcely believe it, yet it is very probable. We can expect them in mid-August fairly definitely. How often have I pictured the joy when the telegram arrives to say that I have returned safely! (...)

When I now think of life at home, it seems to me almost unthinkable with its comfort and cosiness. But, do you know, there is one thing that pains me in my soul. My rough, horny fingers will probably never play the piano again, yet I still need music, although I haven't *entirely* mastered it. If only I could just hear a sonata in A major, or Schumann's *Fantasia* or the *Eroica* [by Beethoven]!

But now enough! Soon we will see each other again, safe and sound. With sincere love, your friend and brother, Franz.

[D2]
[13 July] **Sunday**   Since the dogs have to eat, both Shanguja went hunting. We were fishing for salmon all day. Like yesterday, the weather is atrocious with a strong avagnanirn. The two men did not come back until about 11 with 3 old and 4 young caribou. So I will not get away tomorrow, since nothing has been made ready. (and 1 seal.)

[14 July] **Monday**   In the morning I explained to [Padli] Shanguja that I want to travel tomorrow and told him to get everything ready today. The dogs will be fed tomorrow. The weather is still the same. During these two days the ice up here has dried off almost completely, and the stream has swollen enormously. The fast ice is now disappearing very quickly. It is still blowing strongly up the fiord

[15 July] **Tuesday**   Headland between Nudlung and the next fiord [no name]. Last night it snowed; this morning it rained initially, then clearing up. The wind is somewhat less[,] but it did not die completely until [we were] this side of the high cape before the glacier that lies up above. I took Sh. and his 2 caribou with me; the other sledge did not start off until much later. In the past few days the ice has become very dry so that today we did not encounter any water at all where the dogs were swimming recently. The ice is now very bad for the dogs' feet, which become badly cut up. At many places the ice is honeycombed to a depth of almost 6 inches and is again forming mauja. The cracks and floes of the fast ice had been rearranged for the first time. Glaciers calving into the fiord.

[16 July] **Wednesday**   Kikkertalukdjua [K'exertalukdjuax]. Around 10 we started off again, but made only slow headway, since the dogs must have some food and hence we had to hunt. But near the long island [no place name] Sh. got a caribou, but was unable to get any seals. It was not until evening that Kikkerton Sh. got one. Fog and rain in the morning,

clearing later. In the fiords behind Kikkertalukdjua there are large glaciers that reach down to sea level and are said to produce icebergs about
80' high.

[17 July] **Thursday** Manitung. Although the Eskimos had completed
their travel preparations in good time today, I was ready even earlier and
went ahead as far as the corner of Kikkertalukdjua to get some bearings.
Since it became fairly clear. I at long last got a quite decent view into the
fiord. From Pagnirtu [Pangnirtung] to Nedlukseak [Nedluxseax] and
from there to N[ucha]tauchin [Nuxatoaxsin] it – the ice – is largely covered with water. But then we made fairly rapid progress along the coast
and we camped for the night near the eastern tip of Manitung. Sh. Kikkerton found an old grave with implements, from which I took a stone
pot. From up on the hill the others spotted a lead which, we hope, will
allow us to make rapid progress tomorrow.

[18 July] **Friday** Kangeeakdjung [K'angeeaxdjung]. Now we are only
about two hours from Kivitung. Although I erred by half an hour, we got
away at 10. It was quite thick, but a lead provided us with dry, fast going to
Alikdjua. There we found Ikeraping's and Nachojassi's tupik. I[keraping]
sold us some walrus meat. When they spotted the tupik the dogs dragged
[the sledges] into deep water in a crack in the fast ice. Although Sh.
would gladly have stayed[,] I insisted that we travel farther. After Attereel-
ling I fell half into a crack because the fall ice, though dry, is also hard.
From here to the mainland there is quite a lot of water. But the grounded
ice was so thick that we could find our way through the pack ice formed
two years ago only with difficulty. When we subsequently stopped, it
cleared up somewhat and we could see that we had already detoured
around the point [of K'angeeaxdjung].

[19 July] **Saturday** Kivitung. Early in the morning it cleared up a little
and we found ourselves far beyond the northern point of Kangeeakdjung.
Although we made only slow progress, we had already reached Kivitung by
about 1 o'clock; there, to my great joy, we found the tupik undamaged.

The Eskimos are still at Idjuniving (Tudnirn). The ice here is now covered with water. In the afternoon Sh. again went hunting seals with his
harpoon and brought back 2. We pitched the small tupik and stowed
most of our things in it.

At K'ivitung: Waiting for the Whalers, July–August 1884

Completion of the Cartographic Work

[D2]

[**20 July**] **Sunday**   Today I was thoroughly lazy; some reading and writing filled the day. In the evening Tyson, Bob, Tessigang and a couple of boys came to visit. I bought a nettiavinirg [I. *natsiaviniq* = young seal (male or female) in its first summer] and 1 seal. Nuvukdjua has stayed at Padli; Sh. [Padli-Shanguja's] mother has come with Bob and will arrive here tomorrow. Shangin [Shanguja] has taken 8 seals.

[**21 July**] **Monday**   Arranging and transcribing things all day. I cannot locate a mistake in my calculations with reference to Padloping. In the morning Sh. went hunting young seals with his entire family. Around noon Bob's kuni, Shanguja's mother and [gap: name left out] arrived here and erected 2 tupiks. The fog finally disappeared and in the afternoon the weather was superb. At 9 I walked across the harbour again to take a look at the floe edge, and was back by 12. It appears to be about 15 miles away.

[**22 July**] **Tuesday**   A very fine day. Around noon an E wind began blowing; it appears to be fairly strong farther out. In the evening it became a SE wind. I hope that it will break up a lot of ice. On the basis of the cloud shapes Sh. thought that there was a strong uargang [I. *uangnariktuq* = northwest wind, land wind] yesterday at Ichalualuin [Exalualuin], while there was a strong wind farther out. In the evening Iwi was here and I ordered a small kayak [miniature model] from him. From Tyson I bought 4 nettiavinirn skins and a piece of ugjuk [bearded seal] leather. I am now starting to collect words seriously.

[**23 July**] **Wednesday** Around noon Shangin went out seal hunting and did not come back until 4 a.m. I bought 4 nettiavinirn skins from Jack, who had stayed here last night. Sh. obtained 3 young sealskins for a pair of pants. I have been collecting some words again, writing and lazing.

[**24 July**] **Thursday** The dogs were fed in the morning. I got Sh. to describe for me the geographic configuration between Maktartidjennak and Narpang [Narpaing]. I bought some young seal meat from Tessigang. In the evening Wilhelm threw a stone at poor Waldmann [one of the named dogs] and almost killed it; I'm afraid the poor animal will die. The ice appears to be very broken up in the past few days. Sh. has gone with his wife, Tessigang, Apitang and [gap: name left out] to Koeinilli [Koainilling] to fish for trout. (...) The sun has disappeared behind a hill. [The arctic day is coming to a close.]

Boas did not make any entries on 25 and 26 July.

[ww]
25 July [**Friday**] Today the weather was very fine, with little wind; what we need now is a lot of wind. Whenever somebody goes out of the tubik, he first glances at the floe edge. The water on the ice is now changing greatly and the fast ice is becoming very bad. Towards evening the Dr. went to Kiwittung [K'ivitung] to look around and Schangu went with him to fish in a pond on the headland. They came back at 11.30; Schangu had caught 4 trout, of which Attelschuling [a dog] had eaten one; this led to a thrashing.

26 July [**Saturday**] After coffee I went out to the pond to fish; it was very warm and there were many flowers over on the other side, so I decorated my hat with them. I was there until noon and caught 2 trout. After we had eaten lunch we fried the two trout. In the evening Schangu and Teschiwan [Tessivang] came back. Schangu got a caribou and his son shot a young one. The Dr. was sketching mountains and glaciers inland today. [He was drawing maps.]

[D2]
[**27 July**] **Sunday** Got up late. Unfortunately it is still fine weather. Since Wilhelm was too lazy in the [afternoon] I climbed .. [the hill at K'ivitung used as a lookout for ships]. [The text breaks off here in the middle of a word and the entry for this date is not continued.]

[WW]
(...) The Dr. saw the smoke from a ship.

[D2]
[**28 July**] **Monday**   Moved. This morning we packed everything up. With Shangin's and my team I can move everything at once. Shangin, his mother, Bob and Ikeraping are all moving with me. Today there was a little avagnanirn which we hope will drive out the ice. Unfortunately the floe edge is still very far away. In the afternoon it became completely clear. The tupik is now handsomely erected, with my book trunk inside. Unfortunately Ikeraping's reports about the mountains do not agree well with Shangin's; I now have to get the two men together again; thus far I trust Shangin more although many things are dubious in his information too.

[**29 July**] **Tuesday**   Shanguja [Padli] is here and has been telling me all sorts of things; Kikkerton Sh. says he wants to go to Padli tomorrow and from there to Kikkerton [whaling station] in the fall. Hence I will quickly question him about the necessary things, especially the country of {Tudjan} Tudnunirn [Tununirn]. Sh.P. [Shanguja Padli] is travelling to Idjuniving to buy furs. During yesterday evening there was an uagnanjang; today there is a strong avagnanirn. At noon I climbed the first hill at Kivitung, but when I could not see enough from there, I climbed to the cairn on the highest hill. The floe edge is now about 4 miles from Kangeeakdjung. Really beautiful blue water for the first time. A wide expanse of water towards Manitung with an ice-blink beyond; only a slight strip of water to the E. Interviewed Sh. in the evening.

[**30 July**] **Wednesday**   Sh. went to hunt seals with the Idjuniving Esk., who want to come here in the morning. Bob and Tessigang went south, since they want to fetch tupik poles from Kikkertaujak [K'exertaujang]. But they came back in the evening because there is a very wide crack off Amaroktelling [Amaroxtelling] and they are both afraid there may be a strong avagnanirn, preventing them from getting back.

Sh.K. [Shanguja K'exerten] set off at noon. I gave him percussion caps, tobacco, powder as well as small items for Eisik and Keppignangu and a letter for Mutch. He expects to meet Pakkak at Kitingajung. In the afternoon Wilhelm went up the hill while Ikeraping was here telling me stories. Apparently the floe edge has been driven farther up. The crack that extended from Kangeeakdjung yesterday has closed today; and the crack towards Tudnirn has opened in this direction. There is now much ice to the WNW; a little water from NE to east. Sh. came back tonight, having caught nothing.

[WW]
(...) When we had our evening coffee – we don't have tea any more, also our sugar is gone – I went to the lookout. I took a flag along which I placed on top of the hill. The floe edge was close; there was a lot of water. (...)

Ethnographica, Dictionary, and Stories: Last Notes

[D2]
[**31 July**] **Thursday**   At 5.30 this morning Kudlukulu [bitch] was at the door howling that she had driven a fish hook into her foot. As a result we tried to pull it out, but finally gave her to Shanguja who operated on her. We slept until 8.30. Around 12 the wind which until then had been a bad avagnanirn, swung round to being an iküschuk [I. *iki'rtsuq* = sea wind (FB)] which brought thick fog.

In the afternoon Sh. and Ikeraping were again telling me stories, and then played nuglarpok [I. *nuglu'pok* = stabbing game (FB); I. *nulluktaqtut*] with all the women and children of the camp. The nuglaktuk [I. *nulluktaq* = a bone with holes; sticks] hangs from 3 racks for drying skins, which stand between my tupik and Sh.'s; next to them lies my sledge on which everybody stands. In the meantime tricks were demonstrated; for example Padlu's little daughter ran on her knees, then with Shanguja and Ssegdloaping jumped into a box from circles; then she turned somersaults etc. Then there were jumping competitions and ball games [Boas 1888:565ff].

In the evening transcribed everything possible, except Kaudjukdjuak's story [Qaudjaqdjuq; see story in Boas 1888:628–33]. The weather is now very thick; cold and almost no wind. I really wanted to go up the hill but because of the fog I naturally stayed down here. I hope that when it clears I will find the ice very shattered. Where might the floe edge be by the 3rd [August]? [Marie's birthday, when she would turn 23 years old.]

[**1 August**] **Friday**   Imakra [Inuktitut?] got up late. Thick fog, clearing occasionally. Have been thinking a great deal about the floe edge and resting. Watched 1 dubious piece of ice off Tudnirn all day. Unfortunately, in the evening we finally discovered the old floe edge off Kivitung again. Shanguja [Padli] has been telling me all sorts of things about customs associated with birth and about the fall festival as well as the plan of the kaggi [Boas 1888:600]. Jack, Akkudlu and Tyson's son-in-law arrived in the evening. Akkudlu brought a seal with him. In the evening the Inuit were playing ball in front of my tupik. [WW: .. After we had our evening coffee, I played ball with the natives.] Ikeraping told me a story; Bob brought a ssakatan [I. *saketa'n* = roulette (FB)]. I continued packing my ethnographic collection.

[**2 August**] **Saturday**   Very thick weather. Shanguja is travelling to Kangeeakdjung to hunt ugjuit [= bearded seals]. I hope he also finds a ship during the 4 days he will be there. Iwi, Shorty, Tyson and Padlu arrived. Shorty has borrowed my sledge and in the evening came back with a tupik. Now the camp is at full strength. I believe Ikeraping and Tessigang are away with a boat, perhaps also to Kangeeakdjung. Iwi has made an elegant kayak [miniature] and was telling me only stories in the afternoon. Quite thick weather in the evening.

At noon a ship was guessed at and played out! Since a ship is coming tomorrow evening, got my book in order. ... [There follows an illegible sentence in Inuktitut.]

[**3 August**] **Sunday**   To mark the day [Marie's birthday] it was quite thick again in the morning. Early this morning the dogs were making a hellish row, so I had to give them a sound thrashing. At noon clearing up somewhat. I climbed to the cairn on Kivitung where the flag is still standing. One could see as far as Kachodluin [K'axodluin] but there was thick fog lying all along the floe edge, which in any case is a long way from Kangeeakdjung; beyond it one can see water. I was accompanied by Attishellik, Utuitung, Kinnidliak and Okidliriak. In the evening the fog moved farther inland. Tyson and his wife came close to my tupik in the evening and he told me all sorts of things about Akkudliak [Akuliax; Nile Harbour] and the boaster Kaimerte.

[WW]
(...) After we had coffee in the morning, we counted our bread; 21 loaves and a box full of crumbs. When the bread bag was empty, we tied it up on top of the tubik. Then the Dr. laid stones in front of the door and I cleaned the tubik, opened a can of meat and had duck soup with it. (...)

[D2]

[**4 August**] **Monday**   Thick fog again; in the afternoon it also began raining and it rained all night long. The dogs are fighting now day and night
because of Mika's bitch. Sitting in the tupik, writing up songs and being
lazy. In bed by 8 and again slept through till 8. At night it seemed as if an
avagnanirn had come and the rain ceased; however this morning there
was first a little ikichsuk then okudsuk [I. *oqu'xtsuq* = southeast wind (FB)].

My curletang, which the dogs had half eaten at Kignait, is repaired
again. Our bread bag is now lying empty on top of the tupik, but we have
another 20 pieces coming in a tin box! Shorty is keeping a falcon he has
captured; according to Tyson, Ikeraping has gone with his boat to Nedluchseak [Nedluxseax].

[**5 August**] **Tuesday**   Still foggy. In the afternoon it cleared up a little
and Wilhelm went up the hill to take a look around. He reported that it
was all full of ice[,] whereas it was quite clear outside; he could not identify the floe edge. The ice lay about 7 miles from Kangeeakdjung. I have
completed a copy of my itinerary and tomorrow I shall make a copy of my
map. In the evening I was again in bed by around 8.30. The Eskimos were
out hunting and came back late, but they had killed only 1 seal. In the
evening it was quite thick again.

[**6 August**] **Wednesday**   It is still foggy, and how! I spent the entire day in
the tupik drawing. In the evening the clouds were racing with an avagnanirn with a speed of 0.786. I wish we could have a force-10 wind till the
ice is gone! *Erk!* Shanguja is still not back at 9.45. Fed the dogs in the
morning.

[**7 August**] **Thursday**   In the morning it was still quite thick and raining.
But finally it cleared up, so I climbed the hill. Up there the wind was blowing out of the N. whereas down below it was calm. The ice appeared to be
still lying exactly as it was after the recent avagnanirn. It seems to have
broken up only near Manitung. All the Eskimos were out hunting and
came back fairly early. Angutikan and Neinennak [dogs] have run away. I
have no idea where to look for them. To bed early again.

[**8 August**] **Friday**   Weather clear and sunshine. Got up at 7. In the
morning W.[ilhelm] went over to Kivitung to look for plants[;] I was writing, working and tidying up. During the day a trace of a swell appeared
here, which the Eskimos alleged they had also seen yesterday near

Idjuniving. Now around 8 there *appears* to be some avangnanirn developing, but will anything actually come of it? Iwi brought a kayak and the associated harpoon [model].

[**9 August**] **Saturday**   Fog and snow; all day I was making calculations concerning the Kikkertons [probably the K'exerten archipelago, since calculations for that region pop up in the notebooks at this period], Coffee at 4; in the evening W.[ilhelm] was reading and I was singing in bed. At 1.30 Shanguja came back with the other Esk.[;] he had been at Nedluchseak and brought only 1 caribou with him. He came into the tupik and asked for some tobacco. Today we had a shortage of meat. We then slept until morning. Snow during the night. Yesterday and today there was a severe avagnanirn. Sh. set out when it cleared towards evening. Alikdjua says there is a strong swell near Kangeeakdjung and thin ice.

[**10 August**] **Sunday**   Some okuchsuk in the morning, which rose very rapidly. I took a sun altitude and walked to the lookout cairn. As soon as Sh. and I arrived up there, it socked in. The ice to the northeast is still very shattered, so the floe edge is now about 3 miles from Tudnirn. I have high hopes of getting away, since it now gets dark again at 8 p.m. [WW: .. In the morning we got a caribou leg, liver and tongue. They [the Inuit] had two caribou for us while they were gone.]

[**11 August**] **Monday**   Working. In the afternoon Wilhelm climbed the hill. It seems that the ice has broken up to about 3 miles from Kangeeakdjung and that there are several leads behind Tudnirn. This morning I saw water from here for the first time, but still not right off the tent door. In the evening the Eskimos were playing in Bob's tupik where Tyson's kuni was playing tricks with twine around her head. In the evening playing and jumping with the boys. Sh. was kicking up a row in his tupik all night; so I was unable to sleep while they were singing monotonously.

[**12 August**] **Tuesday**   The Eskimos went seal hunting. I rested in my sleeping bag in the morning. Then we ate and I climbed the hill. There was nothing noteworthy to see. There is little ice outside, but everything as Wilhelm described it yesterday. 6 dogs came running along with me again. Utuatung's nose, which was bad yesterday and the day before, is better today, but I don't know whether it was just congested. Shanguja was still away at 8:15 a.m.; Jack has been ugjupoking [I. *ujjupuq* = hunting bearded seals; anglicized] at a lead near Koeinnilli. Also somewhat near

Iwi's [camp]. Up above there was quite a wind, but almost nothing down here. Iwi will also {make} have the boat [model] ready soon.

[**13 August**] **Wednesday**   Wind and snow last night, okuchsuk; this morning {fog} ikichsuk and sunshine broke through, so the snow will again be melting quickly. In the evening Shanguja told me various stories. Iwi arrived later too, and told me a story about the raven and the duck, which I could understand only with great difficulty. His boat frame, along with oars, is finished [Boas 1888:528]. He is still to make the covering and the mast, as well as the sails [miniatures]. [WW: .. We fill our time with eating; tonight we spent two hours drinking coffee.]

[**14 August**] **Thursday**   In the morning we shared the last piece of bread among us. In the evening a strong okuchsuk began blowing. In the afternoon Wilhelm and I made a disgusting row with tin drums and plates, tattoo, etc. The Eskimos must certainly have thought we were *ankuting*. I have been transcribing the stories and making calculations from around Ananatu [Anarnitung].

[**15 August**] **Friday**   Yesterday evening, while W. was cooking[,] the wind swung round to an avagnanirn. All night long, until 1.00 today we had a gale with snow, so the entire country now looks white. But the ice has still not gone out; however, one can see water clearly from up on the rock, which we keep visiting. If it is not foggy tomorrow, I think we should be able to see the floe edge clearly from Kivitung. I hope that now, finally, it runs from Kangeeakdjung to Tudnirn. In the afternoon it was clear and calm; in the evening I worked on my itinerary.

[**16 August**] **Saturday**   Shangin went hunting with my rifle and did not come back till late. He had shot 2 seals. One can still not see any water from the tent door, but I believe that the floe edge runs out from Kangeeakdjung, but where to, heaven only knows! I have finally identified the mistakes [in my calculations] about Anarnitung and can now begin drafting. I hope that I shall soon get the necessary bearings on Pilektuak and Kachodluing.

[**17 August**] **Sunday**   In the morning drafting and washing. Then I unpacked a box and brought the contents inside so that Wilhelm doesn't always have to fetch the things from behind. The kerosene box now stands in front of the entrance full of food [for the dogs]; the old box contains meat, trade goods and books. Shangin went to Kivitung today and reported that there is little change there. The sky is now terribly black, but there is probably no ice. Yesterday it rained heavily, so a lot of snow has melted again. It rained again this morning too, before another avagnanirn began to blow (quite strongly). The country again looks very beautiful.

[**18 August**] **Monday**   Avagnanirn all blessed day. I wanted to take observations, but since the wind was blowing too strongly, I had to abandon the notion and left my instrument [theodolite] here. I then climbed the hill and saw that the water has finally reached Tudnirn. However, beyond that is still full of ice. But Wilhelm became curious and raced over there in the evening too. In the meantime the wind had died completely. I have been organizing things and working. In the evening Shanguja and his wife were here. We told stories. Iwi and his wife came and brought a boat [model]. The first stars.

[ww]
(...) After coffee I went again to Kivittung [K'ivitung]. Down at the pond I discovered graves; 4 whites [whalers] are buried here. (...)

Whalers in Sight

[D2]
[**19 August**] **Tuesday**   In the morning I wanted to climb the hill with Wilhelm to take bearings on Kachodluing, but it became overcast so I did not go. I drafted and calculated. In the afternoon W. climbed the hill on this side, but saw nothing except the last sledge, which came driving in towards the evening to announce that there was a ship in sight. Nachojassi. Since I still have to close up my tupik, and don't want to travel there at night, I stayed here. Padlu went out alone with Saudloaping and Apitang. I shall follow tomorrow morning. In the evening Shanguja pitched his new tupik.

[**20 August**] **Wednesday**   Woke at 5. By 7.30 everything was ready and we set off. Sh., Wilhelm, myself and Padlu's daughter. The entire Tyson family was ahead of us. When we were in Kangeeakdjung, we could only see the ship's masts away off in the distance as it steamed around there. Soon dense fog rolled in, and we lost the ship completely. Shorty drove back along the floe edge. At noon he announced that it is the *Arctic*, but that he was unable to go aboard, since the ship was still about 4 miles away. The fog soon dispersed again, but an avagnanirn with snow began, so I had to stay at home. In the evening I was drafting and making notes.

[FB/MK]

(...) Oh, Marie, just imagine how I felt when last night, as it got dark, Shanguja suddenly came into my tupik and told me a ship was coming. An Eskimo who had been out hunting seals this afternoon had spotted it. A sledge left yesterday evening to try to locate it, and we are now, at 5 o'clock[,] making preparations for breaking camp.

Yesterday we were not even thinking about a ship. There wasn't a breath of air stirring and the ice had not changed at all. I had been working until it grew dark, then played the concertina and sang, our usual activity when it got dark. I saw Wilhelm's face as his blood (like mine too) went to his heart. What news will I hear from home now? What things may have happened? (...)

I hope I can go aboard today; if the ice is not too badly broken up, we will probably manage to get out to her. We have still not seen the ship. Wilhelm is now coming with the trunks, and then we will be off!

With this entry Boas ends the letter-journal that he began for his fiancée, Marie Krackowizer, on 23 June 1883. Not until he was crossing from St John's to New York via Halifax on board the Ardandhu *in September 1884 did Boas again manage to write to her (see below).*

[D2]

[**21 August**] **Thursday**   Today the Eskimos went with 5 sledges and Jack's boats to the little water hole at Kangeeakdjung to hunt walrus. In the morning I climbed to the cairn to look for the ship, but saw nothing. There was nothing but mountains to be seen. I came back at 11, and the sledges not until 12. In the afternoon Wilhelm went up the hill on this side, while I drafted. By noon a lot of ice must have been eroded along the numerous leads near Tudnirn and been drifted away, because in the afternoon we could see it [the water] from the tupik for the first time. The sledges came back in the evening. Sh. had 3 walrus, Tyson 1 and Iwi 1. [WW: .. the meat was given to our dogs.]

[**22 August**] **Friday**   In the morning I wanted to come up here on the hill to take some s[outherly] bearings. But in the meantime it became overcast, so after 45 minutes I turned back without achieving my goal. Soon the sun disappeared completely. I dozed away the greater part of the day; Cumberland Sound [map] is finished; I still have to draft Tupir-bikdjureitung [Tupirbikdjariaitung] and Padli, then the minor details of the maps are finished. The Eskimos want to stay at Kangeeakdjung today. In the evening Shorty came back, having shot 2 walruses and 2 seals. I bought meat from him. [ww: .. In the afternoon I boiled our clothes to rid them of lice.]

[**23 August**] **Saturday**   Woke at 6.30; unfortunately it is cloudy again so I can still not get my bearings. I finished my map and now have to make one more copy in order to send it off with a ship. In the afternoon I slept terribly soundly, and did not wake again until evening. Shorty did not go anywhere today.

[**24 August**] **Sunday**   Since it was clear in the morning Wilhelm and I set off up to the cairn. There was a little iküschuk, so the fog came in very fast and concealed Kachodluing and Kikkertuktjuak, so I got only a miser-able bearing on Ssettiksun and Kikkerluktjuk [K'exertalukdjuax], as well as a latitude.

The sledges came back after noon. We fed the dogs. Sh. had 3 walrus. He now wants to go hunting caribou. Tessivang is still not back from salmon fishing. Iwi has finished the tupik poles and will have the whole thing ready tomorrow [a miniature].

Another 2 days have passed while we have waited in vain for the dear! ship. Kanga tikipin? [I. *Qanga tikipit?* = When will you arrive?]

Leaving the Inuit and the Arctic, August–September 1884

With the Wolf to K'armaxdjuin and St John's

[D2]

[25 August] Monday Jean Mayen [*Jan Mayen*]. It cleared in the afternoon and I was about to go up the hill when S. arrived with the news that Kimalo [Shanguja's wife] had seen 2 ships. We immediately set off at 1 o'clock and by 6 had safely reached the ships which are lying at the floe edge. As we were getting across a lead 3 men and a passenger, Mr. Yeaman, also a white man, came up to us. The latter took me with him to the Nova Semlja [*Nova Zembla*]. Her captain was Mr. Gregory [actually Captain David Kilgour of Dundee; McGregory was captain of the *Cornwallis*, according to Lubbock 1937]. Capt. Tujor [William Douchars, Fay Terrace, Broughty Ferry, Scotland] of the *Jan Mayen* had messages for me. They are not original letters, but how delighted I am. Only the fact that there is nothing in Papa's handwriting causes me fear and anxiety. I discussed with them that it would be best to leave now.

[26 August] Tuesday Kivitung. *Wolf* [steamer from St John's, Newfoundland]. Early this morning the *Wolf* and *Cornwallis* appeared. Captain Burner [of the *Wolf*; John Burnett, 18 Ferry Road, Dundee, Scotland] was immediately prepared to take me with him. He had received my letter at Niachonanjan [Niaxongnang]. I went ashore as quickly as possible to fetch my things. I set off at 10 and by 12 midnight I was back. There is a German-speaking doctor on board the *Cornwallis*.

The Captain wants to go to Cape Searle tomorrow [K'axodluin; Nuvuktlirn] in order to go into the harbour there as a precaution, to make repairs to the screw and take on water; so we could possibly be in St. John's by 5th or 6th Sept[ember].

Hurray! I've given all my things to the Eskimos.

[**27 August**] **Wednesday**   In the morning I visited both ships [*Jan Mayen* and *Nova Zembla*] and said goodbye. They want to leave today too. The last Eskimos. Gave Sh. a letter to take to Kikkerton. Then we set off. Quite a lot of ice. In the evening it grew foggy, but at 5 we made fast to the headland. *Jan Mayen* and *Nova Zembla* must be almost off C. Broughton. I slept on the captain's sofa.

[ww]
(...) .. the *Wolf* sailed at 9.30 [a.m.].

[D2]
[**28 August**] **Thursday**   My parents' wedding anniversary. In the morning it cleared up. The two ships [*Jan Mayen* and *Nova Zembla*] came over and brought mail for the captain. Then we steamed away. Much ice. Had to stand off the land. Around 4 p.m. we set a SSW course along the land. Fairly clear weather; perhaps we'll be able to get into Exeter [Sound].

[**29 August**] **Friday**   Exeter [Sound] (Kangmaadjuin). Got under way at daybreak. We are able to steam close along the coast and can see that Durban Har. is open, but there is still a lot of ice here along the coast. The farther south we go the clearer it becomes. There is little ice off Exeter [Sound]. In the afternoon we arrived off the harbour. Eskimos were sighted; in fact it is Aranin and Mummiachia from Ssaumia. They, and also the children, recognize me again despite my European clothes.

The *Arctic* was here a few days ago and had bought all the bear pelts except for 1. I had to do a lot of interpreting. When we arrived there was no snow left on the land. By the afternoon the screw had been repaired and some casks of water had been taken aboard. There will probably be a major encampment here next winter.

[**30 August**] **Saturday**   Exeter [Sound]. In the morning I went ashore and recorded the time and the latitude. The latitude determination was a good one. I gave Aranin, who had lost his dogs[,] my two animals [which Boas had intended to take home]. During the morning 2 dogs that had run away in April came running up to him; they were very fat. Sessirang's wife is very sick and has deteriorated badly since spring. I can give them

quite a lot of news about Cumberland Sound and Kivitung. In the afternoon the ship was being painted.

This is Boas's last entry in Diary 2.

[WW]
31 August [Sunday]   Due to the ice the ship hove to for the night.

On the night of 30–1 August the Wolf *left Exeter Harbour and headed for St
John's, Newfoundland.*

[WW]
1 September [Monday]   Quite windy in the morning; a gale in the
evening, which lasted all night; the Dr. and I were seasick.

*With this entry Weike ended the diary he had begun on Sunday, 10 June 1883, in
Minden i. w., which right to the end he had kept faithfully under the guidance of
'Herr Dr' Boas. Wilhelm then left the Arctic and the Inuit forever, on board the* Wolf.
The Wolf *headed for St John's, Newfoundland, where she arrived on Monday,
7 September 1884. On the inner back cover of Diary 2, Boas recorded the texts of
the telegrams he sent after his arrival in St John's.*

[Telegrams]

[7 September, Monday]   Sophie Boas. Minden Westfalen Marienstr. Both
returned safely. Address Atlantic Hotel. Letters and clothing. New York.
    Boas. Minden. Westfalen. Marienstrasse. Both safely returned. Answer
Atlantic Hotel. Letters and clothing. New York. Franz.
    Marie Krackowizer. New York. 16 East 60th Street. Returned safely.
Wednesday [9 September] to New York. Franz.
    Berliner Tageblatt. Berlin. Just returned. Travelled Cumberland Sound
and coast Davis Strait from C. Mercy to C. Raper. Boas.

[FB/parents]
St John's, **8th September 1884 [Tuesday]**   (...) I have truly escaped all
dangers safely and can send you a few sincere greetings of welcome from
here, since the mail leaves tomorrow and since I am fully occupied here.
    On the 26th of last month 2 ships arrived at the floe edge near C.[ape]
Hooper [K'ivitung is intended; Cape Hooper is Nudlung], but about 6
German miles from where I was camped; however, I was able to travel out

to meet them quite quickly with my sledge. How happy I was to receive copies of your letters which had travelled via Dundee! I knew then that as of May you were all well. (...)

Oh, dear parents, if only you could experience the joy, after the isolation[,] to be among people for the first time again, and now, in a few days, to be able to hold my fianceé in my arms. After such a long period everything sweeps over me so overwhelmingly that I can scarcely get my bearings. I hope you are not angry that when the *Wolf* came I [decided] to first travel aboard her to America to my Marie, and left the Dundee ship [*Nova Zembla*]. If only I had replies to all my messages. I should like so much to know how you all are! (...)

You won't believe how lonely it is up there in the frozen north, how deeply one feels that only living together with loved and loving people can make one happy. How much I would like to have you all here instead of all the strange faces, to see you and hear your dear voices. But instead of that I am besieged by newspaper reporters, who want to suck me dry, but all of whom I have declined. I do not want to relate today what I have done; you will see it shortly in the [*Berliner*] *Tageblatt.* I myself have been as healthy as a horse and have safely survived all the dangers and privations of the climate and starvation. In December Wilhelm froze his left big toe and as a result had to stay at the Scottish station for 3 months. Otherwise he too was healthy the whole time.

I was on very good terms with the good Eskimos and they never allowed me to suffer from hunger if I gave them tobacco. The winter, when all the dogs died, was a very difficult and anxious time for me[,] because I could see no opportunity for travelling and did not know whether ships would come to the Sound. But ever since I had my team things have always gone quite well for me; the only problem was that I had to leave all my things, provisions and all, in the country [at the King-nait-Padli pass] and have arrived here with only the absolutely essential things – without clothes or anything else.

I have arranged for money to be cabled to me from New York and have outfitted myself with the help of the ship's owner [Thoburn, owner of the *Wolf*]. On Thursday [10 September] a steamer [*Ardandhu*] is leaving for New York, and I shall travel aboard her. (...)

On Board the Ardandhu to New York

Boas and Weike travelled on board the Ardandhu *from St John's via Halifax to New York, where they arrived on 21 September 1884. On board ship, Boas wrote letters to Marie and to his parents, in which he summarized the past few weeks and reflected upon his experiences.*

[FB/MK]
[**11 September, Friday**]   (...) I was unable to get to Iglulik because all the dogs had died, yet I am quite content, because I have been able to map Cumberland Sound and the coast of Davis Strait, and have brought back very interesting ethnographic material. Even if occasionally I experienced very difficult and hungry times, I easily endured it all and am now as cheerful as ever. (...) *'Forward, I'm waiting for you!'*

[**16 September, Tuesday** from Halifax]   (...) I won't send you my diary; it is lying in my trunk, the only one I have saved, and I shall give it to you in New York. (...)

[FB/parents]
On board *Ardandhu*, **20th September** [**Sunday**]   (...) We are now only about 50 nautical miles from New York and in very calm water. Since I probably won't get around to writing to you tomorrow, I want to take the opportunity today and to tell you about things from 1st August onwards. I had stopped writing letters at that point because of a strange feeling that news from home was very close. Whenever I tried to sit down to write something, my thoughts began to wander to all that might have happened at home and what the content of the latest mail would be, and I could never assemble my thoughts to write to you. At that time I attempted to think of home as little as possible, because such thoughts were beginning to torture me. Whereas previously going home and being at home had been our constant topics of conversation, now we gave this up completely and discussed only the floe edge. You knew that I had come back from my last sledge trip on 20th July.

We took advantage of the next few days to rest and to feed up because, although we had certainly had enough to eat since 12 July in terms of caribou meat and salmon, we still looked forward to finding a piece of bread and coffee again. I found all my things intact [at Pamiujang near K'ivitung]. The Eskimos were now living on Idjuniving, which lies about 3 nautical miles from Pamiujang. But they all came over to Pamiujang again when they heard that I was back.

On the 30th and 31st [of July] finally all of them had moved and the encampment consisted of 8 tents, all near the narrow strait between Kivitung and Pamiujang. I was now diligently occupied in collecting stories and expanding my vocabulary; I also had toys and other items made for me, but I could not proceed too quickly with this, since I had to give the Eskimos tobacco or something else for everything and my reserves had shrunk drastically. The ice still extended far, far from land. I had hoisted your flag, dear Toni, up on the hill where there was a [flagstaff] so that any ship that might be passing would see it. Apparently in previous years by about this time, i.e. early August, there was practically no more ice to be seen here; but now it extended about 15 miles off Kangeeakdjung and despite many squalls it was reluctant to break up.

On 2 August the weather was foul, but we greeted it with joy, and on the 3rd., Marie's birthday[,] I climbed hopefully to the top of the flag hill, 1400' high, to spy out the floe edge, but I could see nothing very comforting. You can't imagine how we watched the floe edge, how every slightest change was noted and how after every storm we hoped that it would have moved closer, but we were always disappointed.

Our bread bag now hung almost empty outside the tent and the last 20 pieces of bread, weighing 5 lb, were carefully shared out so that they would last another 10 days. But we were not suffering from want since the Eskimos were catching enough seals and the excellent *Carne pura* soups were keeping us well nourished.

From Padli onwards Shanguja, a young Eskimo with 3 wives and 1 child[,] had attached himself closely to me and I had arranged with him that he would always provide me and my dogs with meat, for which he always received tobacco and matches and anything else he needed. He pitched his tent right next to mine; his wives worked for us and, along with other Eskimos, often visited me in my tent. On 2 August Shanguja had gone north with one wife to hunt caribou and returned on the 9th. Since the weather had been bad the whole time, he brought little back with him.

All this time I was working on a copy of my itinerary, which I planned to send off with a different ship from the one I myself would travel on; now it occurred to me here, you should send it to me to New York and the book 'Literature of the Polar Regions' [Boas's Notebook with excerpts], which is at home.

From 3rd to 6th August it was continually dense fog; when it cleared up on the 7th I was up at the lookout, but could see nothing new. You can't imagine how cheerless the ice had begun to seem to me when no change had occurred; as I was coming back I noticed that one of the cracks in the fast ice had now been pushed quite far apart; there was some swell, and I hoped this would break the ice up, but again I was disappointed.

On the 9th it was blowing strongly and now, finally[,] one could see some effect on the ice. About 4 miles of ice had broken up and was now drifting rapidly southward. Since there was a gale on the 10th too, on the 11th I sent Wilhelm up the hill. He found the ice all shattered; the floe edge was about 10 miles from Kangeeakdjung and 3 from Idjuniving. Thus we lived from day to day in this fashion, hoping for a change that refused to come.

On the 14th we shared the last piece of bread. But you should not imagine that we were in a depressed mood at this stage. We had enough to eat and amused ourselves as best we could. There was no point in harbouring thoughts about whether the ship would come or not, and we made the best we could of the situation. I played ball with the Eskimos, and jumped and ran with them and made a hellish racket in our tent.

On the 15th the first snowstorm raged again and the entire landscape was now white. The ice had now broken away from there to the island of Idjuniving, but, just as before, remained as far as Kangeeakdjung. I often climbed the 90-minute route to the top of the hill to take a bearing that I absolutely had to have, but was unable to obtain one because the sun was always obscured.

On the afternoon of the 19th Wilhelm was up the hill, but was unable to spot anything new and it was a sledge that arrived from Kangeeakdjung in the evening that brought the first news that there was a ship in sight. At first I wanted to go out there immediately, but after some deliberation I stayed put since I still had to pack up all my things.

A sledge went out, taking a message from me. But the good Eskimo was unable to reach the ship which he recognized as the *Arctic*. He travelled all through the night after it, but got only to within ... 4 miles of it.

At 5 next morning we too set out, but saw only the above-mentioned Eskimos returning and three distant masts of a ship disappearing into thick fog. Hence we had to turn back, depressed. But I was still in good heart since I knew that there were ships on this coast and that it was unlikely that I would not see a single one.

So we put a good face on a bad situation and continued to live as we had been doing, but now hoping by the day for another ship. Since we had seen on our way out across the ice that there were many walrus in a small polynya off Kangeeakdjung, the Eskimos now went out with a boat and next day killed 6. From now on they were out there every day and thus I could learn little from them though I seized every opportunity to do so.

On the 25th I was just about to go up the hill when Shanguja arrived with the news that his wife had seen two ships. In an instant the tupik was

sealed up, because I was already prepared for this, the team was harnessed and my dogs, which had done nothing for weeks, raced off like
the wind.

That evening I could not travel fast enough although we were covering
at least 5 miles per hour. We set off at 1 [o'clock] and by 2.30 we were at
Kangeeakdjung; from there we headed out to the floe edge to where the
ships had been spotted. The going was rather unpleasant due to large
leads, but we reached the ships safely around 6 o'clock. A lead about 30'
wide, which we would have to cross, lay between us and the ships. Naturally the man in the crow's nest had long since seen our sledges and
numerous dogs, and 3 sailors came towards us, to the other side of the
lead, as well as another white man who turned out to be a passenger [Mr
Yeaman]. With their help we got across the lead.

You would think I would have been able to speak English right away;
quite involuntarily nothing but Eskimo came out of my mouth instead of
English. But it was an inexpressible joy! The passenger was the owner's
son who had come out to hunt. Neither he nor the captain of the *Nova
Zembla* [David Kilgour] (the first ship we had encountered) had any
inkling that we were here, but they were very friendly towards us. Immediately afterwards the captain of the second ship, *Jean Meyen* [William Douchars, *Jan Mayen*], came over and brought me a letter. Can you imagine
my delight? He had not expected to find me here, since the letter was
addressed to Cumberland Sound. Right there I simply scanned the sheets
to learn whether you were all well and postponed the rest till later when I
would have some peace.

Since the Cpt. invited me to stay on board, I did so and discussed with
him the best way of getting home. I told him that I wanted to stay here as
long as possible, but did not want to miss the opportunity of getting
home. They pointed out to me that ice conditions were very unfavour-
able, because from Pond's Bay to here the fast ice was continuous, and
that as soon as this broke up there would be no prospect of a ship getting
in to C. Hooper [near K'ivitung] where I was staying. So I arranged with
Cpt. Kilgour that I would sail with him, because he wanted to head home
immediately, but I said that I first wanted to see the *Wolf*, from St. John's,
since I would like to transfer to that ship because I hoped to go to America with her.

That night we slept aboard the *Jean Meyen*, and the first news, when I
awoke in the morning [26 August] was that a third ship, the *Wolf* was
approaching. I was absolutely delighted. We immediately walked over to
the other ships. Cpt. Burnett of the *Wolf* was also very obliging. He had

seen the Eskimos at C. Raper, with whom I had left a letter for these captains, and had read my message. But since he had heard and knew of nobody being here to explore, he had therefore taken the message for a joke from a doctor. He immediately said he would take me and wanted to leave next morning. Thus I immediately travelled back to land and quickly finished packing and I was back on board by 12 midnight. Naturally I was very tired, because the night before I had been unable to sleep for excitement.

In the morning [27 August] we indeed got under way, once the other ships had said goodbye. When fog set in that night the captain moored to the ice. Next morning [29 August] we sighted the *Nova Zembla* and *Jean Meyen* again as we steamed southward. Since the ice was lying fairly close, we made only slow progress, and on the 29th ran into Exeter Bay. The captain had to take on fresh water and to make repairs to the screw.

As I had surmised there were Eskimos here whom I had seen in winter near C. Mercy. I assisted in the conversation between the captain and them, but he was unable to barter very much because the *Arctic* had been here a few days before us and had bought all their furs. The Eskimos were really amazed because I could now speak Eskimo much better, and we chatted about old friends and everything that had happened in Cumberland Sound in the interim. Quite accidentally I told one poor man that his son, whom he had given to a childless couple, had died! We were there for two days and three weeks ago today I saw the last Eskimos.

On the night of the 31st we weighed and headed rapidly south. Since we had foul weather the entire way, I was almost constantly seasick and thus was very glad when we finally reached St. John's on the 7th. We had a serious collision with an ice floe in fog and ... found a leak in the bulkhead. We had 5' of water in the hold and were making 5 inches of water per hour, but they were able to keep it under control with the pumps. There were many large icebergs all the way to St. John's but we got into the harbour unhindered.

What joy it was to see the first green patches on the land and the first houses. Everyone in St. John's was very obliging towards me; the only problem was to try to escape the reporters. Mr. Thoburn, the ship's owner, helped me in every way and directed me to the right source to get some money, because I had to fit us out completely. When we had come aboard the ship we had only our skin clothing. For the first few days Cpt. Burnett lent me some of his clothes but by Tuesday evening [8 September] we were completely fitted out anew.

I had hoped that a ship would be sailing for New York on Wednesday [9

September], but I was mistaken. There was only one sailing for Liverpool and I sent you a letter and the [*Berliner*] *Tageblatt* a report by it. In these past few days I have had enough to do, and now I must finish this letter. We are dropping anchor and the cabin is full of people. Tomorrow morning [21 September] we'll be going into New York.

Hurray!

Your Franz

With these sentences Boas concluded the notes he had kept for fifteen months – records which in their abundance of information and data, reflections, and analyses would take shape in numerous scientific and popular publications in both German and English in subsequent years.

Weike returned alone to Germany and to Minden i. W. by ship in late September 1884 after an absence of almost sixteen months. Soon afterwards he married Mathilde Nolting, and continued to work for the Boas family. In 1886 he moved with Boas's parents and sisters to Berlin, where he stayed until his death in June 1917.

From New York, Boas made his way first to his fiancée, Marie Krackowizer, at her family's summer cottage on Lake George in upstate New York, meeting her on 23 September 1884. Then he set about developing his scientific career in the United States, working in New York and Washington, DC, before returning to Germany for a year. He arrived there in late March 1885, when he was at last united with his family after an absence of almost two years.

Appendix 1
Dog Names

Dogs occupied an important place in the social and economic organization of the Inuit, who invariably gave them names. During his sojourn Boas was dependent on dogs in order to carry out his investigations. The epidemic of 1883–4 greatly reduced the number available to him. It was only in May 1884, after great effort, that Boas was able to assemble a full team for his journey to Davis Strait, and only then did the names of his dogs begin to appear in his journal (June–August 1884). The names given below are the ones mentioned by Boas and Weike (ww).

Angutikan
Attelschuling
Kudlukulu, a bitch
Neinennak
Neinessuak
Pegbing (or Pöbing in ww), a bitch that produced nine pups on 4 June 1884 at
    K'exertalukdjuax. Of these, Boas raised some and wanted to take two back to
    New York; but on 30 August he gave them to Aranin, whom he'd met at
    K'armaxdjuin, because he had lost his dogs.
Pilulak (ww)
Waldmann, almost killed by Weike, who gave him a thrashing on 24 July 1884.

Appendix 2
Names of Ships and Boats

All names of ships and boats cited in the text are listed here alphabetically. The names used by Franz Boas in his writings are identified by (FB). Data and information on individual ships and boats are derived partly from Boas's diaries and partly from various sources (Barr 1985; Boas 1885; Goldring et al. 1984; Lubbock 1937:462; Ross 1975, 1985; Sherman 1986).

Alhambra. American expedition ship, dispatched to evacuate Adolphus Greely's expedition in 1884 (see *Proteus*)

Antelope. Whaler, Naujateling, Cumberland Sound 1866. USA

Arctic (FB). Whaler, 522 tons, Captain Adams, Scotland; cruising off K'ivitung, Davis Strait, August 1884

Ardandhu (FB). Passenger steamer on which Boas and Weike travelled from St John's via Halifax to New York, 10–21 September 1884

Catherine (FB). Supply ship, Peterhead/Dundee; Captain Abernathy; owner; Crawford Noble, K'exerten; in Cumberland Sound 7 September – 3 October 1883

Cornwallis (FB). Whaler, Captain McGregory, Scotland; K'ivitung, Davis Strait, August 1884

Germania (FB). Three-masted sailing vessel of the German Polar Commission 1882–3; Captain A.F.B. Mahlstede (Hamburg); voyages: 28 June – 24 October 1882; 20 June – 17 October 1883; in Cumberland Sound 1 August – 18 September 1882 and 28 August – 16 September 1883

Helgoland (FB). Tug that assisted the *Germania* in the Elbe estuary, 20–2 June 1883

Irene (FB). Sailing ship that lay near the *Germania* in Jonashafen, Hamburg, 20 June 1883

Jan Mayen (FB). Whaler, 319 tons, Captain William Douchars, Dundee/Broughty Ferry; K'ivitung, Davis Strait, August 1884

Lizzie P. Simmons (FB). Whaler, 89 tons, New London, Connecticut; owner: C.A. Williams. Captain John Roach (of Montreal); sources indicate J.W. Buddington as captain; wintered in Cumberland Sound 1877–8 and 1881–4; lost off Greenland

Marie (FB). Sailboat and rowboat that Boas brought with him from Germany, fall of 1883; remained with James Mutch at K'exerten

Nova Zembla (FB). Whaler, 255 tons, 25 February – 31 August 1884, Captain David Kilgour, Dundee; owner; Mathew; K'ivitung, Davis Strait, August 1884

Proteus. American ship that was to have evacuated the Greely expedition in 1883 but was crushed by the ice in Kane Basin

Oxford. Whaler, Naujateling, Cumberland Sound 1869. USA

Red Lion (FB). Whaler, St John's, probably in Cumberland Sound, 1882

S.B. Howes (FB). Whaler, Naujateling, Cumberland Sound 1873. USA

Thetis (FB). Whaler, 492 tons, Dundee, Scotland; Davis Strait, August – September 1883

Wolf (FB). Whaler, Captain John Burnett; owner, Robert Thoburn, St John's Newfoundland; K'ivitung, Davis Strait; Boas and Weike sailed aboard her from K'ivitung to St John's, 28 August – 7 September 1884.

Glossary

The glossary contains all the foreign words that occur in Boas's and Weike's diaries. They consist of a limited English vocabulary with Scottish influences and influences from other languages, as well as words from Inuktitut, the language of the Inuit of the Eastern Canadian Arctic. At the time of his sojourn, Boas knew English fairly well, but he had difficulty in particular with the Scottish accent and dialect of James Mutch and others; the English of the Inuit, predominantly men, who had worked together with the whalers for years, was certainly coloured by their accent and dialect. The polyglot crews of the whaling ships added words of different origin to the vocabulary used in Cumberland Sound.

The manner in which Boas used English words in his diaries allows one to conclude that he spoke mainly English with the Inuit. Words in Inuktitut occur more often from May 1884 onwards, when Boas was becoming increasingly comfortable in Inuktitut; moreover, from that date until the end of August 1884, he did not encounter any English-speaking partners. The orthography of Inuktitut is mainly phonetic and was later corrected and standardized by Boas with the help of Henrik Rink (Copenhagen) according to Kleinschmidt's method (Kleinschmidt 1851). Apart from a few illegible words, all the Inuktitut expressions could be identified. Boas's spelling in the original and in the variations is reproduced here and has been compared with his published version (Boas 1894) and with the modern standardized orthography for the Eastern Inuit languages (Schneider 1985). Words identified WW are derived from Wilhelm Weike's diary.

English Words

Oxford English Dictionary and Webster	*Franz Boas*
beef	Beef
beefsteak	Beefsteak
blubber	Blubber
cakes	Cakes
	Kegs (ww)
corned beef	Corned Beef
cairn(s)	Cairn(s)
crack(s)	Crack(s)
crazy	crazy
cooney	Kuni(s)
cooper	Küper, Kuper
gimy	gimy
lemon juice	Lemon Juice
main boom	Mainboom
mile(s)	Miles, mile
molly	Molly(s)
mutton	Mutton
natives	Natives
pannikins	Pannekes
piccaninny	Pikkanini
pidgin English	Pigeon Englisch
pilot	Pilot
plug	Plok (ww)
rock(s)	Rock(s)
shawl	Shawl
slipper	Schlipper
stockings	Stockings
team (dog team)	Team
teetotaller	Teatotaler
terns (bird)	Turns
whaler	Waler

Inuktitut Words (Eastern Canadian Arctic)

Words in quotation marks were Germanized by Boas as verbs and are given here in anglicized form. Words in brackets are derived from Schneider (1985) and are compared with the word used by Boas.

Boas 1883–4	Boas 1894	Schneider 1985	Translation (Franz Boas)
akalerit			gets up
angekok	a'ngekoq	angakkuq	shaman
'to ankut'	–	anguqtuq	to conjure
appuu	apun	apput	snow
avagnanirn	avagna'nirn	[avunnganiq]	north wind
avangnanirn			
(*see* avagnanirn)			
cammings			
(*see* cummings)			
comings			
(*see* cummings)			
courletang			
(*see* curletang)			
cumans (ww)	–	kumak	louse
cummings	ka'ming	kamik	skin boots
curletang	qudlita'q	qulittaq	skin jacket
doctoraluk	doctoraaluk	great doctor	
doctoradluk			
(*see* doctoraluk)			
erk!	oh!		
idjua(n)	idjung	itjuq	peat, moss
iglu	igdlu	illu	snow house
ikaggan	–	ikkaruq	reef
ikichsuk			
(*see* iküschuk)			
ikuchsuk			
(*see* iküschuk)			
ikirn	ikirn	ikiq	open water, strait
iküschuk	iki'rtsuq		sea wind
imirk	imiq	imiq	fresh water
innuit	innuin	inuit	people
ipputit	(ipun)	(iputi)	oars ready!

Inuktitut Words (*continued*)

Boas 1883–4	Boas 1894	Schneider 1985	Translation (Franz Boas)
kaggi	qagi	qagi	singing house
kagmang	q'agmang	qarmaq	sod house
kajak	q'ajaq	qajaq	kayak, man's boat
kaumang			
(*see* kagmang)			
kayak			
(*see* kajak)			
kakkak	q'aqaq	qarqaq	mountain
kanga	qu'anga	qanga	when
kautak	kautaq	kautaq	stone hammer; diorite
kilauju	kilaut	qilaut	drum
kikkiten			
(*see* kikkertons)			
kikkertak	qi'qertaq	qikirtaq	island
kikkerton(s)	qiqerten	qikirtait	group of islands
kikkertins			
(*see* kikkertons)			
killak	qi'laq	qilaq	sky
kingawa	qi'ngua	kingua	fiord head
kodlunak	qa'dlunarn	qallunaq	white man (large
	(qa'dlu)	(qallu)	eyebrow)
köolu	kadlu	kallu	thunder
koffilirputit	–	kaapilirputit	brews coffee
kolitans (ww)			
(*see* curletang)			
komachiadlu	komakiadlu	-	annoyed
kommings			
(*see* cummings)			
koudschuguk	qaudjaqdjuq	–	songs, singing
mana	mana	mana	now
'manilary'	manilara'dlu	maniilaaraaluk	rough pack ice
mauja	mauja	maujaq	soft snow
maujadluk	mauja'dlu	maujaaluk	mass of snow
mitik	mi'tiq	mitiq	eider duck
naikerneiak(?)	nia'qonaujang	niaquunjaq	headlike
nauja	nauja	nauja	gull

Inuktitut Words (*continued*)

Boas 1883–4	Boas 1894	Schneider 1985	Translation (Franz Boas)
netshillik	neti'ling	natsilik	with seals
netsirn	net'irn	natsiq	seal
nettiavinirg	net'iaviniq	natsiaviniq	seal in first summer
nettiavinirn			
(*see* nettiavinirg)			
nettirn			
(*see* netsirn)			
nigpei	nigirn	nigiiq	east wind
nuglaktuk	nuglu'ktaun	nulluktaq	perforated bone
nuglarpok	nuglu'pok	(nulluktaqtut)	stabbing game
nuna	nu'na	nuna	mainland
nuvukulu	–	nuvukuluk	small point
nu'wuja'	nuvu'ja	nuvujaq	clouds
okuchsuk			
(*see* okudsuk)			
okudsuk	oqu'xtsuq	[urqu]	southeast wind
pagnir	pa'ngnirn	pangniq	bull caribou
po'adlu'	poadlu	pualu	glove
Sininirmiut	siri'nirmiut	siqinirmiut	people of the sun
ssakatan	saketa'n	–	roulette
ssiko	si'ko	siku	ice
takirn	takirn	tarqiq	moon
tarriok	ta'rioq	tariuq	sea water
tavunga	(takuvunga)	takuvunga	I see
tellirrua	tali'rua	taliruaq	flipper
tikipin	(tikipoq)	[tikiputit]	you come
torngasuck	to'rngaqsuq	tuurngasuq	like a guardian spirit
tubik (ww)			
(*see* tupik)			
tudnik	tuniq	tuniq/tuniit	ancestors of the Inuit
tupik	tu'piq	tupiq	tent
turgnang			
(*see* turgnak)			
turgnak	to'rngaq	tuurngaq	guardian spirit
uagnanjang			
(*see* uargang)			

Inuktitut Words (*concluded*)

Boas 1883–4	Boas 1894	Schneider 1985	Translation (Franz Boas)
uargang	ua'ngnang	uangnaq	northwest (land) wind
udlumi	–	ullumi	today
udluriak	udlu'riaq	ulluriaq	star
ugiuk			
(*see* ugjuk)			
ugjuk	u'gjuk	ujjuq	bearded seal
'ugjupoked'	ugjukpok	ujjupuq	hunted bearded seals
ujarak	ujarang	ujarak	stone
uman	u'men	uumma	heart, life
umiak	umi'aq	umiaq	women's boat
unicartua	unika'artua	unikkaatuaq	stories
utos	u'toq, o'toq	uuttuq	seal on the ice
zyninnirn(ing)	siri'nirn	siqiniq	sun

References

Abel, Herbert, and Hans Jessen
1954   *Kein Weg durch das Packeis: Anfänge der deutschen Polarforschung (1868–1889)*. Bremen: Carl Schünemann

Abbes, H[einrich]
1884a   Die Eskimos des Cumberland-Sundes: Eine ethnographische Skizze. *Globus* 46:198–201, 213–18
1884b   Die deutsche Nordpolar-Expedition nach dem Cumberland-Sunde. *Globus* 46:294–8, 312–15, 328–31, 343–5, 365–8
1890   Die Eskimos des Cumberlandgolfes. In Neumayer, (ed.) 1890, 1–60
1992   The German Expedition of the First International Polar Year to Cumberland Sound, Baffin Island, 1882–83. *Polar Geography and Geology* 16, no. 4: 272–304

Admiralty Charts
v.d.   Chart 262, 1847. Chart 2177, 1853. Chart 235, 1875. London: British Admiralty

[Ambronn, Leopold], L.A.
1883   Bemerkungen über den Cumberland-Sund und seine Bewohner. *Deutsche Geographische Blätter* 6:347–57

Andree, Richard
1969   *Geschichte der Berliner Gesellschaft für Anthropologie, Ethnologie und Urgeschichte, 1869–1969*. Berlin

Andrews, H.A., et al.
1943   Bibliography of Franz Boas. *American Anthropological Association Memoirs* 61:67–119

Angmarlik, Allan
1984   Personal communication. Pangnirtung, Nunavut, Canada

Barr, William

1983   Geographical Aspects of the First International Polar Year, 1882–1883. *Annals of the American Association of Geographers* 73, no.4:463–84

1985   The Expeditions of the First International Polar Year, 1882–83. *Arctic Institute of North America Technical Paper 29.* Calgary: University of Calgary

1992   Background to the German Expedition to Clearwater Fiord, Baffin Island, as Part of the First International Polar Year, 1882–1883. *Polar Geography and Geology* 16, no.4: 265–71

Barr, William, and Chuck Tolley

1982   The German Expedition at Clearwater Fiord, 1882–83. *Beaver* 313, no.2:36–44

Boas, Franz

1883a   Über die ehemalige Verbreitung der Eskimos im arktisch-amerikani-schen Archipel (mit Karte). *Zeitschrift der Gesellschaft für Erdkunde zu Berlin* 18:118–36, plate 2

1883b   Über die Wohnsitze der Neit[s]chillik-Eskimos (mit Karte). *Zeitschrift der Gesellschaft für Erdkunde zu Berlin* 18: 222–33, plate 3

1883c   B. [Boas, Franz]
Neueste Nachrichten über die Eskimos des Cumberland-Sund. (Review of Ludwig Kumlien's 'Contributions to the Natural History of Arctic America, Made in Connection with the Howgate Polar Expedition 1877–78,' Washington 1879.) *Deutsche Geographische Blätter* 6:172–8

1883d   Brief an den Vorstand der Gesellschaft für Erdkunde. *Verhandlungen der Gesellschaft für Erdkunde zu Berlin* 10:476–7

1884   Ssedna die religiösen Herbstfeste. *Berliner Tageblatt,* 16 November, 5–6, second insert

1885   Baffin-Land: Geographische Ergebnisse einer in den Jahren 1883 und 1884 ausgeführten Forschungsreise. Mit zwei Karten und neun Skizzen im Text. *Petermanns Mitteilungen,* supplement vol. 80:1–100

1888   The Central Eskimo. *Sixth Annual Report of the Bureau of Ethnology* 1884–5 [1888]:399–669 (Reprints, Lincoln: University of Nebraska Press 1964; Toronto: Coles 1974)

1894   Der Eskimo-Dialekt des Cumberland-Sundes. *Mittheilungen der Anthropologischen Gesellschaft in Wien* 24, n.s. 14:97–114

1901–7   The Eskimo of the Baffin Land and Hudson Bay from Notes Collected by Capt. George Comer, Capt. James S. Mutch, and Rev. E.J. Peck. *Bulletin of the American Museum of Natural History* 15, no.1 (1901): 1–370, and no.2 (1907): 371–570 (Reprint, New York: AMS Press 1975)

1972   Franz Boas. *The Professional Correspondence by Franz Boas* (44 microfilm reels) and *Guide to the Microfilm Collection of Franz Boas*, vol. 1–2. SR Scholarly Resources Inc. in cooperation with the American Philiosophical Society, by permission of Miss Franziska Boas. Wilmington, DE: SR Scholarly Resources Inc.

Böhm, Hans, and Astrid Mehmel, eds.

1996   Alfred Philippson: Wie ich zum Geographen wurde. Aufgezeichnet im Konzentrationslager Theresienstadt zwischen 1942 und 1945. *Academica Bonnensia* 11. Bonn: Bouvier Verlag

Börgen, C.

1882   Die internationalen Polarexpeditionen. *Deutsche Geographische Blätter* 5, no.4: 283–307

Brilling, B

1966   Die Vorfahren des Professors Franz Boas. *Mindener Heimatblätter* (Sonderbeilage des *Mindener Tageblattes*) 3–4:1–2

Cole, Douglas

1983   'The Value of a Person Lies in his *Herzensbildung*': Franz Boas' Baffin Island Letter-Diary, 1883–1884. In Stocking, ed. 1983, 13–52

1988   Kindheit und Jugend von Franz Boas: Minden in der zweiten Hälfte des 19. Jahrhunderts. *Mitteilungen des Mindener Geschichtsvereins* 60:111–34

1994   Franz Boas: Ein Wissenschaftler und Patriot zwischen zwei Ländern. In Rodekamp, ed. 1994, 9–23

In press   'A Certain Work Lies before Me': The Early Years of Franz Boas. Vancouver: Douglas & McIntyre and Seattle: University of Washington Press

Cole, Douglas, and Ludger Müller-Wille

1984   Franz Boas' Expedition to Baffin Island, 1883–1884. *Études/Inuit/Studies* 8, no.1:37–63

D'Souza, Dinesh

1995   *The End of Racism: Principles for a Multicultural Society.* New York: The Free Press

Dürr, Michael, Erich Kasten, and Egon Renner, eds.

1992   *Franz Boas: Ethnologe, Anthropologe, Sprachwissenschaftler. Ein Wegbereiter der modernen Wissenschaft vom Menschen.* Wiesbaden: Reichert

Études/Inuit/Studies

1984   Dans les traces de Boas: 100 ans d'anthropologie des Inuit/In Boas' Footsteps: 100 Years of Inuit Anthropology. *Études/Inuit/Studies* 8, no.1:3–179

Fischer, Hans

1990   *Völkerkunde im Nationalsozialismus: Aspekte der Anpassung, Affinität und*

Behauptung einer wissenschaftlichen Disziplin. Berlin, Hamburg: Dietrich
    Reimer Verlag

Fitzhugh, William B., and Igor Krupnik

1994   The Jesup II Research Initiative: Anthropological Studies in the North
    Pacific. *Arctic Studies Center Jesup II Newsbrief,* 19 January, 1–8. Washing-
    ton, DC: Department of Anthropology, National Museum of Natural
    History

Gieseking, Bernd

1996–7 Personal communication and correspondence. Kassel and Montreal

Goldring, Philip

1985   Whaling-Era Toponymy of Cumberland Sound, Baffin Island. *Canoma*
    11, no.2:28–35

1986   Inuit Responses to Euro-American Contacts: Southeast Baffin Island,
    1824–1940. *Annual Meeting of the Canadian Historical Association, Histori-
    cal Papers,* 146–72

Goldring, Philip, Elizabeth Snow, and Tim Sookocheff

1984   Arctic Whaling Study: 1984 Site Inspection Report. [Parks Canada]
    465–539

Hall, Charles Francis

1865   *Life with the Esquimaux: A Narrative of Arctic Experience in Search of Survi-
    vors of Sir John Franklin's Expedition from May 29, 1860 to September 13,
    1862.* London: Sampson Low & Marston

Halpin, Marjorie

1994   A Critique of the Boasian Paradigm to Northwest Coast Art. *Culture* 14,
    no.1:5–16

Hyatt, Marshall

1990   *Franz Boas Social Activist: The Dynamics of Ethnicity.* Contributions to the
    Study of Anthropology 6. New York: Greenwood Press

Jacknis, Ira

1996   The Ethnographic Object and the Object of Ethnology in the Early
    Career of Franz Boas. In Stocking, ed. 1996:185–214

Kasten, Erich

1992   Franz Boas: Ein engagierter Wissenschaftler in der Auseinanderset-
    zung mit seiner Zeit. In Dürr et al. 1992, 7–37

Kleinschmidt, Samuel

1851   *Grammatik der grönländischen Sprache mit teilweisem Einschluß des Labrador-
    dialektes* (Reprint, Hildesheim: Georg Olms 1968)

Kluckhohn, Clyde, and Olaf Prufer

1959   Influences during the Formative Years. In The Anthropology of
    Franz Boas: Essays on the Centennial of His Birth, ed. Walter

Goldschmidt. *American Anthropologist* 61, no.5, pt. 2, Memoir 89, 3–28

Klutschak, Heinrich

1881 *Als Eskimo unter Eskimos: Eine Schilderung der Erlebnisse der Schwatka'schen Franklin-Aufsuchungs-Expedition in den Jahren 1878–1880.* Wien: A. Hartleben Verlag

1987 *Overland to Starvation Cove: With the Inuit in Search of Franklin, 1878–1880,* translated and edited by William Barr. Toronto: University of Toronto Press

Knötsch, Carol Cathleen

1992a German Polar Research, the Inuit, and Franz Boas. *The Musk-Ox* 39:267–73

1992b Franz Boas als teilnehmender Beobachter in der Arktis. In Dürr et al. 1992, 57–78

1992c *Franz Boas bei den kanadischen Inuit im Jahre 1883–1884.* Mundus Reihe Ethnologie 60. Bonn: Holos Verlag

1993 Franz Boas' Research Trip to Baffin Island, 1882–1884. *Polar Geography and Geology* 17, no.1:5–54

Krause, Richard A

1992 *Die Gründungsphase deutscher Polarforschung, 1865–1875.* Berichte zur Polarforschung 114. Bremerhaven: Alfred-Wegener-Institut für Polar- und Meeresforschung

Liss, Julia E

1996 German Culture and German Science in the *Bildung* of Franz Boas. In Stocking, ed. 1996, 155–84

Lubbock, Basil

1937 *The Arctic Whalers.* Glasgow (Reprint 1968)

Malinowski, Bronislaw

1967 *A Diary in the Strict Sense of the Word.* New York: Harcourt, Brace & World Inc

Massin, Benoit

1996 From Virchow to Fischer: Physical Anthropology and 'Modern Race Theories' in Wilhelmine Germany. In Stocking, ed. 1996, 79–154

Minden-Lübbecker Kreisblatt

1883 Local-Berichte. Minden. 26 June

Müller-Wille, Ludger

1983a Franz Boas (1858–1942). *Arctic* 36, no.2:212–13

1983b Vorläufige Bestandsaufnahme und einstweiliges Inhaltsverzeichnis der Akten der Internationalen Polar-Kommission, der Deutschen Polar-Kommission und deren Stationen der Nord-, Labrador- Süd-

Expeditionen im Rahmen des Internationalen Polarjahres 1882/83, der Deutschen Südpolarforschung (1898) und des Hilfskomitees zur Rettung deutscher Forscher im Polareis (Spitzbergen, 1913). Unpublished manuscript. Hamburg: Deutsches Hydrographisches Institut, Bundesministerium für Verkehr

1984   Document: Two Papers by Franz Boas. *Études/Inuit/Studies* 8, no.1:117–20

1992   Franz Boas: Auszüge aus seinem Baffin-Tagebuch, 1883–1884 (19. September bis 15. Oktober 1883). In Dürr et al. 1992, 39–56

1994   Franz Boas und seine Forschungen bei den Inuit: Beginn einer arktischen Ethnologie. In Rodekamp, ed. 1994, 25–38

Müller-Wille, Ludger, and Linna Weber Müller-Wille

1984   Cumberland Sound Nuna-Top Inuit Place Name Survey and the Franz Boas Inuit Place Name Collection of 1883–84. Unpublished data and map collection. Montréal: Indigenous Names Surveys, McGill University

Neumayer, Georg von, ed.

1890   *Die internationale Polarforschung 1882–1883: Die Deutschen Expeditionen und ihre Ergebnisse.* Vol. 2, *Beschreibende Naturwissenschaften in einzelnen Abhandlungen.* Hamburg: Deutsche Polar-Kommission

1891   *Die internationale Polarforschung 1882–1883: Die Deutschen Expeditionen und ihre Ergebnisse.* Vol. 1, *Geschichtlicher Theil.* Hamburg: Deutsche Polar-Kommission

Neumayer, Georg [von], and C. Börgen, eds.

1886   *Die internationale Polarforschung 1882–83. Die Beobachtungsergebnisse der deutschen Stationen.* Vols. 1–2. Berlin: Asher

Northwest Territories, Historic Parks

n.d.   *Kekerten Historic Park, Baffin Island, Northwest Territories, Canada.* [ca 1985]

Püschel, Erich

1983   Franz Boas (1858–1942), Amerikas großer Ethnologe, als deutscher Student und Assistent, zum 125. Geburtstag. *Curare* 6:81–4

1988   Franz Boas (1858–1942), Amerikas großer Ethnologe als deutscher Privatdozent. *Curare* 11:141–4

Ratzel, Friedrich

1883   Die Bedeutung der Polarforschung für die Geographie. *Verhandlungen des 3. Deutschen Geographentages zu Frankfurt/Main* 21–38

Renner, Egon

1992   Franz Boas' Historismus und seine Rolle bei der Begründung der amerikanischen Ethnologie. In Dürr et al. 1992, 125–67

Rink, Henrik
   1885   Rink Papers in the Royal Library, Copenhagen. Manuscript Depart-
           ment, no. 2488, Collection Group 9: Eskimoske Sagn og Sange sam-
           lede af Dr. F. Boas paa Baffins-Land. Correspondence and 51 items
Rodekamp, Volker, ed.
   1994   *Franz Boas 1858–1942: Ein amerikanischer Anthropologe aus Minden.* Texte
           und Materialien aus dem Mindener Museum 11. Bielefeld: Verlag für
           Regionalgeschichte
Rohner, Ronald P., ed.
   1969   *The Ethnography of Franz Boas.* Chicago: University of Chicago Press
Ross, W. Gillies
   1975   *Whaling and Eskimos: Hudson Bay, 1860–1915.* National Museum of
           Man. Publications in Ethnology 10. Ottawa: National Museums of
           Canada
   1985   *Arctic Whalers Icy Seas: Narratives of the Davis Strait Whale Fisheries.*
           Toronto: Irwin
Rudolph, Wolfgang
   1968a   *Die amerikanische 'Cultural Anthropology' und das Wertproblem.* Berlin:
           Duncker & Humboldt
   1968b   *Kritische Analyse einer Grundsatzfragen-Diskussion in der amerikanischen
           Ethnologie.* Berlin: Duncker & Humboldt
Schneider, Lucien
   1985   *Ulirnaisigutiit: An Inuktitut-English Dictionary of Northern Quebec, Labrador
           and Eastern Arctic Dialects (with an English-Inuktitut Index).* Québec: Les
           Presses de l'Université Laval
Sherman, Stuart C., ed.
   1986   *Whaling Logbooks and Journals, 1613–1927: An Inventory of Manuscript
           Records in Public Collections.* New York and London: Garland
Smith, Eric Alden
   1984   Approaches to Inuit Socioecology. *Études/Inuit/Studies* 8, no.1:65–87
Smith, William Benjamin
   1944   *The Iliad of Homer.* New York: Macmillan
Stevenson, Marc G.
   1997   *Inuit, Whalers, and Cultural Persistence: Structure in Cumberland Sound
           and Central Inuit Social Organization.* Toronto: Oxford University
           Press
Stocking, Jr, George W.
   1965   From Physics to Ethnology: Franz Boas' Arctic Expedition as a Problem
           in the Historiography of the Behavioral Sciences. *Journal of the History
           of the Behavioral Sciences* 1:53–66

1968   *Race, Culture and Evolution: Essays in the History of Anthropology.* New York: The Free Press

1992   *The Ethnographer's Magic and Other Essays in the History of Anthropology.* Madison: University of Wisconsin Press

Stocking, Jr, George W., ed.

1974   *A Franz Boas Reader: The Shaping of American Anthropology.* Chicago & London: University of Chicago Press (Reprint 1982)

1983   *Observers Observed: Essays on Ethnographic Fieldwork,* vol. 1 of *History of Anthropology.* Madison: University of Wisconsin Press

1996   Volksgeist *as Method and Ethic: Essays on Boasian Ethnography and the German Anthropological Tradition,* vol.8 of *History of Anthropology.* Madison: University of Wisconsin Press

Wenzel, George

1984   L'écologie culturelle et les Inuit du Canada: Une approche appliquée. *Études/Inuit/Studies* 8, no.1:89–101

Weyprecht, Carl

1875   Die Erforschung der Polarregionen. *Mittheilungen der k. u. k. geographischen Gesellschaft zu Wien* 18, n.s. 8, 357–66

Index